Unreal® Tournament Game Programming for Teens

John P. Flynt, Ph.D.

with

Brandon Booth

THOMSON

―――――★――――― ™

COURSE TECHNOLOGY

Professional ■ Technical ■ Reference

Important: Thomson Course Technology PTR cannot provide software support. Please contact the appropriate software manufacturer's technical support line or Web site for assistance.

Thomson Course Technology PTR and the authors have attempted throughout this book to distinguish proprietary trademarks from descriptive terms by following the capitalization style used by the manufacturer.

Information contained in this book has been obtained by Thomson Course Technology PTR from sources believed to be reliable. However, because of the possibility of human or mechanical error by our sources, Thomson Course Technology PTR, or others, the Publisher does not guarantee the accuracy, adequacy, or completeness of any information and is not responsible for any errors or omissions or the results obtained from use of such information. Readers should be particularly aware of the fact that the Internet is an ever-changing entity. Some facts may have changed since this book went to press.

Educational facilities, companies, and organizations interested in multiple copies or licensing of this book should contact the Publisher for quantity discount information. Training manuals, CD-ROMs, and portions of this book are also available individually or can be tailored for specific needs.

ISBN-10: 1-59863-346-5

ISBN-13: 978-1-59863-346-7

Library of Congress Catalog Card Number: 2006906796

Printed in the United States of America

07 08 09 10 11 PH 10 9 8 7 6 5 4 3 2 1

Publisher and General Manager, Thomson Course Technology PTR:
Stacy L. Hiquet

Associate Director of Marketing:
Sarah O'Donnell

Manager of Editorial Services:
Heather Talbot

Marketing Manager:
Heather Hurley

Senior Acquisitions Editor:
Emi Smith

Marketing Assistant:
Adena Flitt

Project Editor:
Jenny Davidson

Technical Reviewer:
Marcia Flynt

PTR Editorial Services Coordinator:
Erin Johnson

Interior Layout Tech:
William Hartman

Cover Designer:
Mike Tanamachi

CD-ROM Producer:
Brandon Penticuff

Indexer:
Larry Sweazy

Proofreader:
Sara Gullion

THOMSON

COURSE TECHNOLOGY

Professional ■ Technical ■ Reference

Thomson Course Technology PTR, a division of Thomson Learning Inc.
25 Thomson Place ■ Boston, MA 02210 ■ http://www.courseptr.com

This book is dedicated to its readers.

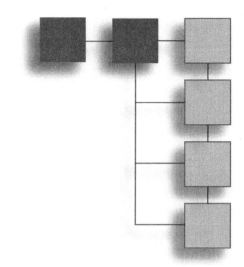

Acknowledgments

To Epic

Although you find a few praises of Epic buried in the text, be aware that a book like this one would not be possible without the tremendous efforts on the part of many very cool people at Epic. They have created a fantastic world and an unequalled game development environment. They have made their work available through the DVD and Internet resources. Many thanks to Mark Rein, the engineers, developers, writers, and others associated with Epic.

Unreal is a registered trademark of Epic Games, Inc.

John

To Emi Smith and Stacy Hiquet for arranging for the publication. To Jenny Davidson, for watching over the schedule and making it happen. Thanks to the many good people at Thomson who attend to the work. Many thanks to Brandon for being a great partner and tolerating my stories about the history of Colorado. Thanks to Marc Rein at Epic for being positive and responding to phone calls and e-mails. Also, thanks to the engineers at Epic who characterized *UnrealScript Game Programming All in One* as a "solid" effort. The good word from the source has meant everything. To Beth Walker, Adrian Flynt, Amy Flynt, Kevin Claver, and others for being helpful and supportive in the Unreal effort. To students at DeVry, NYU, and elsewhere for being themselves. To the folks at SmartDraw who for years now have been generously providing me with tools to create illustrations. Thanks to Marcia for the tremendous technical editing effort. You have made this book possible.

The story told to the player Pawn object in Chapter 8 is derived from a story the religious historian Mircea Eliade recounts in a book titled *Myths, Dreams, and Mysteries* (translated by Philip Mairet; Harper and Row: New York, 1975). The original story is about a wise and revered rabbi who lived near Cracow. In Chapter 10, the lines attributed to Groucho Marx were found at www.quotationspage.com.

Brandon

First and foremost, my thanks go to John for putting in very long hours to make this book possible in such a short amount of time.   Thanks also go to John and Marcia for providing me with this wonderful opportunity.   Thank you to my dear girlfriend, Bonny, for constantly putting up with my busy schedule and for always being there when I need you. Thank you to my wonderful family whose love, support, and guidance have helped me immeasurably throughout the years.   I love you all!   Thank you to all of the other dear friends and people in my life who have believed in me and helped shape me as a person. Finally, thank you to my sweet cat, Buddy, for being playful and helping me remember to always try to have fun.

About the Authors

John P. Flynt, Ph.D., has taught at colleges and universities, and has authored courses and curricula for several college-level game development programs. His academic background includes work in information technology, the social sciences, and the humanities. Among his works are *In the Mind of a Game, Perl Power!, Java Programming for the Absolute Beginner, UnrealScript Game Programming All in One* (with Chris Caviness), *Software Engineering for Game Developers, Simulation and Event Modeling for Game Developers* (with Ben Vinson), *Pre-Calculus for Game Developers,* (with Boris Meltreger), and *Basic Math Concepts for Game Developers* (with Boris Meltreger). John lives in the foothills near Boulder, Colorado.

Brandon Booth wrote his first program at the age of twelve. He graduated from high school with an International Baccalaureate diploma and decided to pursue dual degrees in applied mathematics and computer science at the University of Colorado, Boulder. As a freshman at CU, he wrote a PC game based on the pattern-based card game *Set*. His favorite games include *Final Fantasy, Guitar Hero, Kingdom Hearts, Guild Wars, Unreal Tournament, Half-Life,* and *Worms Armageddon.*

CONTENTS

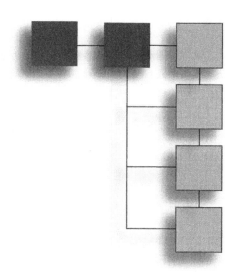

INTRODUCTION

About This Book

This book centers on programming. All of the program examples involve the actions within a map (or level), so you can readily expand on the programs you create during the course of this book to modify the game. This book focuses on the creation of programs using UnrealScript. The programs are often made fairly long and involved so that you have a chance to more fully explore the syntax of UnrealScript and the principles and practices of object-oriented programming. This book is centered on beginning examples of programming, so if you are seeking both an introduction to programming and an introduction to using the Unreal Level Editor, you are likely to find useful information. All programs in this book involve working with the Unreal Level Editor.

If you have been working with UnrealScript on an experimental basis and already know how to do the things this book illustrates, you might still benefit from the book if you have not studied the game or programming in a formal way. This book uses software engineering terms to talk about the activities you undertake as you program through the Unreal Level Editor. It helps you learn technical terms for the actions you perform as you work with the Unreal Tournament class hierarchy. Such terms can prove helpful as you expand your knowledge of the game engine into contexts in which people educated as software engineers or computer scientists lead the discussion.

All the programs involve extending the Actor class or its subclasses. In several instances, you create classes that augment the visible objects. You use these on the basis of association to supplement the actions of objects used directly in the game. Some of these classes, such as the Math class, are purely for illustration. You program and make them work. Others, such as the Story class provide functionality that you might actually take into the maps.

You work with a limited number of classes derived from the Actor class. The goal of the book is not to provide its readers with a comprehensive knowledge of the Unreal Tournament class hierarchy. Instead, the focus here is on introducing readers to how to derive and develop fairly extensive classes that reveal many dimensions about how to work with UnrealScript, inheritance, composition, the Unreal Level Editor Property dialogs, and many fundamental aspects of programming.

This book is not about level design, but since its examples involve levels, every attempt is made to provide step-by-step introductions and discussions of the use of the Unreal Level Editor. If you do not know what the Unread Level Editor is, then this book should allow you to get started. You create basic geometry, introduce a few objects, and then use extended programs to manipulate these things. References are provided to some standard resources for learning how to use the Unreal Level Editor.

Who Should Read This Book

If you are new to either programming or level development, this book is suitable for you. If your interests lie only in the area of level development, not in the area of programming, then there are probably more appropriate books for you. At the same time, even though most of the projects center on programming, much of the discussion concerns the Unreal Level Editor, so it helps to have an interest as a programmer in level editing.

This book addresses the fundamentals of computer programming by allowing you to work with UnrealScript and the Unreal Level Editor. The book uses maps from *Unreal Tournament 2004* in some of its chapters, but most of its contents are based on examples that you create for yourself. Using the knowledge you acquire from this book, you can begin exploring how to program a number of events characteristic of *Unreal Tournament.*

It is not assumed that you have any programming experience. It is assumed, however, that you can access the Internet for information about how to use the Unreal Level Editor. Discussion of such resources is provided in the text. Every effort is made to instruct you about how to use the Unreal Level Editor to supplement your programming activity, and the text should cover most of the actions you need to perform. Still, it remains important to keep in mind that a bit of web browsing might help your level-development activities.

You gain familiarity with how to specialize classes and how to use them on the basis of association. You spend a fair amount of time working with the dialogs that enable you to set properties of various objects. The focus remains, however, on programming, and the assumption from the first is that you want to learn how to program with UnrealScript and in general about programming.

The book equips you to understand how object-oriented programming works. You learn the difference between abstract classes and concrete classes, how inheritance works, and how to override functions from base classes. You examine many features of the UnrealScript programming language. With respect to *Unreal Tournament* itself, you do not play *Unreal Tournament* during the course of this book.

As a renowned programmer once said, when programming is not fun something is wrong, so it should not be inferred from the previous paragraph that this book, as a programming book, represents something that is not fun. From beginning to end, it is hoped that the reader finds in it a friendly, hands-on, and fun introduction to programming using UnrealScript the Unreal Level Editor.

The Advisory

As for readers in general, if you are not familiar with *Unreal Tournament*, it is good to keep in mind that the publishers of the game provide an advisory for it. The gist of the advisory is that people under 17 should not play the game without consulting first with their parents. (See the label for the exact advisory.) That makes the title of this book, which includes the word "Teens," stand out.

Epic provides a "stripped down" version for the educational community. This version of the game engine is made available over the Internet. With just a few minor changes to compensate for the file extensions, you can use this book with the stripped down version.

This book does not make use of the stripped down version, because you can still use pieces of the commercial version to learn about programming without having to involve yourself in the deeper dimensions of gameplay. In this book, your attention focuses on how to derive classes from the classes in the *Unreal Tournament* class hierarchy, how to use features of the Unreal Level Editor, and how to work with the syntax of UnrealScript.

In his documentary film, *Bowling for Columbine* (2002), Michael Moore recounted a story of visiting a missile factory near Columbine High School. Columbine High School is located here in Colorado, where both of the authors of this book were born and live. A few years ago two students entered the high school and injured or murdered others and then killed themselves. Michael Moore reported that he found people in the nearby missile factory unable to view as relevant any connection at all between the acts committed at the high school and the missiles being produced in the factory.

Missiles definitely kill people. Computer games have not been shown in any definitive fashion to kill people or even lead people to do violent things, but it remains that the problem might not be so much the depiction of vicarious violence as it is indifference to violence.

That Epic provides a stripped down version of the game constitutes a particularly forceful and positive message. It is a statement about self-consciousness that might be said to be missing in a huge number of places. Thank you, Epic, Atari, and others for this statement. As mentioned previously, despite the option of going to the stripped down version, this book invites you to purchase *Unreal Tournament 2004* and to work with programming examples that do not necessarily lead you directly into the game.

The Chapters

Chapter 1 provides you with an overview of some of the key activities you might think about attending to as you work with the book. These notions might not make much sense if you are new to *Unreal Tournament* programming, but if you are aware of them from the start, they should make sense soon enough and allow you to derive greater enjoyment as you learn.

Chapter 2 is likely to prove a little irritating if you already have experience with the Unreal Level Editor. It helps you acquaint yourself with the level editor. It asks you to experiment with moving around in the viewports and working with the mouse. The exercises are based on classroom experiences one of the authors has had getting people started with the somewhat complex activity of negotiating navigation in the world space of the viewports.

In Chapter 3, you begin learning about the code editor (or script editor), the Actor class hierarchy, and the basic syntax of UnrealScript. You create a class derived from the Trigger class. You use a level from the game.

Chapter 4 involves creating a level for yourself and then performing more programming to develop another version of a Trigger class to place in the level. You are introduced to the notion of a class hierarchy, object-oriented programming, and the use of the extends keyword in relation to inheritance.

Chapter 5 marks the beginning of a sustained study of the syntax of UnrealScript. In this chapter, the discussion centers on data types and operators.

Chapter 6 furnishes discussions developing functions and systems of classes. You learn about things like scope and the arguments and return values of functions. You learn about how classes can be characterized as states and behaviors. You develop a system of classes that allows you to dynamically spawn an instance of one class within another and in this way explore the idea of peer classes and class composition.

Chapter 7 offers the first of two chapters that allow you to explore control statements. This chapter concentrates on sequence and selection. It also introduces you to notions concerning abstract classes and functions, function overriding, and the use of such keywords as super. You also explore the use of static arrays, structures, and enumerations.

Chapter 8 ventures into the world of refactoring. In this case, you develop a very long class and then break it into three classes that you then use on a composition basis in addition to investigating the use of repetition controls and dynamic arrays.

Chapter 9 provides you occasions for working with classes you derive from the KActor, Light, and Trigger classes. You also work with functions of the Vector data type and control the movement of a static mesh you equip with physics properties.

Chapter 10 finishes off your work by having you work with a TriggerLight object and an iterator. You also work with such classes as KHinge and KActor to implement some special effects and in the end add some music.

Appendix A includes notes on how to deal with a few activities in the Unreal Level Editor that can help you expand your work to include such activities as using ConTEXT and other editors to develop. You need to go to other books or the Internet for information on external editors. Generally, in this appendix, however, the discussion centers on what you do using the Unreal Level Editor alone.

Appendix B covers how to restore packages.

The CD and Source Materials

On the CD you find all the projects for the book. The material on the CD is also provided on an Internet site. To obtain the code from the publisher's website, access www.courseptr.com/downloads and enter the title of the book.

While you can load the levels and packages and work from there, it is suggested that at most you just use the *.txt files to access code that you might find difficult to correctly type for yourself. Build the levels and packages as you go.

When you access a given chapter folder, you find all the material used in that chapter. This can include the following:

- **Text versions of the source code (*.txt) files.** You find the code in two forms. In the text, all code is identified as residing in *.txt files that you can open with Notepad. It is suggested that you access these files only with Notepad. This way you do not introduce font types that corrupt them. When you open them, notice that they are all set to Courier 12 pt. This ensures that you can copy and paste them into the Unreal Level Editor code window.

- **UnrealScript (*.uc) files.** These files are files that have been exported from the packages you work with. They are the same as the *.txt files. In fact, to make them into *.txt files, all you have to do is change the extension. The same applies to converting *.txt files to *.uc files. Generally, these files are for reference only. If you want to know more about what to do with them, see Appendix A.

- **One or more map (*.ut2) files.** The text instructs you when to create new versions, and you find maps representing the versions for each chapter. To use the *.ut2 files, you must place the *.u files and *.usx files associated with them in the System and Static Meshes directories. If you do not have these files in place, then when you try to run the levels, UnrealEd issues errors.

- **Package (*.u) files.** These all go in the UT2004/System directory. Generally, the best thing to do is to keep them in reserve in case you have problems. Work through the book and create levels and packages as you go.

- **The mesh and texture (*.usx) files.** These are included only when they have been changed from what you find in the default game directories. For example, if a static mesh has been generated using one of the brushes used to create primitive geometry objects, then you find the static mesh and its package in the folder for the chapter in which it appears.

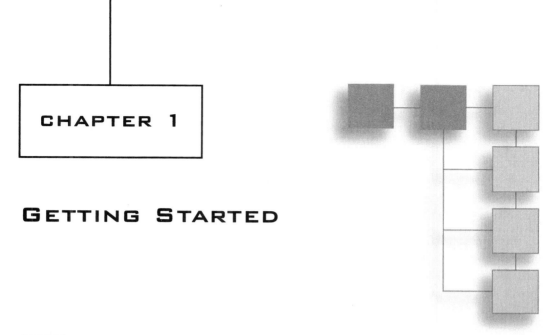

CHAPTER 1

GETTING STARTED

This first chapter primarily focuses on subjects that will be helpful to those who are making their first journey into programming involving Unreal Tournament. When you program for Unreal Tournament, you program with UnrealScript. Most of your programming involves modifying default features of the game. You can use properties dialogs to learn about most of the default features. All such features are defined in the code for the classes that make up the Unreal Tournament class hierarchy, which you can view through the browser that the Unreal Level Editor provides. Through the browser and in other ways, you can access the code that defines the features of the game and add to them. Accustoming yourself to the complexities of the Unreal Level Editor can be an exacting chore, but after you get so you can work with the code and manage the features the code defines, you are well on your way to an endless adventure. In the process, as your efforts take you into the Unreal development community, if you sustain practices that incorporate professional and craft standards, you are more likely to find your explorations fulfilling. Here are a few topics addressed in this chapter:

- What it means to modify the features of a game in core programming terms
- The basic layout of the Unreal Level Editor
- How to proceed initially so that your work is minimally frustrating
- What it means to incorporate craft and professionalism into your work
- Some resources that might he helpful to keep at hand
- A hearty welcome to you if you are new to the game

Development Focus

Figure 1.1 illustrates what might be viewed as a strategy for learning how to write programs you can include in *Unreal Tournament*. If you are just starting out as a programmer, you face a fairly difficult road. *Unreal Tournament* now represents over a decade of development. The development efforts have focused on professional game developers. Tens of thousands of features are at hand to work with. The Unreal Level Editor offers perhaps 5,000 different contact points. Learning how to combine programming and the Unreal Level Editor is a justifiably daunting task.

In this book, the activity of working with the Unreal Level Editor is approached on an elementary basis. No attempt is made to address professional game developers or even people who already know a few things about level design or how to program. The goal is to provide a comfortable beginning for working with the Unreal Level Editor and learning how to write programs using UnrealScript.

As Figure 1.1 illustrates, as presented in this book, these two activities involve familiarizing yourself with three areas of endeavor. One encompasses being able to structure your activities with relation to certain concepts and practices that foster successful development projects. Another consists of understanding the tools (the Unreal Level Editor) used to perform the work. A third focuses on comprehending how core programming activities involving UnrealScript and the Unreal Tournament class hierarchy unfold.

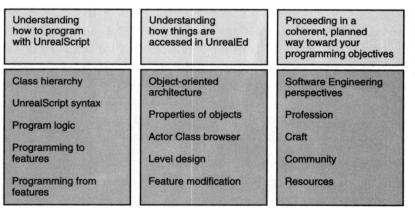

Figure 1.1
Strategies for learning involve understanding the challenge.

Programming

The three activities shown in Figure 1.1 extend over a broad spectrum. When you learn about programming, you concentrate on the syntax of the programming language and the standard ways that computer programming logic can be applied to the programs you write. Much of this activity occurs in isolation from your work with level development. You can, for example, spend hours programming and reprogramming a few lines of code to achieve a given programming objective. When you are looking at and working with lines of code, your success depends on the effort you make to understand syntax and programming logic.

At the same time, to program for a level, you must familiarize yourself with the graphical user interface (GUI) that the Unreal Level Editor provides. To an extent, programming and level development are inseparable. For this reason, throughout this book, you move back and forth between writing and understanding programs and developing level features in which to apply the programs. Your progress as a programmer depends to an extent on your progress as a level developer, so not knowing how to work with the features of the GUI can be costly. The same applies in the other direction. When you do not understand specific features of the syntax of UnrealScript or the Unreal Tournament class hierarchy, you cannot readily modify the behavior of level features. Figure 1.2 illustrates the basic dynamic of these two forms of activity.

Level features

Programming logic

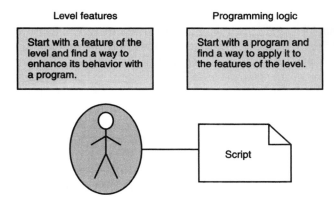

Figure 1.2 Level development and programming activities complement each other.

In the context provided by this book, the work is primarily that of performing simple programming tasks. You find a feature of the game and see what you can do with it, or you write a program that illustrates a standard approach to programming logic and then find a way to fit this program into the level. For example, in one passage, you write programs that use the Rand() function to generate messages you retrieve from an array. You then apply this activity to a Trigger object. When you do this, you follow the path from programming to features of the game. On the other hand, in another passage, you put Light objects in a level and then write a program to iterate through them to turn them on or off. In this way, you proceed from the level to the program.

From a programming perspective, you worry about issues of UnrealScript syntax and the Unreal Tournament class hierarchy. UnrealScript is not the Unreal Tournament class hierarchy. It is a scripting or programming language used to develop the Unreal Tournament class hierarchy. If you have a background that has led you to explore different programming languages, you probably recognize similarities between UnrealScript and such languages as C#, Java, and C /C++. It provides a fairly standard body of syntax that allows you to immediately put to work skills acquired from working with other programming languages.

In this book, your programming activities are confined to work you can perform using the code editor provided with the Unreal Level Editor. Experienced programmers often condemn this editor, but if you are starting out and want to concentrate on getting right into the game, then the best route is through the code scripting window the Unreal Level Editor provides. The authors have found it fairly satisfying to follow this route. The code editor is convenient to use, and from the first it is the best route to follow for debugging. For the 2004 version, of course, the darkness of the background, the miniscule proportions of the font, the lack of a buffer that allows for multiple undo operations, the lack of optional line numbers, the lack of the ability to save off versions of a given file, and a plethora of other irritants might lead you to concur with the condemnations voiced by experienced developers, but it remains that despite the cacophony, if you use the scripting window, you can go right to work and accomplish much.

Tip

Use the default Windows keys (Control + C and Control + V) to copy and paste your scripts into Notepad files from the script editing area. Also, as you'll read later on in the book, remember to set the font style of Notepad to Courier. Otherwise, your code disappears when you try to transfer it to or from the script editing window. When the Unreal Level Editor was developed, the powerful text components now commonly used by application interface developers were not as readily available, so with subsequent releases of the Unreal Level Editor, the complaints voiced by some are likely to vanish.

While becoming familiar with the script editor is in many ways as fundamental to your success as learning to use the features of the Unreal Level Editor that deal with level features alone, it remains that the central focus of your programming efforts is using UnrealScript to access and modify the classes the Unreal Tournament class hierarchy provides. Toward this end, you concentrate on such things as the uses of the var, local, class, and extends keywords. You explore how the use of parentheses with the var keyword turns it into a control that allows you to define a property that is displayed in the properties dialog. Your work with the syntax grows from these items to encompass many others, such as the use of structures, enumerations, access modifiers, control statements, built-in data types, and built-in functions. Hundreds of other specifics come into play. It is a fun, satisfying learning adventure, and as mentioned previously, since UnrealScript resembles other languages, if you have aspirations to follow the path of programming, this is an excellent beginning.

The Unreal Level Editor

When you learn about the Unreal Level Editor, you become familiar with the extensive vocabulary that allows you to name features of a level in relation to the culture of *Unreal Tournament* and its players and developers. The language used is often confusing and cryptic at first, but over time, its meanings become clear.

As Figure 1.3 illustrates, the Unreal Level Editor is designed to allow you to work with the features of the game using an *object architecture*. The term *architecture* in this context refers to the way the software of the game is designed. The architecture identifies everything you work with in the level as an *object*. Each object is associated with a properties dialog. A properties dialog is a dialog just like those you are used to working with when you use any Windows application. It provides fields with field names.

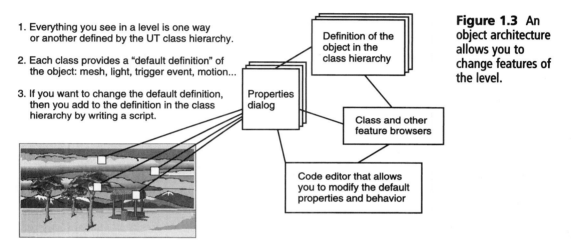

1. Everything you see in a level is one way or another defined by the UT class hierarchy.

2. Each class provides a "default definition" of the object: mesh, light, trigger event, motion...

3. If you want to change the default definition, then you add to the definition in the class hierarchy by writing a script.

Definition of the object in the class hierarchy

Properties dialog

Class and other feature browsers

Code editor that allows you to modify the default properties and behavior

Figure 1.3 An object architecture allows you to change features of the level.

The field names define the object. You can make an object large or small, for instance, by providing values to fields that define such characteristics. The fields in the properties exist because they are defined in the program that creates the object. Each type of object (a light, an event trigger, a static mesh, and so on) is defined by a program. The programs establish how the information you provide in the properties dialog changes the object.

The fundamental notion of an object-oriented architecture is that each object can be viewed largely in isolation from other objects. For this reason, the properties dialog provides a summary view of each object. It tells you what the object does and what options you have with respect to controlling it. At the same time, as a programmer, you can move from the properties dialog to the code and know that in the code you can find the definition of what you find in the dialog.

Properties dialogs are not the only way available to you for controlling objects. As a programmer, your focus is on the programs behind the dialogs. The Unreal Level Editor provides you with a way to modify the programs. There are two general paths to this activity. The first is that you can access the defining program directly from the object. You do this by just clicking on the object. The script editor opens, and you see the code that defines the object.

The other approach is through a *browser*. A browser is one of nine tabs visible to you in a dialog you access from the main menu of the Unreal Level Editor. The browsers represent different categories of objects. For example, you see separate tabs for classes in the Unreal Tournament class hierarchy, meshes, textures, animations, and music. The tab for the classes allows you to view source code. For other things, you do not see source code, only properties that apply to the objects. Such objects usually consist of binary files…files that contain information that defines an object. This information is so dense that it makes little sense for anyone to ever try to read it. Instead, you use tools like Photoshop, SoundForge, or Maya to create the files. You then import them into the Unreal Level Editor and work from there. You select from tabbed browser options to see their properties and use them.

How this happens precisely is the topic of discussion in several chapters to come, but for now the important thing to understand is that where code is involved, you access the code directly from the object or indirectly through the properties dialogs. To work with the code, you open the script editor window. By adding code, you can redefine the behavior of almost any object you see in the game. Among other things, you can add new fields to the properties dialog. You can change the way the information in the existing fields is interpreted. You can do about anything you want.

Working from the object to the code is the primary activity you perform as a programmer. As Figure 1.4 illustrates, the other part of the activity involves working as a level designer. This part of the activity encompasses learning the meaning of the icons in the different

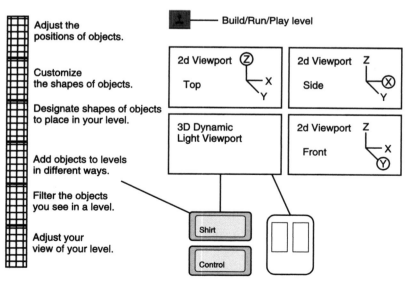

Adjust the positions of objects.

Customize the shapes of objects.

Designate shapes of objects to place in your level.

Add objects to levels in different ways.

Filter the objects you see in a level.

Adjust your view of your level.

Build/Run/Play level

2d Viewport Ⓩ
Top — X / Y

2d Viewport Z
Side — Ⓧ / Y

3D Dynamic Light Viewport

2d Viewport Z
Front — X / Ⓨ

Shirt

Control

Figure 1.4 Icons, the viewports, and the mouse actions, in addition to selections from the top menu, give you easy access to most Unreal Level Editor actions.

Almost every feature is controlled by combination of left and right mouse buttons and Shift and Control key actions. Experimentation is the key.

palettes you see on the left side of the Unreal Level Editor. Among other things, these palettes allow you to create the geometric objects you place in the levels. As you use them, you easily gain competence in their use, but when you first start, be warned that the learning curve is fairly steep.

Using the tools provided by the Unreal Level Editor recurs as a topic many times in this book, but with the exception of Chapter 2, the discussion remains fairly cursory. (See the "Resources" topic in this chapter for information on sources that explain the user interface in detail.)

For now, consider that the main elements of the interface consist of the icons on the left of the work area, the menu at the top, the actions the mouse invokes, and the four viewports. Figure 1.4 illustrates these features. Generally, people begin by applying the navigation skills they use in the game. This activity tends to be a fairly good approach since most learning involves, after all, employing what you know to find analogies that allow you to learn what you do not know. Chapter 2 provides some exercises for absolute beginners, but even there the objective is one only of inducing people who are new to the GUI to try some different experiments with the viewports.

The depiction of the mouse in Figure 1.4 is not intended as an insult to anyone's intelligence. The representation is intended to emphasize the theme that almost every context of activity in the Unreal Level Editor is associated with several (five or more in some instances) combinations of keys and mouse actions. If you are used to Photoshop, Maya, CorelDraw, or any number of other applications, you usually click to open a palette. Then you activate a feature in the palette and use a left-click of the mouse to perform the action. This is not the case with the Unreal Level Editor. Palettes are used, but in the main interface, you find that you can perform some actions only after experimenting at great length with combinations of keys and mouse buttons. This activity might strike you as utterly bizarre at first. Teaching experiences have led one of the authors to warn people to expect a high degree of frustration when they first start using the Unreal Level Editor.

The viewports present another point of interest. You perform most of your work in them. You almost always keep several in view at once. The key to understanding them is to realize that the x coordinates trace movement from right to left or left to right. The y coordinates trace movement from the front to the back or the back to the front, as though you are looking into the distance. The z axis points up and down. Figure 1.5 isolates the views.

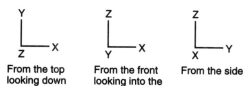

Figure 1.5 Different coordinate views allow you to navigate.

From the top looking down

From the front looking into the world

From the side

In addition to dealing with the basic GUI features, you also work with four activities over and over again:

- **Build geometry.** Building geometry involves refreshing the settings that the Unreal Level Editor maintains of the coordinate positions of all of the objects in your level. This information becomes outdated every time you perform even the smallest action that changes the position of an object. Generally, you find that almost no action you want to perform proves easy to perform unless you first build the geometry of your level. Practice doing this often. If you cannot get something to change, then it is probably because you are clicking on a position in the viewport that no longer corresponds to the geometrically defined position of the object. What you see is not what you get. You need to rebuild the geometry to set things right. Rebuilding is not the same as saving your work. It is instead updating it so that you can see the actual positions of objects in your level.

- **Build lights.** You often need to build the lights. Generally, practice building "changed" lights every time you make a change to your level. Lighting is not as important as geometry as you construct objects in your levels, but unless you refresh lighting regularly, your view of your work can vary enormously from the current state of your work.

- **Save.** The importance of saving cannot be emphasized too much. You save your map. You also save your classes and the packages that contain your code. These are not consistently unified activities. You are likely to come across many episodes in which a programming error causes the Unreal Level Editor to crash. When you reopen the editor, your work is no longer there. The code editor in the Unreal Level Editor is extremely unforgiving. You can lose your work in a moment. You can also corrupt a package fairly easily and lose many hours, days, or weeks of work. The implications of these reversals become clearer in the chapters to come. For now, just remember that as you work with code, it is important to 1) compile changes, 2) save the package, 3) save the level, and 4) make backup copies regularly and consistently.

- **Play/Run the map.** In this book, *playing* a level and *running* a level are synonymous terms. The game is a computer program, so after you compile a program you run it. This book is on programming, so the expression *run* seems more suitable in many of the discussions. For a programmer, compiling, building, and running a program are largely parts of testing. Testing is seeing whether your code works. As for the specifics at hand, one especially important activity is to build the geometry of your levels before you run them. Otherwise, unexpected and undesired results often occur. Train yourself to habitually build the geometry and lighting of a level before you try to run it.

Icons on the top toolbar provide convenient ways to perform such actions as saving your work, building lighting, and building geometry. Chapter 2 and subsequent chapters remind you frequently to perform such actions. As has been said before, the Unreal Level Editor is unforgiving. You lose your work often and painfully unless you get into the habit of working in a precautionary manner. This involves compiling, building, saving, and backing up your work in a practiced way. After a time, you get used to the routine, and things become a lot easier.

Practices

When you learn about practices and procedures, you enter the world of *software engineering*. Generally, one of the reasons people often find it difficult to learn from programming examples produced by hacking is that the examples are not written for others to read. Hacking has often been characterized as a way that programmers who lack professional ethics promote their job security. Whatever the characterization, the hacker is by definition not someone who is part of a community, and so a community that supposedly consists of a group of hackers is not really a community. It is a collection of people who do not want to be accountable to each other.

Software engineering is much more than some kind of battle with hacking. In fact, that is a largely insignificant part of the picture. Software engineering is a form of *craftsmanship* and an extension of an ages-old tradition of guild society. It consists largely of a set of practices and ethical standards you maintain along with others who share a common profession or craft. It allows you to share more readily what you know and to learn more readily what others have to teach. It calls upon you to conduct yourself decently and respectfully toward others in your community, and to do what you can to improve the overall quality of your work and the work of others.

It might be said that in the past Unreal Tournament development culture has been lacking with respect to certain craft and engineering ideals, but this can be said of many programming realms. The fact remains that with each passing day, the foul and accusatory language, the personalized attacks, the hacked and untested code, and other things characteristic of hacker culture are disappearing. As in most other professional settings, on the Internet it is not uncommon to see advisories that use of vicious language will res'' barred access. The Wiki, UDN, and other sites now offer such advisories. People are h ing more cooperative and friendlier.

From craft and engineering follows code and projects that are developed with gr/ tion to coding practices and standards. The goals no longer stop at just maki' or doing it. They now extend to thinking about how to do it, planning it, job well, with an eye to finding channels to continuous improvement.

In the most immediate context, the tools and practices of software engineering allow you to understand how the components of the Unreal Tournament class hierarchy fit together. Using tools such as those provided by the Unified Modeling Language (UML), you are in a much better position to plan your efforts and produce programs that you can test and improve.

A simple definition of engineering is that it consists of an activity of planning to build something and then building it as planned. Everyone has at some time run into games that suffer from lack of engineering. The result is that unpredictable behaviors often lead to things that go wrong when you play the game. What is not so evident is that lack of craft and engineering often make the process of developing a game extremely unpleasant, and what applies to play and development applies also to learning.

As Figure 1.6 illustrates, dissatisfaction with the end product becomes a concern of a craftsperson. Craft involves examining the thing your activity results in. Over the centuries, craft workers have sustained their craft on the basis of the one generation's examination of the products of the previous generation.

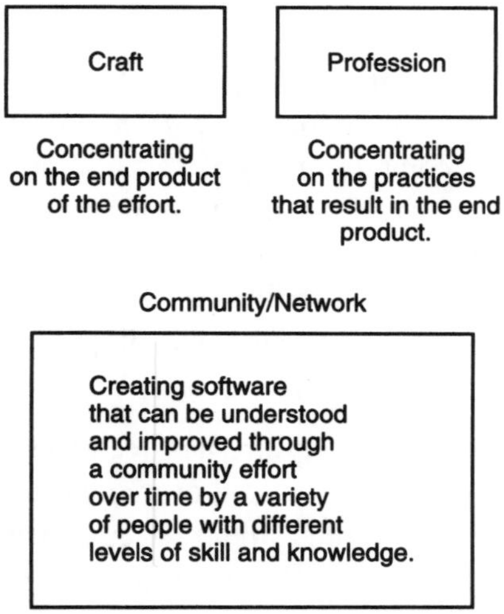

Craft	Profession
Concentrating on the end product of the effort.	Concentrating on the practices that result in the end product.

Figure 1.6 Participating in the development community is an important step.

Community/Network

Creating software that can be understood and improved through a community effort over time by a variety of people with different levels of skill and knowledge.

Profession centers on practices, and for this reason software engineering is at times said to present a sharp contrast to craft. There is some truth to this. Software engineers concentrate on improving processes with the assumption that better processes lead to better products.

Whatever the perspective you take, it remains that when you work as a programmer, whether as a professional, a hobbyist, a student, or a teacher, if you make efforts to develop code that you can understand and that others can understand as well, then you embark on a journey that is likely to carry you a long way.

Resources

Epic has done a wonderful thing by making Unreal Level Editor freely available to the game hobbyist and educational communities. The action parallels those of Sun when it fostered the Java programming language and Microsoft when it released DirectX and then the Express editions of Microsoft Studio and the XNA game development studio. It parallels the development of the Perl community and the proliferation of XML and other technologies.

It remains, however, that the bulk of work with the Unreal Engine has been conducted by professional developers, and for this reason, the documentation and other resources related to the game engine tend to be geared toward people who already know what they are doing and are seeking what amounts to supplemental technical information. For this reason, if you visit the Unreal Development Network, the information you find tends to be descriptive rather than tutorial in content. In other words, how a given function works is described in an abstract, technical way, as though you are able to find in such information the practical, down-to-earth ways that it might be applied. It is sort of like reading a section of a physics textbook on velocity and acceleration to learn about how to use the brakes of your bicycle or car.

This approach to providing technical information tends to characterize sites oriented toward professional developers. It can be highly frustrating for someone who is just seeking to know how to do something simple. For this reason the Wiki pages are often useful. The Wiki pages provide tutorials that are written by a mixture of amateur and professional developers. There are enormous holes in the information available, but exemplary efforts are often present for the areas that are covered.

A growing number of books and Internet sites address programming, level editing, and other topics associated with Unreal Tournament development. Here are a few resources:

- **Unreal Developer Network** (**UDN**). This is the "official" site for the Unreal Engine. It is a wonderful resource, but keep in mind that you have access to it based on your license level. Everyone has some level of access to it. Here is the Internet address: http://udn.epicgames.com/Main/WebHome

- **Wiki Unreal.** This is the most egalitarian realm of the *Unreal Tournament* programming effort. You find many tutorials on starter and more advanced projects. The information you find involves all aspects of game development. The Internet address is http://wiki.beyondunreal.com/wiki.

- **UnrealScript programming basics.** John Flynt and Chris Caviness, *UnrealScript Game Programming All in One* (Thomson, 2006). This book provides a review of the syntax of UnrealScript. It was used in the composition of this book as a reference source. It provides extensive information on setting up an editor called

ConTEXT. Such an editor is usually required if you want to go beyond programs that involve only one class. Although every effort was made to stick with the script editor, keep in mind that ConTEXT was used to develop some of the longer, multiple-class programs in this book.

■ **Level design reference.** Jason Busby, Zack Parrish, Joel Van Eenwyk, *Mastering Unreal Technology: The Art of Level Design* (Sams, 2005). This book is on the Unreal Level Editor, not programming. It is often viewed as a reference book.

These sources of information are mentioned because they were used at times during the composition of this book. The point to keep in mind is that many sources exist, and you can develop your own resource list as time goes on.

Conclusion

If you are only just beginning your work with the Unreal Engine or Unreal Level Editor, you can benefit by taking a little time to review some of the actions that can bring the greatest difficulties and rewards. Among these are starting off with a general grasp of what working with the Unreal Level Editor involves. When you use the Unreal Level Editor, you can develop levels using the GUI features of the Editor and add code that redefines the default objects the Editor provides.

This book concentrates on the programming effort, but to program the features of an Unreal level, you must use the Unreal Level Editor to complement your programming work. This activity usually proves greatly satisfying for most people, but to ensure that progress in learning is steady, it is best to observe a few precautions. One is that what you see depends on how frequently you built the geometry and lighting of your levels. Frequent building makes it so you struggle less as you perform development activities. It is also important to realize that the programs you create are compiled and saved as parts of packages, and the packages exist separately from the levels. Save and make backup copies of your level work and your programming work. The chapters of this book provide many discussions of the specific actions necessary to complete these tasks.

In addition to working with programs and learning how to use the Editor, your work with the Unreal Engine depends to a great extent on participation in a community that consists of professionals, hobbyists, and educators. Deriving the greatest benefits from such a community often depends on contributing to it in a positive way. One key to participation is to keep some of the notions associated with craft and software engineering in the background of your efforts. Working with the sense that every program should be developed with care, as a crafted rather than a hacked effort, allows you to more readily share your knowledge with others and improve on your efforts with the next round of work. Many passages of this book provide discussions of ways that you can bring craft and engineering practices into your work, regardless of your starting place.

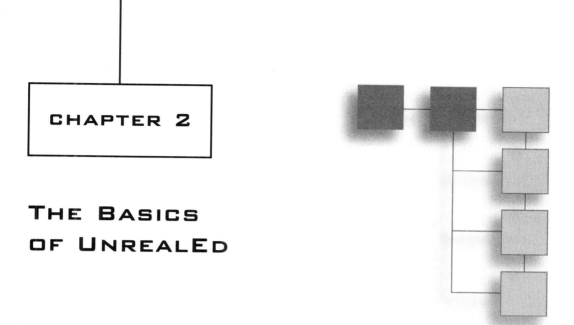

CHAPTER 2

THE BASICS OF UNREALED

I n this chapter you explore or review a number of activities you perform every time you enter into a work session with UnrealEd. Key among these activities are opening a map, navigating through a map, and closing a map. Additionally, you also work with the browser dialog. In this chapter, you do nothing more than become acquainted with the tabs and access options the browser dialog provides. In addition to working with the browser dialog, you also explore how to build and run a map. The map you use in the chapter is of minimum size. Working with a small map allows you to develop a sense of how long it might take to build a much larger map. While loading and running maps are important activities, you also investigate how to change the resolution settings of your display so that you maximize the performance of your computer for programming purposes. Among the topics explored in this chapter are the following:

- Understanding the general layout of the viewports
- Selecting and loading a map
- Navigating 2D viewports
- Navigating 3D viewports
- Building and running a map
- Closing out your work with a map

Unreal Level Editor

The formal name for the software application that allows you to change or modify the features of Unreal Tournament is the *Unreal Level Editor*. Epic apparently thought this title a little pretentious and so they shortened it to *UnrealEd*. You see *UnrealEd* on the marquee, in any event. In other places, Epic calls it *Unreal Editor*. In the editor itself, you see it as Unreal Level Editor.

The level editor has all sorts of nifty options. You probably already know this, but just in case you don't, it doesn't hurt to mention this here. As you'd expect, you can use it to create levels from scratch or modify those you already find in the game. Then you can use it to add lights, bots, ammo, and other things to levels. You can also use it to add code to control the things in your maps.

The Unreal Level Editor works along the lines you'd expect it to work. You begin with a map and then add things to it. When you start with a map, you start with the physical layout of the terrain. You then navigate through this terrain and add objects for the game. Your work begins with a physical layout, not with an abstract body of code.

Note

How you want to label different features of a game you are working with depends on your own preferences. When the difference between a map and a level arises, one distinction to consider is that a level is a map you have loaded with assets. A map can be viewed as the set of meshes (or wire frames) you use to create the essential layout or terrain of a level. A level, on the other hand, contains a map, lights, and other assets that you use to create features of your game world. A level can also contain several maps.

Starting with the physical terrain of the game reflects the fact that developers of Unreal Tournament wanted to make game development resemble the production of a play or a film. One of the first concerns when you produce a film is the setting or the stage. Everything then unfolds within the space the setting or stage provides.

If you work from the level editor your DVD or CD copy of the game provides, you find that the Unreal Level Editor is designed for people who want to *modify* Unreal Tournament. You can add many things to a level. You can add models, sounds, and textures. You can use the UnrealScript scripting language to program the things you add to make them behave in a number of ways. It remains, however, that the Unreal Level Editor does not allow you to develop things from scratch.

It is certainly the case that you can do almost anything you want using the Unreal engine. That is part of the reason the Unreal engine is popular among professional developers. Still, to change the basic game engine, you must acquire a license to allow you to do so. When you buy the game off the Internet or shelf, you work with a limited view of the game engine.

A Starter Session with the Level Editor

To begin a session with UnrealEd, you select Start > Unreal Tournament 2004 > UT2004 Editor. You then see the Unreal Tournament options shown in Figure 2.1. This is what you see if you have installed Unreal Tournament 2004 from the DVD or CD.

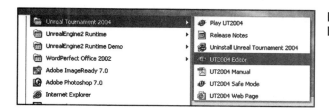

Figure 2.1 Select Ut2004 Editor for UnrealEd.

You then see the window for the Unreal Level Editor. Again, Unreal Level Editor is the formal name for UnrealEd. Epic also calls it the Unreal Editor. You are likely to see the standard set of *viewports*, as Figure 2.2 illustrates. If you are used to Windows applications, then you might know a viewport as a panel or window. In Figure 2.2, the four gray or black divisions of the main UnrealEd window are in the viewports.

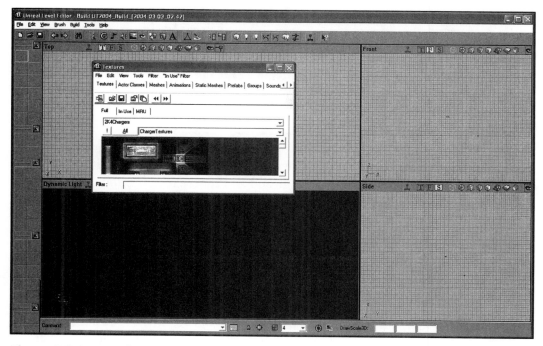

Figure 2.2 You see the standard set of composition frames.

The viewports allow you to view the level or map you are working on in different ways. As you can see from titles in the upper right of the viewports shown in Figure 2.2, the viewports offer you front, side, or top perspectives. The viewport on the lower left of the UnrealEd window is set up to give you a 3D view of your work. It is titled Dynamic Lighting. This title changes according to options you select for it.

You do not see anything in the viewports at first because you need to open a level for viewing. How to open a level is addressed momentarily.

In addition to the viewports, when you first open UnrealEd, you see a dialog. Figure 2.3 illustrates the dialog in isolation. The name in the title bar for the dialog by default reads Textures, but if you click on the tabs the dialog provides, the name changes. For this reason, Epic refers to the tabs in the dialog as *browsers*. You see, for example, a Textures Browser, an Actor Classes Browser, and a Meshes Browser, among others.

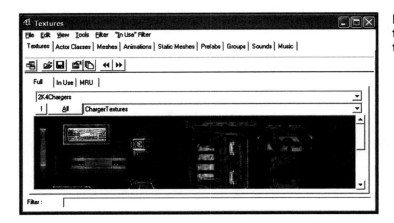

Figure 2.3 You invoke the Textures Browser from the View menu.

As you know, a texture is more or less like a mask, a tent covering, or a suit of clothes for a mesh. The Textures Browser allows you to add and choose textures. You deal later on in this book with the specifics of working with textures. For now, just get used to the notion that a single dialog furnishes you with many browsers, one of which is for textures. To explore the use of the dialog and the browsers, try this routine:

1. First, position your mouse cursor on the right border of the dialog and pull the dialog out so that you see all the tab selections (as shown in Figure 2.3).

2. Then click on the tabs to see the titles in the title bar change. Each tab represents a browser.

3 Now close the dialog. To accomplish this, click the red control box in the upper-right corner of the browser dialog. What browser you have in view does not matter.

4. Then move to the main menu of UnrealEd. Click the View option. Figure 2.4 shows you the browsers you can then access.

5. Select Show Texture Browser. This opens the browser dialog, and you see the Textures tab in focus. Click the tabs as you did in step 2.

6. Then go back to the View option of the main menu. Select Show Actor Class Browser. Don't worry for now what the Actor Class Browser does. That is addressed soon. You see the browser dialog open with the Actor Class Browser tab in focus.

7. If you feel inclined, try the routine a few more times to explore the different browsers. When you finish, close the browser dialog so that you see only the four viewports.

Note

To drive home the point, you can either select different browsers from the View menu or click different tabs in the browser dialog. Later on, you see that you can also invoke browsers from the main toolbar of UnrealEd. UnrealEd provides you different paths to the same set of destinations.

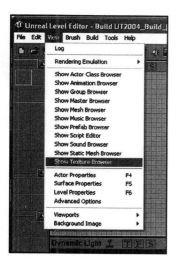

Figure 2.4 The Texture Browser is one among many browsers you find listed in the View menu.

Opening a Level for Your Viewports

UnrealEd allows you to open any level or map for editing. A level consists of a terrain created using a large number of engine *assets*. An asset is almost anything you can name with relation to a computer game: a mesh, a texture, an animation, a map, a musical piece, a sound prop. The list goes on. Likewise, a level consists of a large number of mathematically generated objects that must be regenerated each time you open or change a level.

The result of the combination of the geometry and assets of a level is that the memory and processing power required to open a level for editing varies depending on the complexity of the level. For this reason, in this book an attempt is made to work with fairly simple levels. In addition to being easier to work with for learning purposes, levels that require less processing also allow you to move more quickly through exercises, because you do not have to wait for prolonged periods while the editor compiles your changes.

To open a level for viewing in UnrealEd, select File > Open from the main menu of the Unreal Level Editor.

As Figure 2.5 illustrates, the Open option of the File menu invokes a standard file dialog for Windows. In the dialog, you see a list of files with *.ut2 extensions. In the Look In field at the top of the dialog, you see that the files all reside in the Maps directory. A map can also be called a level. At the bottom of the dialog, in the Files Of Type file, you see that the files are all of a given type. The type is *.ut2.

Depending on the version of Unreal Tournament you are working with, the file type changes. The *.ut2 file type designates maps that are appropriate for Unreal Tournament 2004. In this book, all the maps you work with are of this type.

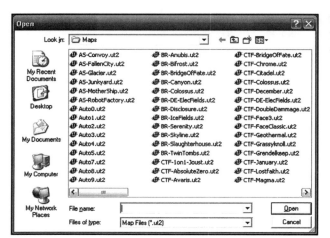

Figure 2.5 Levels reside in the Maps directory.

Select a Map

To open a map for viewing, position your cursor on the View Menu icon on the top left of the Open dialog (see Figure 2.5). Click and select Details as the view option. You then see a list of the maps in the Maps directory with the sizes in kilobytes. As mentioned previously, the size of a map determines the amount of time required for processing, so when you are learning to program, an advantage rests in working with a small map because you have to wait shorter periods of time to view the results of your programming.

In some cases, with large maps, you might have to wait several minutes for UnrealEd to load or process a given map. It is good to know this from the start. Small maps load relatively quickly, so when you see how long your computer requires to load a small map, then you can adjust your expectations as you work with larger maps.

Using Figure 2.6 as a reference, scroll down until you see the CTF-1on1-Joust.ut2 listing. It is one of the smallest maps in the Maps directory. Its size is around 4 megabytes (4000 kilobytes). Click the CTF-1on1-Joust.ut2 map. Then click Open.

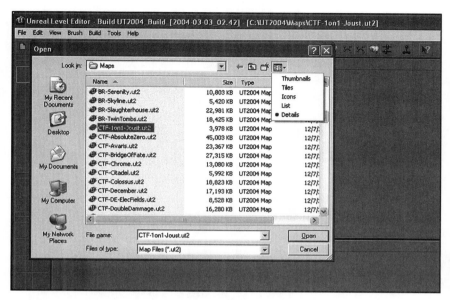

Figure 2.6 Map sizes determine how long they take to load.

After you click Open, the Progress dialog appears while UnrealEd loads the map. You then see different views of the map in the viewports, as Figure 2.7 illustrates. In the lower-left viewport, you usually see the 3D Dynamic Light version of the level. The other three viewports show you 2D views of the level.

The level you access through the CTF-1on1-Joust.ut2 map consists of a set of halls organized so that they resemble an "I". At each end of the long hall you find a statue of the ancient Egyptian god Anubis and a flag. At one end the statue and the flag are blue. At the other end they are red. Figure 2.8 illustrates the layout of the level.

When UnrealEd first opens the CTF-1on1-Joust.ut2 map, you do not see viewport images like those shown in Figure 2.7. This fact provides an occasion for working with some of the controls UnrealEd provides for manipulating objects in maps. The next few sections take you through a few basic exercises. Table 2.1 provides a summary of some of the mouse actions the next few sections review.

Note

The ancient Egyptian god Anubis is the son of the gods Nephthys and Set (or possibly Ra). Nephthys is usually characterized as a goddess of the dead. She accompanies the dead into the underworld. Set is the god of pestilence, drought, conflict, and pain, and generally disrupted peace and anything viewed as healthy. Anubis does not have such a sinister image. He is usually associated with tombs and the dead. He acts as a judge of the dead, as the scales in Figure 2.9 illustrate. Anubis is among the earliest ancient gods. He was the god of the ancient Egyptian underworld.

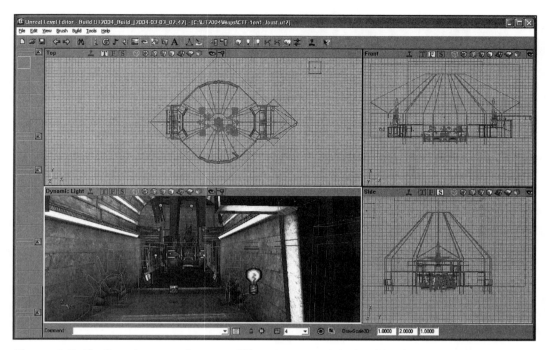

Figure 2.7 The four viewports show you different aspects of the level you have opened.

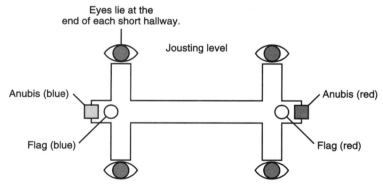

Eyes lie at the
end of each short hallway.

Jousting level

Anubis (blue)

Anubis (red)

Flag (blue)

Flag (red)

Figure 2.8 The CTF-1on1-Joust level consists of halls, flags, and statues of Anubis.

Figure 2.9 Anubis's image is common in ancient Egyptian writings. Image source: http://www.crystalinks.com/anubis.html.

Table 2.1 Viewpoint Motions*

Viewport	Movement	Action
2D	Left or right	Left or right mouse button
2D	Up or down	Left or right mouse button
2D	Forward or back	Both buttons and mouse wheel
3D	Look up	Right mouse button, forward
3D	Look down	Right mouse button, back
3D	Turn left	Right mouse button, left
3D	Turn right	Right mouse button, right
3D	Forward	Left mouse button, forward
3D	Back	Left mouse button, back
3D	Step left	Shift, Right mouse button, left
3D	Step right	Shift, Right mouse button, right

*As you go, you find that one set of actions allows you to perform more than one of these actions.

Manipulating 2D Viewports

Changing your views of 2D (Top, Side, and Front) viewports proves fairly easy. As you change your views, you are changing what might be viewed as the point at which you are located when you work within the map. To change your location, try these steps:

1. Use the left mouse button to click anywhere in the Top viewport. This activates the viewport.

2. Then scroll clockwise using the mouse wheel (pull the top of the wheel back) to pull away from the map. The map decreases in size. Continue until you see all the features of the map, as shown in Figure 2.7.

3. Position your mouse cursor anywhere in the gray grid area and hold down the left mouse button. Move your mouse to the left or right or up or down. Center the features of the level as shown in Figure 2.7.

4. Adjust the Front viewport. Click it to activate it. Once again, scroll clockwise to decrease the size of the map until you see all the features as shown in Figure 2.7.

5 Then hold down the left mouse button and move the mouse to the left or right or up or down to center the features of the level.

6. Adjust the Side viewport. Perform the same actions you performed for the Front and Top viewports.

Manipulating the 3D Viewport

For the viewport that shows you the 3D viewport, your actions are more involved than those you use to manipulate the 2D viewports. To adjust the 3D viewport, you use a combination of keyboard keys and mouse buttons. You turn to the left and right, move backward or forward, or look at the ceiling or floor.

To explore these activities, change the mode of the 3D viewport so you can see its color features. To accomplish this, click in the lower-left viewport (the 3D viewport). Then press Alt + 5. The title of the viewport changes to Dynamic Light.

Alt + 5 switches the mode of viewing so that you see all the meshes and textures in the map with lighting applied.

Alternatively, after activating the viewport, you can click an icon on the toolbar of the viewport to switch to Dynamic Lighting. To accomplish this, click the sixth cube from the left, as shown in Figure 2.10.

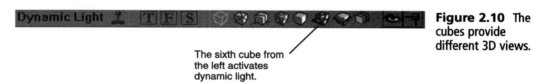

The sixth cube from
the left activates
dynamic light.

Figure 2.10 The
cubes provide
different 3D views.

Turning to the Left and Right

To turn to the right or left in the 3D viewport, click in the viewport to activate it and then press the left mouse button. Move your mouse approximately an inch straight to the left. Let up on the mouse button. Repeat this action a few times.

As Figure 2.11 illustrates, when you perform these actions, it is as though you are standing in one place and turning in a circle on your heels. You rotate in the same direction in which you move your mouse.

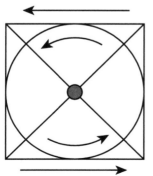

Press the left mouse button
and move your mouse to the
right to turn to the right.

Figure 2.11 You turn
on your heels.

Press the left mouse button
and move your mouse to the
left to turn to the left.

Repeat the left movements until you have gone in a complete circle. Then press the left mouse button and move your mouse slightly to the right. The map rotates to the left. Again, it is as though you are standing in one place and then turning on your heels to the right.

Moving Forward and Backward

To move backward or forward in the 3D viewport, press the left mouse button and move your mouse approximately an inch forward. Let up on the mouse button. When you perform this action, you move directly forward in whatever direction you are facing.

To move backward, press the left mouse button and move the mouse approximately an inch backward. Let up on the mouse button. You move directly backward.

To move in a given direction, you first turn on your heels to the left or the right (as indicated in the previous section). Then you move forward or backward. Figure 2.12 provides a summary view of this action.

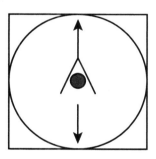

Press the left mouse button and move your mouse forward. You move the direction you are facing.

Figure 2.12 You move backward or forward relative to the direction you are facing.

Press the left mouse button and move your mouse backward. It is as though you are stepping backward.

As an exercise, press the left mouse button and move forward or backward slightly until you are directly in front of the flag. Press the left mouse button and turn so that you see one of the eyes at the end of the short hallway. Then turn so that you face the eye at the end of the other hallway.

Looking at the Ceiling and Floor

To rotate your view of the 3D viewport so you can look up, press the right mouse button and move your mouse approximately an inch forward. As Figure 2.13 illustrates, when you perform this action, it is as though you look toward the ceiling.

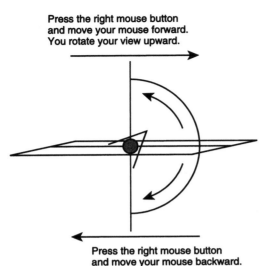

Press the right mouse button
and move your mouse forward.
You rotate your view upward.

Press the right mouse button
and move your mouse backward.
You rotate your view downward.

Figure 2.13 To look up,
press the right key and
move your mouse forward.

To look at your feet, press the left mouse button and move approximately an inch backward. Let up on the mouse button. If you repeat this action, you can continue rotating your view until you are looking straight down. The same applies to rotation upward. The rotation stops as 90 degrees, straight up or down.

Moving Directly to the Left or Right

To move to the right side in the 3D viewport, press the Shift key and the left mouse button. Move your mouse approximately an inch to the right. Release the mouse button. When you perform this action, it is as though you have stepped directly to the left.

Note

Your computer might respond differently to the commands discussed in this chapter. The purpose of the exercises in this chapter is to give you a chance to practice using the editor if you are new to UnrealEd.

Press the Shift key and the left mouse button. Move your mouse approximately an inch to the left. Release the mouse button. When you perform this action, as Figure 2.14 illustrates, it is as though you have stepped directly to the right.

Press the Shift key and the left mouse button.
Move your mouse to the left.
You step directly to the right.

Figure 2.14 Use the Shift and right mouse button to move directly to your right or left.

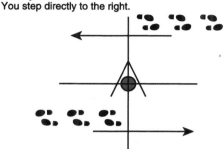

Press the Shift key and the left mouse button.
Move your mouse to the right.
You step directly to the left.

Building and Running

To compile and run the map you are working with, you first open the map you want to work with. In this instance, if you have not already done so, open the CTF-1on1-Joust.ut2 map. After it loads, you have several options. You can build certain features of a map, such as the lights, or you can build all features of the map. In this instance, you want to build the entire map, and to accomplish this, you click the joystick on the top toolbar of UnrealEd. Figure 2.15 illustrates the joystick icon.

Click the joystick on the UnrealEd —
tool bar to run your level.

Figure 2.15 The joystick icon runs the map.

When you first click the joystick icon, you'll see a dialog that proves important during your development efforts. This is the log window. The log window allows you to output messages to confirm operations in your code. As you can see in Figure 2.16, each line in the dialog informs you about the state of the build process. When you add your own code, you can include a call to the Log() function to output your own messages.

Figure 2.16 Log messages tell you about the state of the build.

Figure 2.17 shows you the map after it builds and is running. At this point, since you have made no changes in the map, it behaves just as it would if you were to start it from the default game. The point here is not to add anything to the game but only to go through the routine of accessing and running a map.

Figure 2.17 The jousting level requires a minimal period of time to compile before running.

If you are an experienced player of *Unreal Tournament*, you require no instructions about how to navigate within the game. If you are new to the game, here are the basics:

- To move forward, press the W key or use the arrow key.
- To navigate, move the mouse to the left or right.
- To fire a gun, press the left or right mouse button.
- To exit the game, press Esc.
- The joust involves going down the hall, grabbing the flag, and then returning to your base.
- To get help, press Esc and then click Help.

Note

Running a map involves making it operate for testing or play. This differs from building and compiling. When you build a map, you command the compiler to assemble its code and other assets for compiling. When you compile a map, you tell the compiler to take the code and translate it into the core language of the game engine. When you run your map, you must first build and compile it. If you have made no changes, then you do not need to compile or build your map. You can just run it.

Adjusting Resolution

You are probably thoroughly familiar with setting the resolution for your game. For programming purposes, it is essential to be fairly specific about how you want to display maps to ensure that you can proceed with your development activities without long delays. One approach to this is to reduce the size and resolution of the map display. Toward this end, after you have the CTF-1on1-Joust.ut2 map running, press the Esc key. As you know if you are an experienced player of *Unreal Tournament*, you then see the Configuration window, as shown in Figure 2.18.

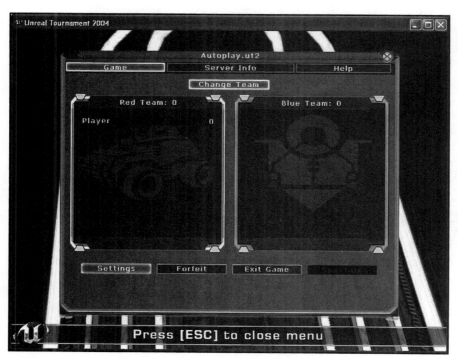

Figure 2.18 Press the Esc key and then click Settings.

In the Configuration window, click the Settings option. This opens the Settings window. In the Settings window, click the Display tab, as shown in Figure 2.19. In the Resolution pane, change or confirm the following settings:

- Set the Resolution field to 800 × 600. To accomplish this, click the drop-down arrow for the field and select the resolution. When the Confirmation dialog appears, click Keep Settings.

- If the Full Screen checkbox is checked, uncheck it. If it is not checked, as shown in Figure 2.19, leave it unchecked. If you have made changes, when the Confirmation dialog appears, Click Keep settings.

- When you finish changing your settings, click Back and then press the Esc key. This returns you to your game.

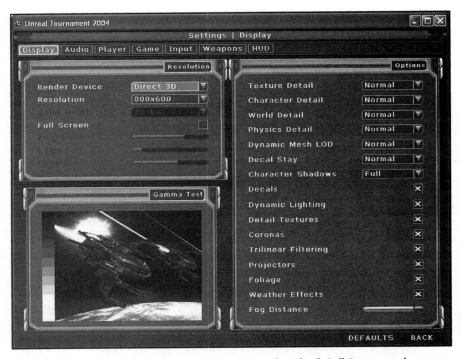

Figure 2.19 Set your resolution to 800 × 600 and uncheck Full Screen so that you can more easily test your work.

Closing a Map and Exiting the Editor

As you proceed in this book, you will often first save one of the maps provided with the game under a name you use for development purposes and then modify the map to accord with your programming projects. In other instances, you create your own maps and add them to the game. In this case, you have not made any changes to the CTF-1on1-Joust.ut2 map, and you want to exit it without saving any changes that might have occurred accidentally.

As you know, to exit the game, you press Esc. You then see the Autoplay dialog. To exit the play session, click Exit Game. You then click Yes in response to the Are you sure you want to quit? dialog. When you are working with UnrealEd, you do not exit everything at this point. You merely return to the editor.

It remains for you to now close out of the map completely. Here are two options:

- To close the map so that you can start developing your own map, select File > New. This action clears the viewports and displays a "blank" map.
- To close the map and exit UnrealEd, select File > Exit.

For these options, if you have made any changes to the map, a dialog queries whether you want to save your changes. Unless you are working with a level that you have saved to a custom name or created for yourself, always click No.

It is certainly the case that you can customize the game and then play it. People do this all the time. Changing a default level of the game so that it provides customized features is what mod development is all about. However, for present purposes, your goal is not to change the default game. Instead, it is to acquaint yourself with a few primary modification activities. After you have acquainted yourself with these activities, you can then proceed to modify integral parts of the game.

Conclusion

This chapter has provided a rundown of some of the topics you explore in depth in chapters to come. In other instances, it has provided a review of a few basic activities you perform every time you conduct a modification session using UnrealEd. Key notions here are that you open a map. You can work with a map under the name you find in the default game configuration, but for learning purposes, you should always rename the maps you work with to avoid problems. In the next chapter, you proceed in this direction. In this chapter, your efforts have been confined to just opening a map and exploring it in the viewports.

An important dialog in UnrealEd is the browser dialog. You can invoke this dialog in a number of ways. It is important enough that when you open a level, it automatically appears in your work area. You can change browsers by clicking browser tabs in the dialog, or you can select browsers from the View menu of UnrealEd. In addition, the toolbar icon allows you to access browsers.

Navigating through a map in UnrealEd provides you work with 2D and 3D viewports of the map. The two types of viewports require different procedures for navigation, but you can master these after a brief period of experimentation. The primary movements in the 2D viewports involve vertical and horizontal movements. The primary movements in the 3D viewports are more complex, involving rotation in addition to horizontal movements.

At the center of much that follows in this book is the notion that you can use math to generate data that you then use to create the events of your game.

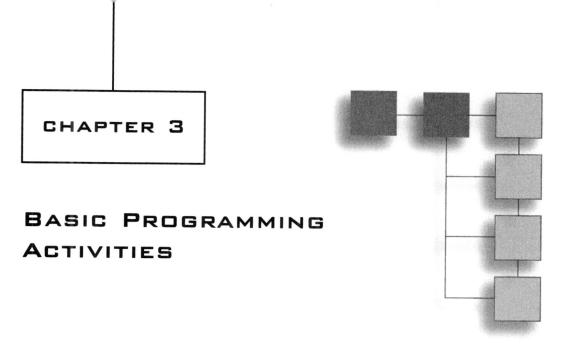

CHAPTER 3

BASIC PROGRAMMING ACTIVITIES

In this chapter, you write your first program to modify a level in Unreal Tournament. To perform this work, you first review a few basics. Among the basics are notions such as classes, base classes, derived classes, and the properties of classes. Given an understanding of these basics, you then examine a few of the classes in the Actor class hierarchy. The Emitter and Light classes are among these classes. For your project you also investigate the Trigger class. This class proves important because you derive a class you create, HelloWorldTrigger, from it. To accomplish this deed, you work with the Actor Class Browser and the code editing window. Using these tools allows you to learn a few things about class signature lines, member variables of classes, and member functions of classes. You also learn how to create and work with a package called HelloWorld. In the end, you can play the level you worked with in the last chapter and see an event that you program become part of the action. Here are a few of the topics covered in this chapter:

- Adjusting UnrealEd so you can more easily write code
- Understanding basics of properties and classes
- Deriving one class from another
- Writing a classical program, HelloWorld
- Compiling and executing your class
- Editing and recompiling code

Starting Points for Writing Code

When you work with Unreal Tournament, you have a number of options open before you. Among other things, you can create your own level and then add features to it, or you can begin with a level and modify the elements it contains. Creating a level from scratch involves a fairly extended body of work, so if you are just starting out and want to see quick programming results, a good course of action is to use an existing level and change a few of its features. Given this beginning, you can then expand your work so that you can explore a wider number of options.

For starters, open the CTF-1on1-Joust.ut2 map. Chapter 2 provides specific details about how to locate, open, and navigate through the map. Consult that chapter if you need a review.

To open the map, select File > Open. You see the Open dialog, as shown in Figure 3.1. Click the View Menu icon on the right to display the details of files. Scroll down the list until you find the CTF-1on1-Joust.ut2 map. Select this map and click Open.

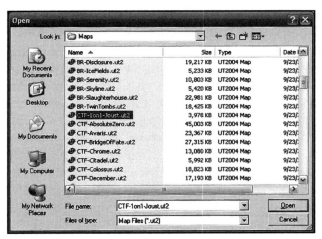

Figure 3.1 Select the 1-on-1 joust map and click Open.

To make it so that you have more flexibility as you work with the viewports, select View > Viewports > Floating. This allows you to view adjustable windows in UnrealEd. Take a moment to resize the windows until they appear approximately as shown in Figure 3.2.

Now enlarge and position the orthogonal viewport as shown in Figure 3.3. You can accomplish such tasks by positioning the cursor on the upper-left corner and clicking the left mouse button. If you click on the title bar of the viewport, you can move it.

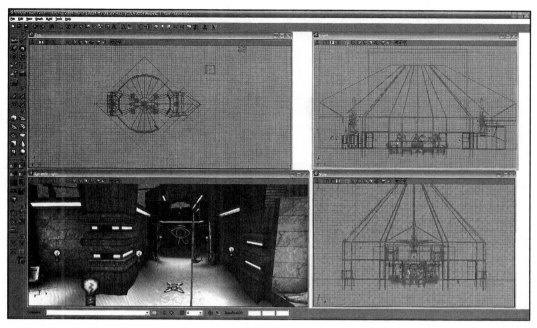

Figure 3.2 Set your viewports to floating to make them easier to work with.

Figure 3.3 Resize the viewport and face the statue from the long hall.

After you have positioned and resized your viewports as shown in Figure 3.3, click the second cube from the right on the task bar for the orthogonal viewport, as shown in Figure 3.4. This action changes the mode of the viewport so that it shows Texture Usage. This mode of viewing allows you to more easily see a few of the entities in the level.

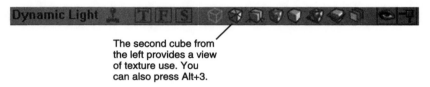

The second cube from the left provides a view of texture use. You can also press Alt+3.

Figure 3.4 Changing the mode to Texture Usage allows you to more easily see what is in the map.

After you have changed the mode of the view of the viewport to Texture Usage, adjust your view until you are facing the statue of Anubis that rests behind the blue flag (as shown in Figure 3.5). You face the statue of Anubis from the long hall of the map. Back away a short distance so that you see the flag and its base. Seven lightbulbs are in the lower part of the map. At the top, you see two smaller, bluish lightbulbs. Just beneath the two bluish lightbulbs at the top, you see a collection of spheres of different colors.

Figure 3.5 Position your view so that you see the statue of Anubis in the Texture Usage mode.

Properties

A property of an entity is something that you can alter to change the entity. Consider a pencil, for example. You can tell one pencil from another by naming the color of its lead. The color of the lead is a property of a pencil. What applies to pencils applies to almost everything you find in a map in Unreal Tournament.

To see how this is so, move your mouse cursor until it is directly over the lightbulb icon in the right front, as shown in Figure 3.5. Select the lightbulb by clicking the left mouse button. Then click the right mouse button. A Light Properties dialog appears, as shown in Figure 3.6.

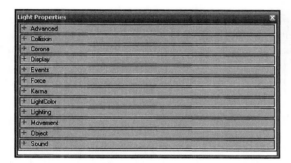

Figure 3.6 A properties dialog identifies actions and values you can designate for a given entity.

A properties dialog exists for almost every entity in a map. When you speak in terms of programming, another term for entity is *object*. The lightbulb icon represents an object. An object is an instance of a *class*. A class is a program that creates a pattern for objects. You can use this program to create many different objects. Each lightbulb represents an object of the Light class.

You see the title Light Properties in the title bar of the properties dialog because the dialog tells you about features of the program that define the Light class. Another term for code that creates a property is *member variable*. You do not see the code for the Light class when you view the Light Properties dialog. The properties dialog only represents the code.

It also sorts the properties into a set of trays. For each tray, there are usually two or more properties. The list for any given tray can be fairly extensive. To see how this is so, click on the tray called Lighting. As Figure 3.7 illustrates, the Lighting tray contains properties that allow you to regulate such things as whether the light blinks, how far its luminosity reaches, and whether it casts shadows. The terms you see that begin with "b" or "LT" directly define what you see in the code for the Light class. These are values you use to directly or indirectly define the properties of the Light class.

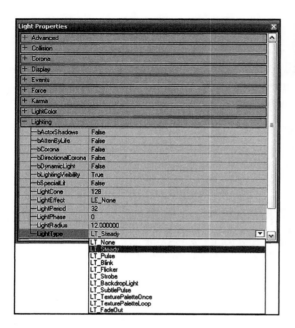

Figure 3.7 Each tray of the properties dialog reveals two or more properties.

To close the properties dialog, click the red control button in the upper-right corner. In the orthogonal viewport, position your cursor on the base of the blue flag and click the left mouse button. You see a StaticMeshActor Properties dialog. As with the Light Properties dialog, this dialog represents the properties of a class. In this case, the class is the class that creates the base of the flag. Its name is StaticMeshActor. The trays of the dialog provide you access to specific properties of the class. As with the properties dialog for the Light class object, each tray might contain a number of properties.

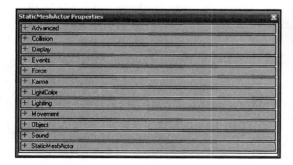

Figure 3.8 A properties dialog exists for the base of the flag, which is an object of the StaticMeshActor class.

Deriving Properties

If you click on the Lighting tray of the StaticMeshActor class, as Figure 3.8 shows, you see many of the properties you saw with the Light class properties dialog. This is so because both the Light and StaticMeshActor classes are *derived* from a common *base class*. The base class is named Actor. The classes are all part of a hierarchy of classes. In this hierarchy, Light and StaticMeshActor are both derived from Actor, and so are all the other classes you work with in this book.

When you derive one class from another, you reuse code. How this happens is discussed extensively in the chapters to come, but for now it is enough to concentrate on the few details Figure 3.9 provides. The Actor class is the base class. The two other classes are the derived classes.

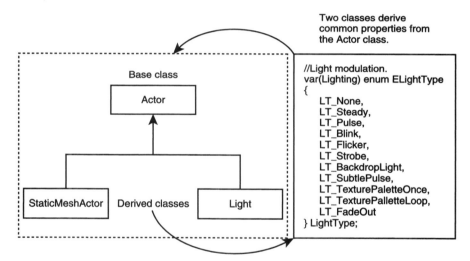

Figure 3.9 Properties are defined in the code for a class.

In the gray box to the side in the figure, you see a small portion of the code you can find in the Actor class. This code sets up the values you can assign to the LightType property. Because these values are defined in the base class (Actor), you can make use of them in all the classes derived from the base class. This applies to dozens of derived classes. Understanding this is at the heart of working with UnrealScript and the Unreal Tournament class hierarchy.

With reference to the sample of UnrealScript code in Figure 3.9, as mentioned before, the code is taken from the Actor class. This code defines values for one of the LightType properties. The mechanism in the code used to define the values is called an *enumeration*.

Discussion of enumerations occurs later in the book. For now, as Figure 3.10 illustrates, it is enough to know that the values acceptable for the LightType property are created using an enumeration in the base class. The Light and StaticMeshActor classes are derived from this class, and this is why you see the same values in the properties dialogs for the Light and StaticMeshActor classes (see Figures 3.7 and 3.10). The two derived classes reuse the code in the base class. Such is the nature of a class hierarchy.

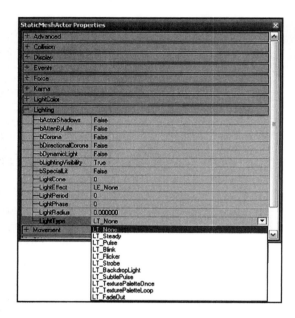

Figure 3.10 A common class, Actor, provides you with a definition of the LightType property.

Class Objects and Distinct Properties

When you create an object, the object is of the type of the class you use to create it. In this respect, then, in the scene you see in Figure 3.5, there are nine objects of the Light type. The base of the flag is an object of the StaticMeshActor type. If you click on the pillars, you find that they are also of the StaticMeshActor type, as is the statue of Anubis. If you click on the flagpole, you find that it is of the xBlueFlagBase class.

If you move up to the top of the two pillars that stand at the arms of the statue of Anubis, you find clusters of orbs. These are objects of the Emitter class. "Emitter" is short for *particle emitter*. You use particle emitters to spray particles at greater or lesser intensities and distances from a given point.

To review activities in Chapter 2, to build and run the map, click the build icon on the main menu and then position yourself in the level so that you are looking at the blue state of Anubis, as shown in Figure 3.11. You see that on the pillars on either side of the blue Anubis statue, emitters are at work creating glowing fields of light.

Figure 3.11 Objects have common properties, but each object maintains its own set of values for its properties.

Emitter objects produce fluctuating clouds atop the pillars on either side of the statue of Anubis. You see changing colors because each Emitter class object possesses its own set of properties. You can add dozens of Emitter objects, each defined with different values for its properties.

All the objects of a given class share the same properties. On the other hand, you can define the properties for each object you create so that property values are unique. This notion is extremely important in the context of object-oriented programming and receives extended discussion in a later chapter.

Programming Hello World

Given the discussion concerning classes, objects, and properties, you are now in a good position to write your first body of code for Unreal Tournament. You can write code to derive your own class. You can create one or more objects of your class. You can define the properties for each of your objects so that its values are distinct. Specifically, you can derive a class from the Trigger class. Then you can use one of its properties, Message, to print text to the screen at given moments in your game play. The text that shows allows you to initiate your coding work according to a revered programming tradition. This tradition calls on you to write a short program that prints "Hello World!"

Classes, Packages, and Renaming Your Map

To write code that you use to control objects in a map, you create a class. The class you create is stored in a package. The package is stored in a special directory. You can access it at any time to modify the classes in it or to add new classes to it.

That is the coding part. The other part pertains to the map. When you create class objects, you place them in a map. When you do this, you alter the map in expected and unexpected ways. Since at this point it is important to be able to preserve the default behavior of Unreal Tournament as much as possible, prior to starting your coding effort, you should save the map you are working with under a name that differs from its default name.

If you have been working with it in the previous sections, the CTF-1on1-Joust.ut2 map is still open. If you have not yet opened it, do so now.

To save this map under a new name, select File > Save As. You see the Save As dialog, as shown in Figure 3.12. In the File name field, type HelloWorld.ut2. Then click Save. After the save operation concludes, you see the title of your newly renamed map in the title bar of UnrealEd.

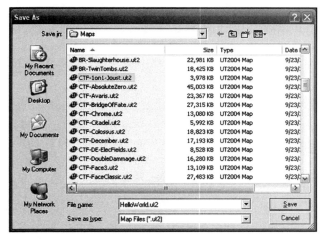

Figure 3.12 Save your map under a unique name.

Trigger Generalities

You have already dealt with such classes as StaticMeshActor, Light, and Emitter. To implement your code for your HelloWorld map, you add an object of yet another class, Trigger. You do not use this class directly, however. Instead, you derive a class from it, in much the same way as the Light and StaticMeshActor classes are derived from the Actor class.

Like the other classes you have dealt with so far, the Trigger class is derived from the Actor class. Unlike other classes, the Trigger class does not provide you with an effect that you can see. Instead, a Trigger object involves an event. The event can involve something you can see. In this respect, a Trigger object works in two ways. In the first way, the object makes it so that some object other than itself changes. For example, a Trigger object can change a Light object. In the second fashion, the Trigger object can itself embody an event.

In the Hello World program, you use the second approach. You tell the Trigger object to produce an effect when the player avatar collides with it. As mentioned previously, the effect consists of issuing a message, "Hello World!". You see this message in the chat field each time the player avatar's movements in the game activate the Trigger object.

The Actor Class Browser

As you saw in Chapter 2, the browser dialog provides you with access to a number of browsers. Each browser is in fact just a tab in a dialog. One of these is for Actor Classes. As mentioned earlier, Actor Classes are the classes in the Unreal Tournament class hierarchy that are derived from the Actor class. These classes are so numerous and important that they merit their own browser.

The Actor Class Browser allows you to perform three important tasks. The first is to create new classes by deriving them from a class in the Actor class hierarchy. Another is to allow you to create packages in which to place your new classes. The third is to allow you to invoke the code editing window. In the code editing window, you code and test your classes. In addition, the Actor Class Browser provides a few menu options that allow you to perform tasks like accessing previously developed classes and packages and saving the new classes and packages that you develop.

To view the Actor Class Browser, select View > Show Actor Class Browser. The browser dialog appears; it should be familiar now from your work in Chapter 2. As Figure 3.13 illustrates, the Actor Class tab displays two fields when you first open it. The top field lists the classes derived from the Actor class. The list is extensive. The bottom field lists all the *packages* that contain these classes.

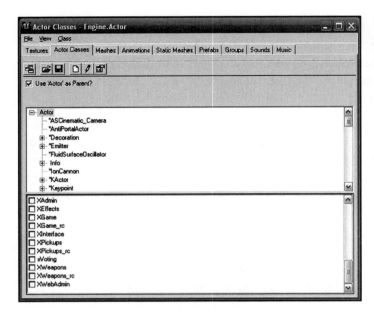

Figure 3.13 The top field displays the classes derived from the Actor class.

A package is analogous to a directory. Among other things, a package allows you to store the code you create for a given map in one place. It also allows you to group together many classes that work together to provide an event to any number of maps. Any class you develop must be contained by a class, so you must either create a package when you create a new class or add the class you create to an existing package.

To show that a given package contains a given class, you join the name of the class to the name of the package with a period. The class you are about to create is named HelloWorldTrigger. It is in the HelloWorld package. To indicate that the HelloWorldTrigger class is in the HelloWorld package, you type HelloWorld.HelloWorldTrigger. This convention proves important as the complexity of your programming projects grows and you begin to create different packages, each of which might contain several classes. In some cases, the classes in the different packages have the same names. You can access them and distinguish them without problems using the "fully qualified" package name.

Deriving a Class and Creating a Package

Your mission in the current context is to create a class called HelloWorldTrigger. You must also create a package for this class, HelloWorld. To proceed with this work, you use the Actor Class Browser to derive your class from the Trigger class. The Trigger class is derived from the Actor class.

To start this activity, if you have not done so, from the UnrealEd main menu, select View Actor Class Browser.

In the Actor Class Browser, select View from the main menu and then uncheck the Show Packages item. You then see only the field containing the names of classes derived from the Actor class, as shown in Figure 3.14.

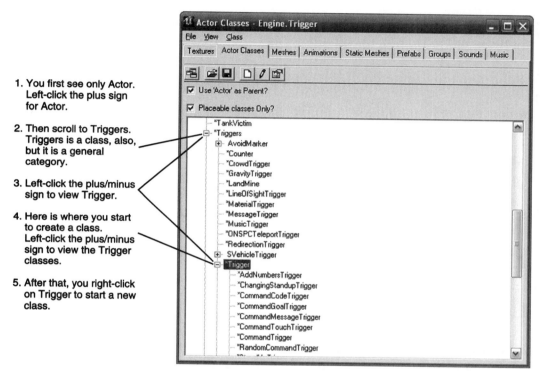

1. You first see only Actor. Left-click the plus sign for Actor.

2. Then scroll to Triggers. Triggers is a class, also, but it is a general category.

3. Left-click the plus/minus sign to view Trigger.

4. Here is where you start to create a class. Left-click the plus/minus sign to view the Trigger classes.

5. After that, you right-click on Trigger to start a new class.

Figure 3.14 The Trigger class is found in the Triggers category of classes.

In addition to changing the appearance of the tab so that you see only class names, as shown in Figure 3.14, verify that the checkbox for the Use 'Actor' as Parent? field has been checked. If it is not checked, then click to check it.

Then scroll down until you see Triggers. After that, scroll a little more until you see the Trigger class. Triggers is a category of classes. Trigger is a class.

To derive a class from the Trigger class, right-click on the Trigger class. As shown in Figure 3.15, you'll see a popup dialog. In this dialog, select New.

After you select New, you see the New Class dialog, shown in Figure 3.16. In the Package field of the New Class dialog, type HelloWorld. In the Name field, type the name of the class you want to create, HelloWorldTrigger. Then click OK.

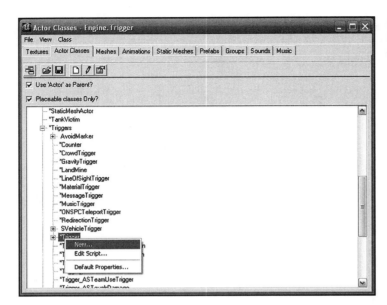

Figure 3.15 Select New from the popup dialog.

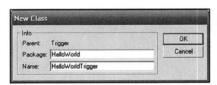

Figure 3.16 Name the package and the class in the dialog box.

As soon as you click OK in the New Class dialog, you see the UnrealEd code editor. Figure 3.17 illustrates the editor. The title bar identifies the class and package you are creating: HelloWorld.HelloWorldTrigger. The blue pane on the right of the window provides you with an area in which to type your code. The white pane on the left of the window provides you with names of any classes you visit when you click on the list of classes in the Actor Class Browser. In Figure 3.17, three classes have been clicked on at some point:

- **Actor.** The Actor class is the primary class in your class hierarchy. Click Actor in the left pane to view the code for the Actor class. If you do not see Actor, then momentarily activate the Actor Class Browser, scroll to the top of the class list, and click Actor. Then click Actor in the code editing window. In this way, you can visit the code for any number of classes. For the Actor class, use the code editor window scroll bar to scroll through the class. As you can see, the code is extensive. Do not try to change the code.

- **Trigger.** The Trigger class is derived from the Actor class. You derive your class from the Trigger class. Click on the Trigger item to view the code for the Trigger class. Use the scroll bar that appears with the code to scroll through the code. Do not try to change the code.

- **HelloWorldTrigger.** HelloWorldTrigger identifies the class you are creating. Click on the HelloWorldTrigger item to activate the code editing window for this class. As shown in Figure 3.17, when you click on this item, the blue area becomes an active editor.

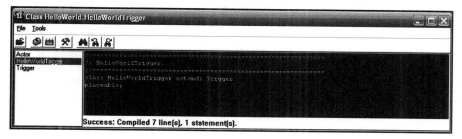

Figure 3.17 The code editor allows you to view and edit code for base and derived classes.

Comments for Code

The Actor Class Browser generates a few lines of code automatically. As Figure 3.17 illustrates, you see the following lines:

```
//==========================================
// HelloWorldTrigger.
//==========================================
class HelloWorldTrigger extends Trigger
  placeable;
```

Regardless of what class you start with, you see roughly the same set of lines. The three top lines are comments. You include comments in your program for your information only. The compiler ignores comments. To indicate that you want the compiler to read a line of code as a comment, you use one of two approaches. You can begin the line with two forward slashes at the start of the line, as is the case with the code in Figure 3.17.

You can also create comments by using a forward slash and an asterisk. In this case, you can comment out several successive lines or a term within a line. This form of comment requires beginning and ending characters. Here is an example:

```
/*
  Here are a few commented lines
  of code
*/
```

You should always comment your code. While styles of comments differ, it is generally a good idea to write complete statements. Programmers often capitalize the first word of a statement. They often do not include a period if the statement consists of only one sentence.

Compiling or Checking Your Syntax

As a general rule, at least when you are first setting out on a coding project, always establish a firm starting point by performing what is known as a *sanity check*. A sanity check allows you to know whether your compiler and the primary set of code you are working with compile correctly. Toward this end, click the second icon from the right on the code editor. Refer to Figure 3.18.

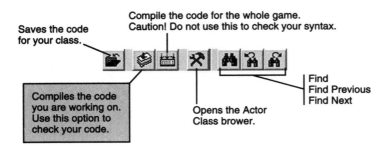

Figure 3.18 The second icon from the right allows you to check your syntax.

The term *syntax* refers to anything you include in a file. As a general rule, it is a good practice to check your syntax after adding a few lines of code. Avoid the practice of typing many lines and then trying to discover what is wrong. If you type a few lines and then compile, you can more easily discover the problems with your code.

If your code contains an error, then the compiler generates an error message. When you click the second icon in from the left in the code editor, the code that is automatically generated contains no errors, so you see a message similar to the one shown in Figure 3.19.

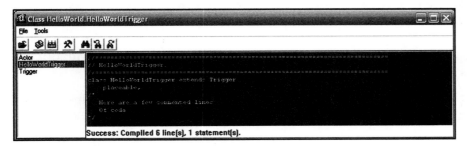

Figure 3.19 Click the compile icon and see whether your code contains syntax errors.

On the other hand, if the syntax of your code contains defects, then you see an error message. In Figure 3.20, to create an error message, the code sample omits the closing syntax for the comment.

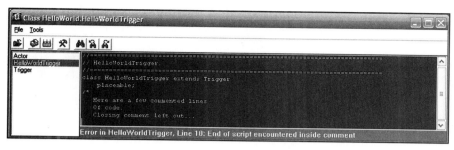

Figure 3.20 An error report tells you that your code contains a syntax error.

Error messages are often cryptic at first. However, after you work with a given programming language for a while, you usually get so you can tell what messages refer to. In Figure 3.20, for example, you see this error message:

```
Error in HelloWorldTrigger, Line10: End of script encountered inside comment
```

If you reason a little, you can discern the meaning. If a script (your program) ends inside a comment, then the comment must not be correctly terminated. A comment has a beginning and an end, and it occurs inside of a script. It must be the case that you have not properly terminated your comment. That is, indeed, what has happened.

Note

The message also provides a line number. This bit of information is useful in some ways. Unfortunately, the editor does not provide you a way to go to the line number. If you become desperate while working on a long script, highlight your code, use Control + V to copy it to the Windows clipboard, and then paste it into Notepad. You can then select Edit > Go to find the line using the line number. When you use this approach, highlight the code in Notepad and format it so that it is of the Courier New font and 12 points in size. This way, you can paste it back into the code editing window of UnrealEd.

Signature Lines

After the comments that introduce your new class, you see the code that creates the class. This is known as the *signature line* of the class. In Figure 3.17, you see two lines of code for the signature line. These lines could also be shown as one line:

```
//Class signature line
class HelloWorldTrigger extends Trigger placeable;
```

The signature line is a statement. A statement is a unit of syntax that you terminate with a semicolon. You can continue a statement over several lines, but if you do not include the terminating semicolon, the compiler issues an error.

The signature line of your class should be the first line of active code. You can precede the signature line with comments.

The first term in the line is class. This is a keyword. A keyword is a word that is reserved as a feature of the syntax of a programming language. When you use the class keyword, the word immediately following it is the name of your class, in this case, as you know, HelloWorldTrigger.

The next term, extends, proves fairly complicated to fully explain, but generally it is the key term involved in deriving one class from another. Like class, it is a keyword of the UnrealScript programming language. When you derive your class from the Trigger class, you *extend* the Trigger class. When you extend something, you add features to what is already there. That is precisely what deriving one class from another involves.

The term Trigger should be pretty clear by now. That is the name of your immediate base class. You derive HelloWorldTrigger from the base class Trigger. The Trigger class, to repeat previous observations, is in turn derived from the Actor class.

The final term in the signature line is also an UnrealScript keyword. The keyword placeable defines your class so that you place it in the game.

Defining a Class

When you type the code for a class, you *define* a class. As you have read in previous sections, you might also refer to such activity as the *implementation* of a class. The terms are synonymous in many ways, but as subsequent chapters reveal, to implement code generally involves about anything you do as a programmer. When you define a class or a part of a class, however, you perform a fairly specific set of actions. This receives more discussion later on. For present purposes, however, either term works.

When you define a class, you start with a signature line, as the previous section detailed. What you type after the signature line of the class becomes part of the class. You develop only one class in a given file. In the current context, the blue pane is a single file. As mentioned before, you can have an unlimited number of classes in a package.

To implement your HelloWorldTrigger class, first click the compile icon to perform a sanity check on your syntax. (Remember, the compile icon is the second icon in from the left. See Figure 3.18.)

Next, click in the blue pane, press Enter to set the cursor on a new line. Add the new code given in the following code sample. Figure 3.21 illustrates the appearance of the text pane after you enter your code.

```
//══════════════════════════════════════════════════
// HelloWorldTrigger.
//══════════════════════════════════════════════════
class HelloWorldTrigger extends Trigger placeable;
    //#1
    //Override a function from the parent class
    function PostBeginPlay(){
        //#2
        //Call a function from the parent class
        Super.PostBeginPlay();
        //#3
        //Assign a value to a member variable of the parent class
        Message = "Hello World!";
    }
```

Note

Beginner's point. Compile periodically as you go. Work line by line, but before you type the lines following comments #2 and #3, type the shell of the function that contains them. These lines are as follows:

```
Function PostBeginPlay(){
}
```

The opening and closing curly braces create a syntactical unit, so you need both of them if you are not to create a compiler error. Type this shell, compile to check your syntax, and then add the lines that go between the curly braces.

In the line trailing comment #1, you create a *function*. More remains to be said about this in subsequent chapters. For the present context, note that the term `function` is an UnrealScript keyword. `PostBeginPlay()` is the name of a function. In this instance, the function is one that you can find in a base class. You redefine (*override*) it in the current class. This topic receives much more attention later on.

At comment #2, you call a function from a base class. The `Super` keyword allows you to do this. You can call a function from a base class if the function you call is defined in the base class in a way that allows you to call it. A function defined in this way is said to be part of the *interface* of the base class. This is a key feature of object-oriented programming, and you can read much more about this, once again, later on.

The `PostBeginPlay()` function attends to a number of setup activities for your trigger. It makes it so that when your player avatar collides with your `HelloWorldTrigger` object, the event you anticipate can take place.

In the lines following comment #2, you once again make use of a feature of the base class. In this case, you are using a property. If you are thinking about the earlier discussion in this chapter, you are right on target. In this instance, instead of using the Properties dialog, you perform your work directly within your code.

Message is the name of the property. As a programmer, as mentioned previously, you can refer to such a property as a member variable. The equals sign is known as an *assignment operator*. You assign the expression "Hello World!" to the member variable Message. When you assign the expression to this member variable, you can then retrieve it later on. In this instance, the game retrieves the expression, allowing you to print it over and over again whenever a collision event occurs.

Figure 3.21 Type the code for your HelloWorldTrigger class and compile often.

Saving and Adding Your Class and Package

After you type the code shown in Figure 3.21, you must save your work. To save your work, first compile your HelloWorldTrigger class one more time and confirm that the compiler issues a Success message similar to the message Figure 3.21 illustrates.

Then, select View > Show Packages in the Actor Class Browser. You see the lower field of the Actor Class Browser. Scroll until you see the HelloWorld package. Put a checkmark next to HelloWorld, as shown in Figure 3.22.

After that, select File > Save Selected Packages. This saves the package and in the process your file. However, at this point, you have not yet completely saved your work. Proceed to the next section.

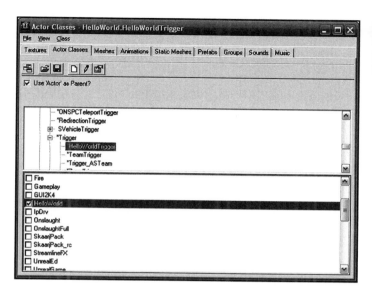

Figure 3.22 After clicking to put a checkmark next to HelloWorld, select File > Save Selected Packages.

Note

Do not close out of your map prior to placing an object of your newly created class in your map. If you do so, then UnrealEd does not save the work you have done to create the package and the class. It will be necessary for you to start over.

Placing a HelloWorldTrigger Object in Your Map

In the previous sections, you created and saved a class and a package for the HelloWorldTrigger class. It remains, however, that if you do not place an object of the class you have created in your HelloWorld map, when you close your map, UnrealEd does not save your work.

For this reason, you must now add an object of the HelloWorldTrigger class to your map. When you place an object of the type HelloWorldTrigger class in your map, you create an *instance* of your class. An object is an instance of a class.

At this point, to make the HelloWorld map visible, click in the orthogonal viewport of UnrealEd. (This viewport is shown in Figure 3.5.)

Now click the Actor Class Browser to activate it. Scroll to your HelloWorld package in the lower pane, as shown in Figure 3.23. Click HelloWorld. (Do not click the checkbox.)

Then in the upper pane, navigate to Triggers > Trigger > HelloWorldTrigger and click HelloWorldTrigger.

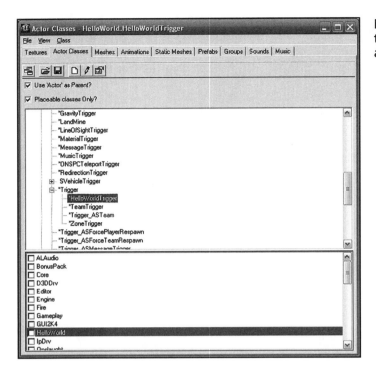

Figure 3.23 Select the class you want to add to your map.

Now move to the orthogonal viewport of your map. As before, position yourself so that you are facing the blue statue of Anubis. Click on the second icon from the left in the toolbar to change the mode of the viewport to BSP. See Figure 3.24.

Just in front of the right foot of the statue of Anubis, right-click. As shown in Figure 3.25, this action opens a dialog. Toward the top of the dialog, you see an option that reads "Add HelloWorldTrigger Here". Select this option. An instance of your HelloWorldTrigger class appears in your map.

As Figure 3.26 shows, the instance of your HelloWorldTrigger class is represented by a box with a switch. This icon represents any object of any class you derive from the Trigger class.

Note

To adjust the position of the icon that represents your HelloWorldTrigger object, first click on the icon itself. To move it forward or backward, first click on the icon. Then press the Shift key and click and hold the *left* mouse key button. Move up or down and the icon will move forward or backward. To move the icon left or right, first click the icon. Then press the Shift key and click and hold the *right* mouse key button. Move left or right.

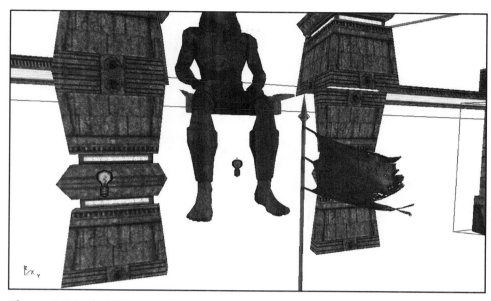

Figure 3.24 The BSP mode allows you to see icons more clearly.

Surface Properties (2 Selected)	F5
Edit	▶
Add HelloWorldTrigger Here	
Add Static Mesh: '2k4ChargerMeshes.ChargerMeshes.HealthChargerMESH-D5'	
Add Path Node Here	
Add Player Start Here	
Add Light Here	
Select Surfaces	▶
Select All Surfaces	Shift+S
Select None	Shift+Z
Extrude	▶
Bevel...	
Apply Texture	
Reset	

Figure 3.25 Place an instance of the `HelloWorldTrigger` class in your map.

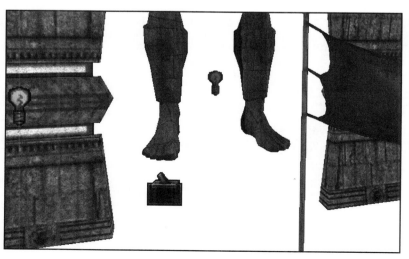

Figure 3.26 A box with a switch serves to identify all triggers.

Trigger Property Settings

The icon representing your HelloWorldTrigger object is now in your HelloWorld map. It rests just in front of the statue's right foot. To view the properties dialog for your newly created class, left click the trigger icon to open the properties dialog.

Besides confirming the existence of your class, you can also check one of its properties. The property you want to check determines whether the trigger can be activated by a collision event. As Figure 3.27 illustrates, to find this property, click the Collision tray. Verify that the corresponding value for bCollideActors is set to True.

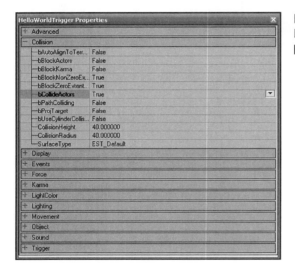

Figure 3.27 Set the bCollideActors property to True.

After you have verified the bCollideActors property is set to True, close the HelloWorldTrigger Properties window.

At this point, to save your work, from the UnrealEd top menu, select File > Save.

At this point, you can close the Actor Class Browser and the code editing window for your class.

Compiling and Testing Your Code

You have developed a class and positioned an object of your class in the HelloWorld map. Now you can test the performance of the object. To accomplish this task, click the Play Map! icon on the main UnrealEd toolbar. UnrealEd builds and compiles your map.

After the game is running, to invoke the HelloWorldTrigger event, navigate down the hallway to a position in front of the blue statue of Anubis. Approach the right foot of Anubis (the left foot as you face the statue). Move the gun back and forth. As you approach, after a few tries, you see the "Hello World!" message as shown in Figure 3.28.

Figure 3.28 As you approach the right foot of Anubis, you collide with your `HelloWorldTrigger` object and see the "Hello World!" message.

Editing Your Code

After you develop a body of code, you often return to it to add to it or modify it. To see how you can accomplish this task, assume that you want to add words to the message your class object issues. The new message reads "Hello World of Unreal Tournament."

There are several approaches to editing your code. One involves starting from the Actor Class Browser. This is the approach you are likely to use if you open UnrealEd for a new work session. The other involves working directly with a given class object in a way that does not require you to start from the Actor Class Browser. You are likely to use this approach if you have a work session started and are testing your code as you go.

Accessing Code from the Package

Suppose you are resuming a work session after closing out of UnrealEd. You want to access a class in a package you have created.

To use this approach, start by opening the Actor Class Browser.

Then in the Actor Class Browser, select File > Open Packages.

As Figure 3.29 shows, you see a list of *.u files. These are files that contain code for various packages. In this case, you see one called HelloWorld, which is the package you created. In this package is the HelloWorldTrigger class. Select the HelloWorld.u file and click Open.

Figure 3.29 The *.u file identifies code for packages.

After you click open in the Open Class Package dialog, the fields in the Actor Class Browser are refreshed. Click the Actor tree and navigate to the Trigger class and find HelloWorldTrigger. Then click HelloWorldTrigger to open the code editing window.

You can now enter new code for your class. Here is the altered version of the code:

```
//==============================
// HelloWorldTrigger.
//==============================
class HelloWorldTrigger extends Trigger placeable;
    //#1
    //Override a function from the parent class
    function PostBeginPlay(){

        //#2
        //Call a function from the parent class
        Super.PostBeginPlay();

        //#3
        //Assign a value to a member variable of the parent class
        Message = "Hello World of Unreal Tournament!";
    }
```

In this code, you alter only the last line, making the message "Hello World of Unreal Tournament!"

To check your syntax, click the second icon from the right, Compile Changed Scripts. After the script compiles, leave the code editing window open for now.

Then go to the lower field of the Actor Class Browser and click the checkbox next to the HelloWorld package. After that, select File > Save Selected Packages.

Since you have already placed an instance of the HelloWorldTrigger class in your HelloWorld map, you can immediately test your work. To do so, click the compile icon in the toolbar of UnrealEd. Your map compiles and executes with the new version of your code. Play the level and invoke the action. As Figure 3.30 illustrates, you see your new message.

Figure 3.30 Your changes create a new message.

Editing Starting with the Icon

Suppose that you are intensely involved in your map development and spot something you want to fix immediately, without fussing around with the Actor Class Browser. To accomplish this, you need only to find the icon for the class that you want to edit and right-click on it.

Toward this end, find the icon for your HelloWorldTrigger class in your HelloWorld map. Right-click on it. As Figure 3.31 illustrates, this opens a dialog. Toward the bottom of the dialog you find the Edit Script option.

When you select this option, the Actor Class Browser and the code editing window open. Use the same approach you used in the previous section to alter your code. First, edit and

Figure 3.31 Click with the right mouse button on the `HelloWorldTrigger` object and select Edit Script.

compile the code using the second icon from the right in the code editing window, Compile Changed Scripts. In this instance, you might change the text to "You have violated Anubis's sanctity. Back off!!!"

After you alter and compile the code, check the `HelloWorld` package and select File > Save Selected Packages. You can then recompile the map to see your changes.

Conclusion

If you are new to programming and UnrealEd, then this chapter might have struck you as something along the lines of a whirlwind tour of a fairly complex game editing environment. That is largely what it was. In this chapter you explored notions that involved both programming and using the editor. Working in both worlds might seem a little daunting, but the more you learn, the more you *can* learn. Essential programming concepts in this chapter included those of deriving one class from another, defining a class, and working with member functions and variables. You also used the Actor Class Browser and the code editing window. You developed a class called `HelloWorldTrigger`, which you placed in a package called `HelloWorld`.

The work you have performed has been fairly limited, but at the same time, it provides a powerful beginning. When you derive one class from another, you begin an activity that underlies everything you do when you work with the Unreal Tournament class hierarchy. UnrealScript and the fairly vast collection of classes allow you to do almost anything you want to do, but in every instance, to reach this power, you must first derive your class from a base class. In this chapter, you dealt only with the `Trigger` class. You can now begin work on many other classes.

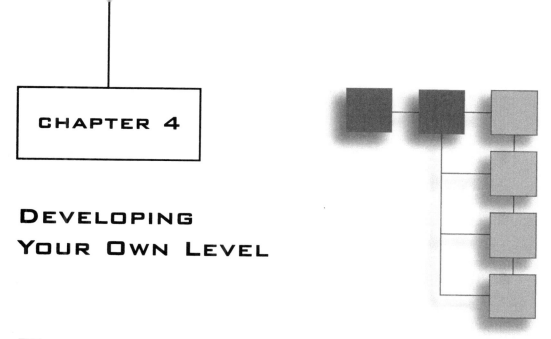

CHAPTER 4

DEVELOPING
YOUR OWN LEVEL

In this chapter, you follow a path that diverges from the path you followed in Chapter 3. In this chapter, you create a level from scratch. The level you create remains simple, consisting of a cube that you define with Light, Trigger, and PlayerStart objects. This simple scenario allows you to further expand your skills, so that you see the essential elements of a level and how you build activities necessary as you add lighting or geometry to a level. You work with a cube brush (or pattern) to add a geometric form to a level. You also work with a sheet object. You then add textures to the geometric forms, and these give your level a theme. Here are a few of the topics covered:

- Adding a cube to a level to create a chamber
- Selecting a texture package
- Applying textures to different surfaces
- Using a sheet entity to create a floor tile
- Adding PlayerStart and Light objects
- Specializing a Trigger object and placing it in your level

Creating a Working Area

In the last chapter, you worked with the CTF-1on1-Joust.ut2 and added a trigger. In this chapter, you follow a different approach, one that involves creating a work area from scratch. Toward this end, you create a cubic area.

To create a cubic work area, select File > New from the main menu of UnrealEd. UnrealEd refreshes the viewports so that you see only the basic grid features. Then select File > Save and save the new map as Ch04Area. Figure 4.1 illustrates the situation at hand.

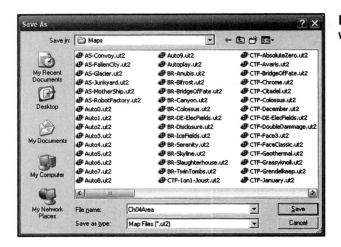

Figure 4.1 Save your work as Ch04Area.

If you do not see the four viewports, from the main menu of UnrealEd, select View > Viewport > Configure. Then select the option on the left. This displays the three 2D viewports and the Dynamic Lighting viewport.

Now you add a cubic area (a room) to your map. To create a cubic work area, right-click on the Cube Brush icon in the brush primitive area of the toolbox on the left margin of the UnrealEd window. Figure 4.2 illustrates the brush primitive area and the Cube Brush icon.

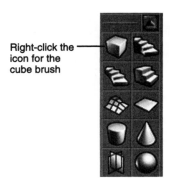

Right-click the icon for the cube brush

Figure 4.2 Right-click the Cube Brush icon in the brush primitive section of the toolbox.

When you right-click the Cube Brush icon, you see the CubeBuilder dialog, as shown in Figure 4.3. Click the fields and change the values as follows:

- Height   600
- Width   1000
- Breadth   1000

Do not change the other field values. Figure 4.3 illustrates the values you supply to the fields of the CubeBuilder dialog. When you are finished, click Build. You see the red wire brush or frame for the cube appear in all four of the viewports.

Next, left-click the Subtract icon in the constructive solid geometry area of the toolbar, as shown in Figure 4.4. This carves out a hollow cube from the space of your map.

When you click the icon for geometry subtraction, in the Dynamic Light viewport you immediately see the hollow cube with the default textures applied to it. Figure 4.5 provides

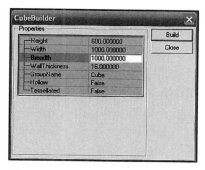

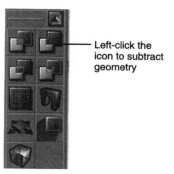

Left-click the icon to subtract geometry

Figure 4.3 Set the Height, Width, and Breadth values of the cube brush.

Figure 4.4 To carve out a cube from the space of the map, click the Subtract icon on the constructive solid geometry palette.

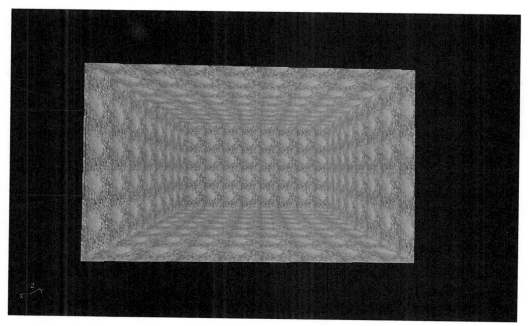

Figure 4.5 When you first view the cube, click to the far wall to give it focus.

a view of the initial cube. In this view, you are looking into the cube from a position outside it. If you do not immediately see the default textures applied to the cube, click on the Textured icon, the fourth icon from the left in the Dynamic Light toolbar.

To explore the cube from the inside, press the left mouse button and move forward, into the center of the chamber. Then press the right mouse button and move your mouse to view the four interior walls and the ceiling and floor.

Position, Lights, and Starting Point

The size of the chamber you have created is roughly six times as high as a character in the game, so to position the camera so that it is more in line with what you might see from the point of view of the character, move to the side 2D viewport. Use the mouse wheel to size the cube brush so you can see its entirety.

As a point of review, the viewport for the side and other views provides you with two wire frames. One is yellow when you click it. The other is red. The red wire frame is a pattern (brush) that you can use to generate any number of meshes or geometrical forms. The pattern is used whenever you click the Build button in the CubeBuilder dialog.

In this instance, you are working with only one geometrical form, so your use of the cube wire frame is limited. You can move it aside by clicking on it with the left mouse button and holding down the Control key. This allows you to move it out of the way. After that, work with the yellow wire frame, which represents the geometrical object you see in the Dynamic Light view.

Camera Preliminaries

To reposition the camera, left-click the Eye icon in the yellow box, which represents the camera. The icon turns green. With the camera selected, press the Shift key and click the left mouse button to move the camera down until you have positioned it roughly as shown in Figure 4.6. Do this in all of the 2D viewports. When you click in the Dynamic Light viewport again, you see the camera view adjusted to accord with the new position. Use the motions mentioned previously to explore the chamber.

PlayerStart Objects

To make it so you can build your chamber, add PlayerStart and Light objects. Generally, you create only one instance of a PlayerStart class when you define a level. A PlayerStart object allows Unreal Tournament to know where to establish the focus of the level when you first activate it. On the other hand, you often create a number of Light objects.

Side Viewport

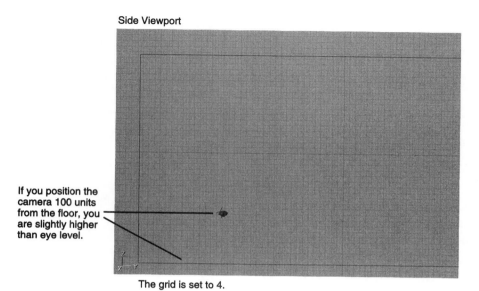

If you position the camera 100 units from the floor, you are slightly higher than eye level.

The grid is set to 4.

Figure 4.6 After you select the Camera icon, press Shift and left-click to position the camera at eye level.

To add a PlayerStart object, work in the Dynamic Light viewport. Move forward into the chamber until you can see three of the walls, as shown in Figure 4.7. Then right-click and select Add Player Start Here. Representing a PlayerStart object, a Joystick icon appears in the location you have designated in the chamber (see Figure 4.8).

The joystick appears roughly in the center of the floor area, as Figure 4.8 illustrates. To reposition the Player Start icon, click on it to select it. Then hold down the Shift key and the left or right mouse button to move it to the sides or forward or backward. Move it so that it is toward the front of the chamber. This gives you a longer perspective on the room when you initialize your session of play.

To make it so that your player avatar is firmly positioned on the floor level, right-click the Player Start icon and select Align > Snap to Floor.

After adding the PlayerStart object, perform a build to adjust the geometry of your level. When you add features to a level, they are often not appropriately positioned relative to each other. Performing a build of the geometry allows you to adjust them. Figure 4.9 illustrates the position of the Build Geometry icon. Click the icon to perform the build. Notice, also, that icons allow you to perform builds of lighting. You use these later in the current chapter.

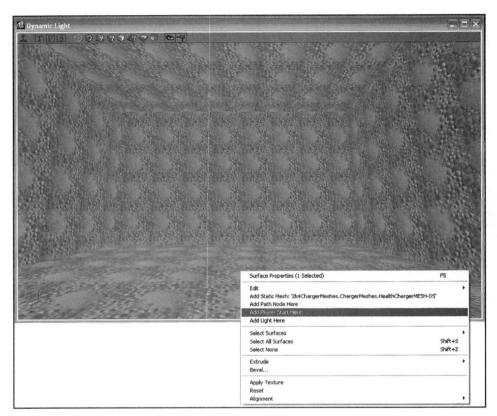

Figure 4.7 Right-click and select Add Player Start Here.

Figure 4.8 To build the level, you must first place a player icon in it.

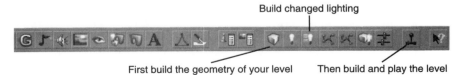

Figure 4.9 Before trying to test play your level, click the Build Geometry icon on the main menu toolbar.

When you do not build your level, the geometry can make it so that your player avatar is accidentally buried in a wall. When you start to play your level, the player avatar is immediately killed. This prevents you from being able to navigate in your level to test it. If you encounter this situation, exit the play mode and in the edit mode click the Build Geometry icon on the main menu toolbar.

The Command Line

If you have not done so, build the geometry of your level and then click the Play Map icon to play it. Navigate around the chamber and observe the behavior of the gun. After you have completed your testing session, press the tilde key (~) to invoke the command prompt. When you invoke the command prompt, you see only the lower half of your level.

The command prompt for Unreal Tournament allows you to issue a number of test commands. Among other things, you can use it to type commands that immediately exit you from your test session. Accordingly, to exit the session, type **exit** at the prompt. (Alternatively, you can type **quit**.) You can type lowercase or uppercase characters.

When you press the Enter key, the game immediately terminates and returns you to your editing session. Figure 4.10 illustrates a test session after you have typed the tilde key and the exit command.

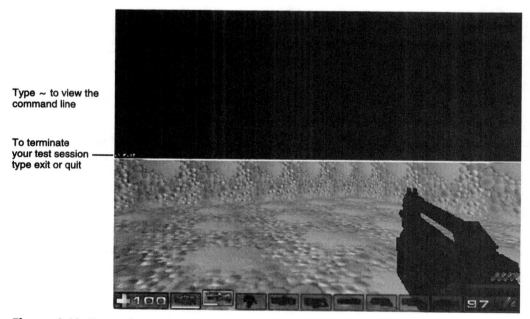

Type ~ to view the
command line

To terminate
your test session ——
type exit or quit

Figure 4.10 Type **exit** or **quit** to return to the editor from a session of testing.

Lighting

In addition to adding a PlayerStart object, you must add a Light object to your map. Unless you add a light, when you try to play your map, you see only what the flashes that accompany the firing of weapons allow you to see.

To add a Light object, right-click in the middle area of the ceiling. Select Add Light Here, as shown in Figure 4.11. As you have seen before, a lightbulb represents the Light object.

Figure 4.11 Right-click and select the Add Light Here option.

What applied to the geometry of your level also applies to the lighting. You must build it after you implement. As Figure 4.9 shows, the icons you use to build lighting for your level are located immediately to the right of the Build Geometry icon. One icon builds all Light objects in your level. The other builds only those you have newly added. Click the Build Lighting icon. After you click the Build Lighting icon, the appearance of your level changes fairly significantly, as Figure 4.12 illustrates.

As a final lighting task, left-click the Lightbulb icon and open the Light Properties dialog. In the dialog, open the LightColor tray and set the properties to these values, as shown in Figure 4.13.

LightBrightness	150
LightHue	43
LightSaturation	144

Figure 4.12 Click the Build Lighting icon on the top toolbar.

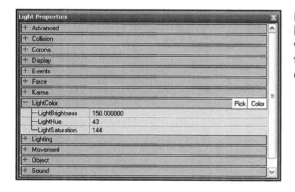

Figure 4.13 Set the light properties to values that increase the brightness of the chamber.

To recompile your lighting, click the Build Changed Lighting icon on the top toolbar. This icon is the second on the left from the Build Geometry icon.

Surface Textures

To provide variety in the appearance of the walls, floor, and ceiling of the chamber, you apply textures to surfaces. A texture is a 2D image that provides a surface for almost any geometrical form you create in your levels.

To apply textures, select View > Show Texture Browser from the top menu. (Alternatively, you can click the Texture Browser icon.) In the Texture Browser, select File > Open. You see the Open Texture Package dialog, as shown in Figure 4.14.

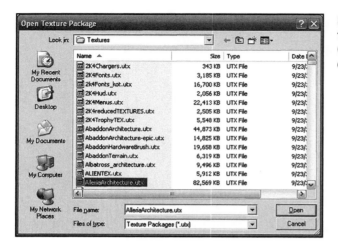

Figure 4.14 Select the texture from the Open Texture Package dialog.

The Open Texture Package dialog displays a list of texture collections. The *.utx extension identifies each collection. Each *.utx file contains one or more textures and represents a specific theme.

Click the AlleriaArchitecture.utx file. Then click Open.

When you click Open, you include the textures in the AlleriaArchitecture group in the list you can immediately access using the browser. After you open the AlleriaArchitecture texture group, any textures that you use in your level remain available to you during subsequent development sessions. To access those you have not yet used, you must reopen the group.

To see all the texture groups that have been used, click the Full tab. Beneath the tab, click the top drop-down list. This list shows you the texture groups. The list you see does not include all the texture groups in the Textures directory.

To examine the AlleriaArchitecture texture group, select AlleriaArchitecture from the top drop-down list, as Figure 4.15 shows. Within the texture group, you can view categories of textures. The lower of the two drop-down lists provides the categories of the textures. Among the categories are Walls, Ceilings, and Floors. After you select a category, you use the scroll bar to view the individual items in a category. The title of each texture appears at the bottom of the texture as you scroll through the list.

To apply textures to the wall, floor, and ceiling surfaces of your level, perform these operations:

- In the Dynamic Light viewport, click on one of the walls of your chamber. The lighter color indicates that you have selected it. Then right-click. You see a drop-down menu. From the Select Surfaces option, select Adjacent Walls. If you then turn the camera on the walls of your chamber, you can see that all the walls are selected.

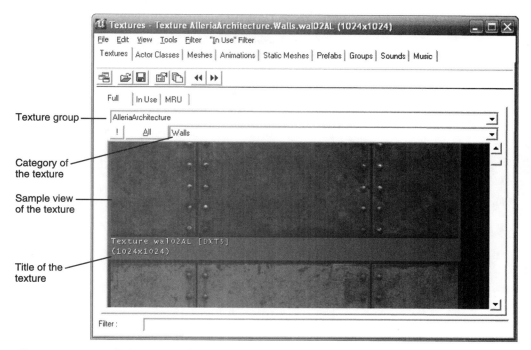

Texture group

Category of the texture

Sample view of the texture

Title of the texture

Figure 4.15 Scroll to view all of the items in the category.

- Now move to the Texture Browser. Select Walls from the lower of the two drop-down lists. Scroll through the Walls textures until you see wal02AL. Click the sample view of the texture in the Texture dialog. This applies it to the four walls.

- To apply a texture to the ceiling of your chamber, click on the ceiling surface. Then in the Texture Browser, select Ceilings from the lower of the drop-down lists. Scroll to cel02AL and click the sample view of the texture in the Texture dialog.

- For the floor, select Floors from the lower of the drop-down lists. Scroll to flr02AL and click the sample view of the texture in the Texture dialog.

After you have applied the textures, click the Build Changed Lighting and Build Geometry icons on the top toolbar of UnrealEd. These actions refresh your work and give you a proper view of the level with its textures, as Figure 4.16 illustrates.

After clicking the Build Changed Lighting and Build Geometry icons, click the Play Map icon. Figure 4.17 illustrates the appearance of your map after the game starts.

Figure 4.16 The textures have been applied to the walls, floor, and ceiling.

Press [Fire] to join the match!

Figure 4.17 Textures from the AlleriaArchitecture texture group give your chamber a unique appearance.

Enhancing Your Level

You have created the basic features of a map. Among these features are a geometrical form that you subtracted from the space of the map, a PlayerStart object, and a Light object. To create the geometrical form (a cube), you used the cube brush. You added textures to the floor, walls, and ceiling of the cube. Now you are in a position to enhance the cube. One enhancement is to add a sheet to the floor to mark the place for an event. A second draws on your work in Chapter 3, where you learned about Trigger objects.

As in Chapter 3, you can create a trigger by *specializing* the Trigger class of the Unreal Tournament class hierarchy. *Specialize* is another term for what you do when you inherit or extend a base class. You add attributes or functions to the base class object that define it in a narrower way. Making a Trigger object issue the expression "Hello World!" was one form of specialization.

Adding a Pad and Decoration Texture

Before proceeding with the work of adding a trigger, first place a tile on the floor of your chamber. This tile provides you with a place in which you can position a trigger. To add a tile, first right-click the Sheet icon in the brush primitive area of the toolbar on the left of UnrealEd. (See Figure 4.18.)

A sheet is more or less equivalent to a tile or a rug. In this case, you want it to be large enough to accommodate a texture with a distinctive decoration. Accept the default size of the sheet, which is 256 by 256, as Figure 4.19 illustrates.

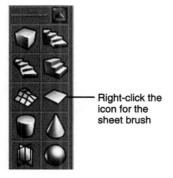

Right-click the icon for the sheet brush

Figure 4.18 Right-click the Sheet icon to add a tile.

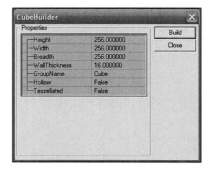

Figure 4.19 The default size of the sheet is 256 by 256.

To create the sheet, you *add* it to your level. When you created the cube for your chamber, you subtracted a geometrical form. Adding a geometrical form differs from subtracting a form; instead of cutting away space from the map, you are creating an entity that fills space. You use the Add button on the toolbar to add geometry, as Figure 4.20 illustrates. Click on the Add icon in the constructive solid geometry area of the toolbar to add a sheet to your level.

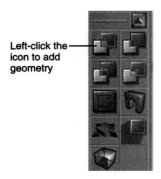

Left-click the icon to add geometry

Figure 4.20 Click the Add button to add geometry.

You work with the Top, Front, and Side viewports to position the sheet. Imagine that you are facing the chamber. Figure 4.21 illustrates the three viewports with the sheet in them. To move the sheet, press the Shift key and left-click on the geometric form. Place the sheet against the back wall, to the right. Place it flush with the floor.

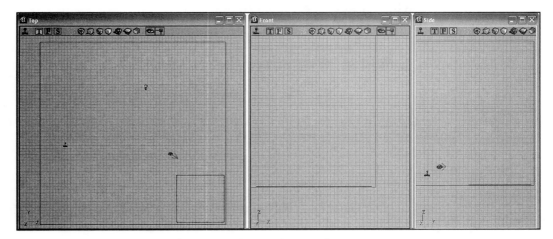

Figure 4.21 Place the sheet flush to the floor in the right far corner.

To select a texture for the sheet, open the Texture Browser. In the browser, select File > Open and the AlleriaArchitecture.utx file. Then in the lower of the drop-down fields, select Decorations and the JumpPad texture, as shown in Figure 4.22.

Click on the sheet and then on the texture to assign the JumpPad texture to your sheet. The result is that the sheet displays a distinctive circular entity in the corner of your chamber, as Figure 4.23 reveals. Click the Build Geometry and Build Changed Lighting icons to refresh your level. Then click the Run Map icon to test your level.

Figure 4.22 Select the JumpPad texture from the AlleriaArchitecture group.

Figure 4.23 You see a tile with a circle in the corner of the chamber.

Working with Versions of a Level

Iterative and *incremental* approaches to development are at the basis of most approaches to extending programming projects. When you iterate, you do something over and over. When you increment, you add something each time you iterate. Most programmers work in an incremental, iterative way. They do things over and over again, and they add details one at a time.

Iteration involves two types of activity. The first is to add an element and then build to see if everything still works. The second involves your overall project. With your overall project, you save successive *versions* of your work. As Figure 4.24 illustrates, you might save the level as LevelV01, LevelV02, and so on. Each version represents a single work session or a significant portion of a single work session.

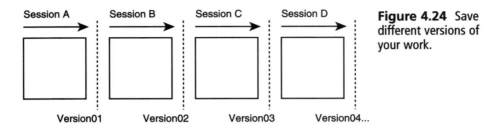

Figure 4.24 Save different versions of your work.

If you commit several hours to a given work session, you might save your work to a new version after the first hour or so. Saving versions provides a way to avoid losing a great deal of work if something goes wrong.

In the current context, you created a basic geometrical form with player start and lighting functionality added. You then added a tile to the floor. Such work represents a fairly significant body of work (at least for beginners), so saving this work to a new version proves a good idea.

Accordingly, if your Ch04Area level is not open, open it. Then select File > Save As, and save it is Ch04Area02.ut2. Click the Play Map icon and verify that your new version compiles. Exit the play session by using the tilde (~) and typing **quit**.

Defining a Trigger

In this phase of your development activity, you develop a `Trigger` class. As you did in Chapter 2, you specialize the `Trigger` class. To begin this work, select View > Show Actor Class Browser. In the class tree, navigate to Actor > Triggers > Trigger. Right-click on Trigger and select New. The New Class dialog appears, as shown in Figure 4.25. Name your new package `Ch04Area`. Name the class you derive from the `Trigger` class `StandUpTrigger`.

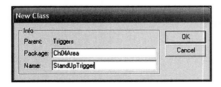

Figure 4.25 Create a new package and a subclass of the `Trigger` class.

Click OK in the New Class dialog. This action opens the code editing window. You see the signature of the `StandUpTrigger` class definition. (See Figure 4.26.)

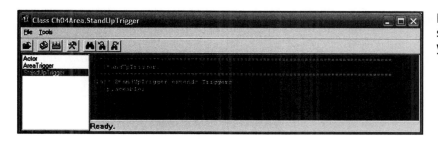

Figure 4.26 You see the signature of your new class.

In the code editing window, implement the code for the StandUpTrigger class so that it reads as follows:

```
//━━━━━━━━━━━━━━━━━━━━━━━━━━━━━━━━━━━━━━━━
// StandUpTrigger.
//━━━━━━━━━━━━━━━━━━━━━━━━━━━━━━━━━━━━━━━━
class StandUpTrigger extends Trigger placeable;
//#1 Declare a member variable
// so that it appears in the properties dialog
var (Message) string StandUpMessage;
function PostBeginPlay(){
    Super.PostBeginPlay();
//#2
// Assign the value to the parameter
    Message = StandUpMessage;
}
```

In the lines following comment #1, you define a member variable for the StandUpTrigger class. The member variable (or property) is named StandUpMessage. At the same time, you use the var keyword to broaden your definition of the variable so that it can appear in the Properties dialog under a given tray. In this instance, the name of the tray is Message.

When you accompany the var keyword with parentheses, the word you place between the parentheses becomes the name of a tray. If no such tray exists, then the compiler creates a tray of the name you have designated. If a tray by this name already exists, then the member variable appears in the named tray.

You can add several member variables to a given var tray. To add a variable, you assign it to the tray using the assignment operator. In the code trailing comment #2, you assign the StandUpMessage variable to the Message tray.

Click the Compile icon (the second from the left) to compile the script for the class. Then save the Ch04Area package. To accomplish this, if necessary, first select View > Show Packages. Then in the lower field, find the Ch04Area package and click the checkbox. After that, select File > Save Selected Packages.

Adding the StandUpTrigger to Your Level

To add an instance of your newly created StandUpTrigger class to your level, first access the Actor Class browser and click to set the focus of the StandUpTrigger, as Figure 4.27 shows.

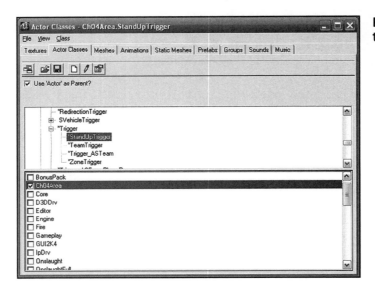

Figure 4.27 Select the StandUpTrigger.

After you select StandUpTrigger from the class list in the Actor Class Browser, move to the Dynamic Light viewport. Navigate to a position above the circular entity and right-click. Select Add StandUpTrigger Here. Then, as Figure 4.28 illustrates, move to the Top viewport and position the trigger in the approximate center of the sheet.

To provide your trigger with a statement for the StandUpMessage property, click the Trigger icon to open the properties dialog. As Figure 4.29 illustrates, you now see the Message tray. Click the Message tray to see your StandUpMessage property. To the right of the property name, you see a field. Type **Stand up and be counted** in this field.

Additionally, as shown in Figure 4.30, find the Trigger tray and click it. As Figure 4.30 illustrates, assign **1.0** to the RepeatTriggerTime property. Assign **2.0** to the ReTriggerDelay property. Setting these values makes it so that you can eliminate the occurrence of multiple messages when you trigger the event that corresponds to the StandUpTrigger object. Even if you activate the trigger several times in a row in intervals of less than a second, two seconds elapse before your message is refreshed.

Click the Build Geometry and Build Change Lighting icons on the top toolbar. Then select File > Save to save your work. Now click the Run Map icon and test your level. Figure 4.31 provides a view of the message you see when you invoke the trigger event.

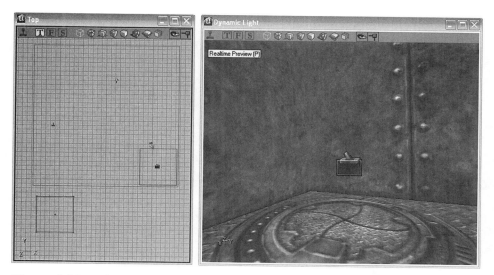

Figure 4.28 Position the `StandUpTrigger` object directly above the circular entity.

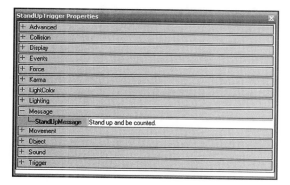

Figure 4.29 Set the `StandUpMessage` property.

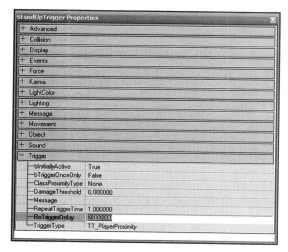

Figure 4.30 Set the `ReTriggerDelay` and the `RepeatTriggerTime` properties.

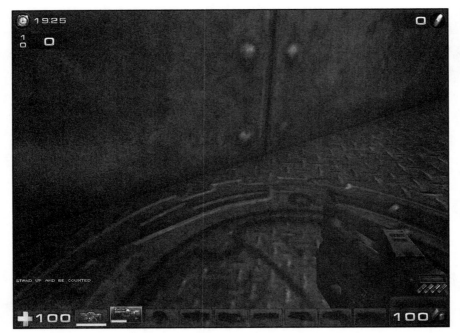

Figure 4.31
You see a message when you invoke the trigger event.

Conclusion

In this chapter, you have implemented a level from scratch and developed it iteratively through two versions. In the first version, you created the geometry and lighting for the level. In the second iteration, you added a specialized `Trigger` class, `StandUpTrigger`. In the `StandUpTrigger` class you use the `var` keyword to create a `Message` tray to hold a property, `StandUpMessage`. The member variable you use to define this property is of the `string` type. Because you define it using the `var` keyword, the property in the properties dialog, you can set it by typing a text message into the field that corresponds to it.

To the forms of your level, you added textures. The textures allow you to set themes and establish purposes for the geometrical forms. For the walls, floor, and ceiling of your level, you use the textures of the AlleriaArchitecture group. This group possesses a strong metal theme. In this group you also find a Decoration texture, which allows you to create a tile on the floor of your level that makes it easier to locate your trigger.

Developing a level in an incremental, iterative way allows you to add and test features as you go. If your work generates problems you cannot overcome, then you can revert to the previous version and try again. In this chapter, your two versions of the Ch04Area level allow you to first add a cube and sheet and apply textures to them. You then work on adding a specialized Trigger object. Although the work involved in these two phases of activity is limited, the pattern you establish when you perform your work iteratively and incrementally proves highly beneficial as your projects grow in complexity.

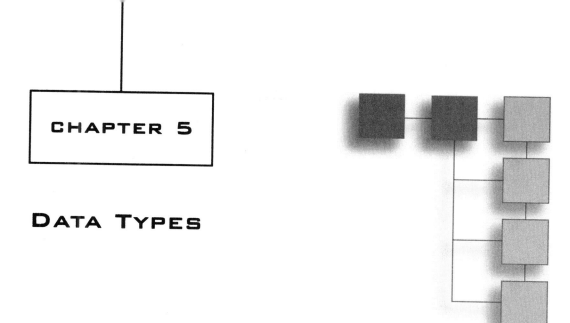

CHAPTER 5

DATA TYPES

The goals of this chapter are to expand on the discussion of the code provided in the last chapter and to lay the groundwork for work in the next chapter. Through each revision of your code, you add a few new elements and create the opportunities for exploring different features of the Unreal Tournament class hierarchy and the UnrealScript programming language. In this chapter, you deal with issues of scope and accessibility and the use of different data types. The focus is on primitive data types, although some mention is made of abstract data types, which you have been exposed to as you have worked with specializing the Trigger class. Primitive data types are sometimes called built-in data types. You employ data types to define identifiers or variables. These are generally known as operands. Operators make it possible to do things with operands. In light of this, you view the standard operators for both primitive and abstract data types. In the end, you work with concatenation operators, which are designed to work almost exclusively with data of the string type. By implementing the CommandTrigger class, you are able to put concatenation to work to join and display a message. What you do in this chapter remains largely preliminary. In later chapters, you put operators and data types to work in a large number of ways. Here are a few topics covered in this chapter:

- Examining variables in close detail
- How the public and private keywords control access
- Distinguishing class from function scope
- Applying primitive data types of identifiers
- Naming conventions and requirements for identifiers
- Looking closer at the operators used for all data types

Another Version of the Working Area

Start by saving the work you completed in Chapter 4 to another version. For the current session, save your Ch04Area02 as Ch05Area01. To complete this task, first open Ch04Area02.ut2. Select File > Save As from the main menu. Then type the new name in the File name field and click Save, as shown in Figure 5.1.

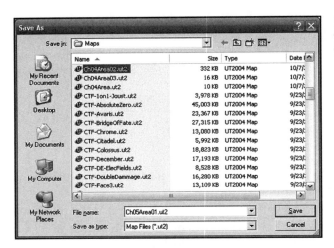

Figure 5.1 Save your work from Chapter 4 toCh05Area01.ut2.

To set up the level so that you can work with a new type of Trigger object, create a second jump pad. Recall that you implemented a sheet mesh and then added the jump pad from the Decorations group of the AlleriaArchitecture texture file. You can now reuse this work by duplicating it. To duplicate your jump pad, move to the top viewport and right-click the existing jump pad. Then from the drop-down menu, select Duplicate.

After you have duplicated the sheet entity, you can then press Shift and the left mouse key to move the duplicated jump pad upward in the top viewport, as Figure 5.3 illustrates. Position it in the adjacent corner of your cube. You can then move to the side viewport to adjust the jump pad so that it is visible above the floor.

After you have positioned the new jump pad, click the Build Lighting and Build Geometry icons on the top menu to make it visible. Figure 5.4 shows you the Dynamic Light view of the two jump pads. The Trigger icon hovers above the jump pad you created in Chapter 4.

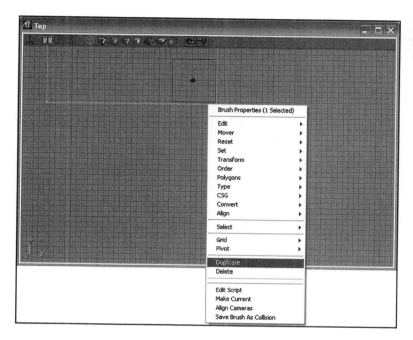

Figure 5.2 Right-click the existing jump pad to duplicate it.

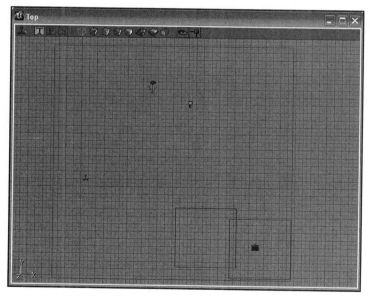

Figure 5.3 Use the Shift key to move the duplicate jump pad.

Figure 5.4 The jump pads are the same except for the trigger.

Revisiting the Code

To add features to your code, start by accessing the Actor Class Browser. Open the Ch04Area package, and access the StandUpTrigger class. Navigate to the Trigger class and right-click on Trigger. In the New Class dialog, enter **Ch04AreaU** as the name of the class. This is the name of an existing package. UnrealEd recognizes the old package so it adds the class you are creating to it. It does not overwrite the existing package. For the name of the class, type **CommandTrigger**. Click OK.

The shell of the class is created and the code editing window opens. You see the name of the new class in the signature line. To make use of some of the code you have already written, click the Compile Changed Scripts icon and then close the code editing window for the CommandTrigger class.

Then right-click and select Edit Script to open the StandUpTrigger class for editing. In the code editing window, select all the code for the class. To select the code, position the cursor at the top of the edit area and hold down the left mouse key. Trace over the lines from top to bottom. UnrealEd highlights the selected lines. When you reach the end of the code, release the left mouse key. The lines remain highlighted. Then press Control + C to copy the lines into the Windows clipboard.

After you have copied the lines, close the code editing window for the StandUpTrigger class. Open the code editing window for the CommandTrigger class. Click to position the cursor in the lines following the signature line of the CommandTrigger class and press Control + V. Windows copies the lines into the edit area. Now delete the signature and comment lines for the StandUpTrigger class, so that your code appears as follows:

```
//========================================================
// CommandTrigger.
// See CommandTriggerV1.txt
//========================================================
//#1
class CommandTrigger extends Trigger placeable;

//#2
var (Message) string StandUpMessage;

function PostBeginPlay(){
    Super.PostBeginPlay();
   Message = StandUpMessage;
}
```

As a review point, preceding comment #1, you change the name of the class as identified in the opening comments. A reference to the text file for the source code resource file is included. The compiler does not read commented code, but such code helps you identify the class when you access it. You also change the name of the class in the class signature line. As the line following comment #1 shows, you change the name of the class to CommandTrigger. The class still specializes (through the extends keyword) the Trigger class. The placeable keyword designates that an object you create with the class can be placed in the game.

It is not necessary to change anything in the remainder of the code. In the lines following comment #2, you declare a member variable of the string type. You define this variable so that it appears in the Message tray of the Properties dialog. The class contains an overridden function, PostBeginPlay(). This is a function that you inherit from a base class. You also use the Super keyword to call a version of the PostBeginPlay() function that resides in a base class. Much more on such topics as function overriding and the use of base classes will be presented later.

Click the Compile Changed Scripts icon and check for errors. If you encounter an error, then check your code against the sample to ensure that you have not accidentally deleted the wrong line or inserted an error. In this way you use code you have already written to create a new class. There are easier approaches to doing this, but for now, you can use the functionality of the Actor Class Browser and the default Windows key actions to move code from one class to another.

Variables and Accessing Them

A closer examination of the use of variables allows you to work more readily with many programming tasks. Toward this end, for review consider once again that in your CommandTrigger class, you create a variable called StandUpMessage. When you create this variable, you use the var keyword. You follow the var keyword with parentheses. Inside the parentheses, you type the term Message. The combination of the keyword, the parentheses, and Message makes it so that you see the Message tray in the properties dialog. You also see the StandUpMessage variable associated with it.

You use the var keyword to create class member variables. A class member variable is a variable that you identify with all the activities of a class. You can see how this is so if you consider a couple of applications of the var keyword.

In one application you use the var keyword to define a variable that appears in the properties dialog. The properties dialog is created by a set of classes that exist separately from your class. When you access the StandUpMessage variable using these classes, it is *visible* to those classes. Figure 5.5 illustrates a situation in which the StandUpTrigger variable is visible to other classes.

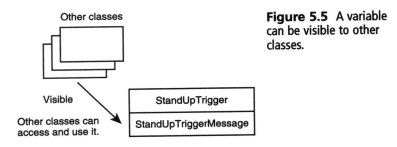

Figure 5.5 A variable can be visible to other classes.

You can also use the var keyword to define variables that you cannot use outside of your class but that you can use anywhere inside your class. Such a variable is still a class member variable. However, if you try to assign a value directly to it from outside the class (using the properties dialog or other approaches), you are not able to do so. Such a variable is visible only within the class.

Scope

Visibility is a technical concept you apply to all the variables and functions you include in your class definitions. Visibility has to do with *scope*. Scope, simply defined, is what you can see or use given that you are working in a certain context, such as that of a function, a class, or a package. Two of the most important keywords relating to the scope of classes in UnrealScript are public and private. These keywords control how the elements in your programs can be *accessed*. They are sometimes referred to as *access modifiers*.

When you define a variable so that it is visible only within a class, the scope of the variable is private. When you define a variable so that you can access it from other classes, then the scope of the variable is public. Figure 5.6 illustrates how the public and private keywords affect the scope of variables or functions. A private variable can be accessed only within the class. A public variable can be accessed both within the class and from other classes.

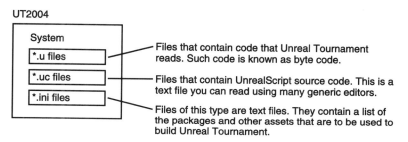

Figure 5.6 Access modifiers control the visibility of variables and functions.

By default, when you define a variable using either var or var( ), the variable you define is public. The keyword var does not alone make the variable public. Instead, by definition, unless you specifically identify the scope of a variable you create as part of your class definition, it is public. However, when you formally define a variable or a function, you do use the keywords public and private. In this way, you show clearly the scope you want to control access to the variable or function. To explore the issue of scope further, add lines to your CommandTrigger class so that it appears as follows:

```
//================================================
// CommandTrigger.
// See CommandTriggerV2.txt
//================================================
class CommandTrigger extends Trigger placeable;

    //#1 Scope of the class but visible outside
    var (Message) public string StandUpMessage;
    var (Message) public string CommandMessage;

    //#2 Scope of the class but visible only inside
    var private string DefaultMessage;

    function PostBeginPlay(){
      Super.PostBeginPlay();

      //#3 Scope of the function, which is also
      // inside the scope of the class
      DefaultMessage = "Move yet again.";
      Message = StandUpMessage;
    }
```

In the line accompanying comment #1, you add a second member variable to the class. The name of this member variable is `CommandMessage`. As mentioned previously, you use the `var` keyword to define the variable as a class member variable. At the same time, you also use the `public` keyword in your definition of the variable. Use of the `public` keyword explicitly defines the variable as one that you want programmers to be able to access outside the class, through the properties dialog or otherwise.

It remains that if you did not include the `public` keyword, you could still access the member variable from outside the class. You have seen how this is so in previous work with your class. As mentioned before, to make your intentions clear as a programmer, you use the access control word to define your variable.

In the parentheses that follow the `var` keyword, you type `Message`. When you use the `var` keyword to designate a message, you are formally defining the variable as one that can be used outside the class.

In the lines accompanying comment #2, you create a third variable, `DefaultMessage`. Your definition of this variable differs from those of the previous variables. With this definition, you use the `private` keyword along with the `var` keyword. You do not follow the `var` keyword with parentheses. The `private` keyword makes it so that you cannot access the `DefaultMessage` variable outside the scope of the `CommandTrigger` class. Also, when you do not use the parentheses to associate `Message` with the variable, the variable does not appear in the properties dialog. Generally, outside the class, it is not possible to know of the existence of the `DefaultMessage` variable.

Scope Concerns

The `DefaultMessage` variable is `private` and so is not visible outside the `CommandTrigger` class. It remains visible inside the class, however, and you use it there. A few lines after defining this member variable, you assign a line of text to it: "Move yet again." The fact that you define the variable in one place and use it in another proves to be fairly important. You define it in the scope of the class; you use it in the scope of a function.

Classes have scope and so do functions. The scope of an UnrealScript class is the file in which you create the class. The scope of an UnrealScript function is restricted to the area described by the opening and closing braces of the function. Consider the `PostBeginPlay()` function:

```
function PostBeginPlay(){
  // line left out
  //#3 Scope of the function, which is also
  // inside the scope of the class
  DefaultMessage = "Move yet again:";
  Message = StandUpMessage;
}
```

The function keyword designates the start of the definition of the function, just as the var keyword designates the start of the definition of a class variable. The name of the function is PostBeginPlay. The opening and closing parentheses following the name of the function provide you a way to introduce information to the function. (This topic is discussed in detail later on.) After the opening and closing parentheses, you find an opening curly brace ({). The opening curly brace is the start of the scope of the function. A few lines of code follow, and then you find a closing curly brace (}). This marks the end of the scope of the function. The area between the opening and closing braces is called the *function block.*

As Figure 5.7 illustrates, when you put lines of code in a function block, you partially seal them off from the rest of your program. If you are writing code for the PostBeginPlay() function, you cannot access a variable you have defined in the NextPlay() function. On the other hand, if you are working within either the PostBeginPlay() function or the NextPlay() function, then you can access variables defined in the scope of the class. This is why you can make use of the DefaultMessage variable within the PostBeginPlay() function to assign a line of text to it.

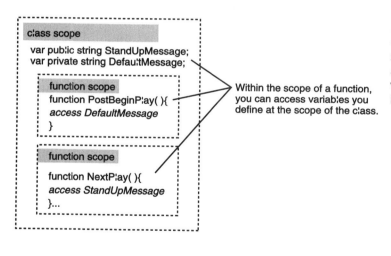

Figure 5.7 When you define a variable at the scope of a class, you can access it from anywhere within your class whether it is public or private.

Data Types

Class scope and function scope are key concepts in object-oriented programming, so they are elaborated in several passages of this book. Another key concept is that of *data types.* UnrealScript provides you with two primary ways of defining the values you use. One is through *primitive data types.* The other is through *abstract data types.* Figure 5.8 provides a summary view of these two categories of data.

The Trigger class is an abstract data type, as is the CommandTrigger class you derive from it. You create abstract data types using the class and extends keywords. In this and previous chapters, you have already developed several abstract classes. Much more discussion of this

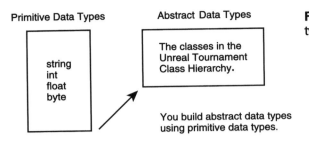

Primitive Data Types

> string
> int
> float
> byte

Abstract Data Types

> The classes in the
> Unreal Tournament
> Class Hierarchy.

You build abstract data types
using primitive data types.

Figure 5.8 You work with
two basic categories of data.

activity remains. For now, it is befitting to give some attention to the humbler variety of data. The primitive data types consist of such data types as int, float, string, and byte. Table 5.1 provides a summary discussion of the primitive data types.

Table 5.1 Primitive Data Types

Data Type	Description
bool	This data type allows you to deal with two basic values: true and false. The terms true and false are keywords in UnrealScript. false has a numerical value of 0. true has a numerical value of 1. You can assign true, false, 0, or 1 to a variable of the bool type. By convention, Unreal Tournament programmers prefix a small "b" to the name variables of the bool type. For example, bLightIsOn.
byte	This data type allows you to store numbers up to 255. A byte value cannot be negative.
int	This data type handles numbers between –12147483648 and 12147483647 if you are working with a 32-bit processor. Integers do not include decimal points.
float	This data type handles numbers in the same range as integers, but they also include decimal points.
string	This data type handles collections of characters. You identify strings with double quotes.

Conventions for Naming

In the CommandTrigger class, you define three variables of the string type. Since UnrealScript is not case-sensitive, you can designate the name of a data type with capital or lowercase letters. By convention, programmers usually type the keywords that designate the primitive data in lowercase, as shown in Table 5.1. On the other hand, they capitalize the names of abstract data types (Trigger, Actor, and so on).

When you create a variable, at a minimum you combine a data type keyword with an *identifier*. An identifier is the word you use as a variable. The terms *variable* and *identifier* are largely synonymous. The difference is that a variable is a term to which you have assigned a value. An identifier is just a term you have declared to receive a value.

Conventions apply to how you name identifiers. Many programmers capitalize the names of identifiers that designate abstract data types—for example, `Trigger`, `MeshObject`, `DamageType`, and so on. If an identifier for an abstract data type consists of more than one word joined with others, all the words are capitalized.

For the identifiers relating to primitive data types, two conventions are common. One is to start the name of the identifier with a lowercase letter. If the identifier consists of two or more words, then words after the first word are capitalized. For example, you might use either `DefaultMessage` or `defaultMessage` as the name of the `CommandTrigger` variable. When you adopt a convention, it is generally considered a good programming practice to observe it throughout your code.

One other convention is to use Hungarian notation. This is where the use of the prefix b for identifiers of the `bool` type originates. Such notation originated with a famous programmer associated with Microsoft who developed naming standards for data types. Different versions of this notation have evolved over time, and in many cases, programming style manuals say not to use them. Still, it remains that they come in handy at times, and many programmers still use them.

Naming Practices and Syntax

Whatever convention you adopt, it is a good idea to observe the practice of naming your variables, functions, and classes in meaningful ways. One approach involves mnemonic naming conventions. In other words, you name an identifier so that when you read it you get a clue about what it does. Likewise, avoid using single letters or expressions of two or three letters to name identifiers.

Here are a few examples of identifier names that reflect questionable programming practices:

```
int m;
Trigger A;
int xisksneoisls;
string CrappyStuff;
float mmmmmmm;
```

You can grasp intuitively why some identifiers reflect questionable practices. If you name an identifier `m` for an integer, you have no idea what `m` means. If you name a class `A`, you are in the same situation. What does the `A` class do? If the programmers at Epic had named the `Actor` class `A`, would that have been helpful? Likewise, using identifiers like `CrappyStuff` is fun, but if you read your code a year latter, it is almost a certainty that you will find such names irritating and possibly nauseating. As for identifiers that are based on creative neologisms, the problem is that since they are not based on common dictionary words, to use them, you must learn wholly new words. The identifier xisksneoisls might have potentials in a science fiction or fantasy context, but try typing it without errors three times in a row.

Other practices are dictated by the compiler. As you might expect, you cannot use a keyword (also known as a reserved word) as an identifier. Use of symbols as a part of an identifier can also create problems. Likewise, try to avoid using numbers at the ends or beginnings of your identifier names. Here are a few problem situations:

```
float 000997;
Trigger TouchTrigger03;
string  ?!PillarName;
int Joy=Ride;
float class;
```

The list of possible error situations extends indefinitely, but using a number with no characters to name an identifier makes it impossible for the compiler to recognize your identifier as an identifier. Numbers are numbers. Identifiers need to contain at least one character. The Trigger example is a little harder to explain, but the gist of the matter is that the compiler does not like file names that end with numbers. Remember that a file name must be the same as the class it contains. If that's so, then you can see why there is a problem. If you want to include a number, then you might use Touch03Trigger.

Starting an identifier with symbols such as ! and ? can generate compiler errors because the compiler tries to read the meaning of the symbol. The same applies to use of symbols within a name. The compiler does not process spaces, so if you use Joy=Ride as an identifier, the compiler reads this statement as an assignment operation in which you are assigning the value stored in Ride to the variable Joy. As for the use of a keyword such as class for an identifier name, the compiler cannot recognize the keyword as anything except a keyword, regardless of how you might qualify it with other keywords, such as float.

Declaration

To declare an identifier, you precede the identifier with a keyword that designates the data type of the identifier. Technically, when you declare an identifier, you just associate it with a data type. To associate an identifier with a data type, you precede the name of the identifier with the name of the data type. This creates a variable that can hold a value that conforms to the data type.

You can add other qualifiers when you declare an identifier. For example, as the use of public, private, and var are illustrated, you can precede the name of the identifier with a keyword to designate the scope of the variable or its intended use. In addition to public, private, and var, local is a commonly used keyword used to provide access and scope information. The local keyword allows you to designate identifiers at the function scope. Here are some examples of how to declare variables:

```
//declare an integer identifier
var int NumberOfTries;
var float AmountOfCash;
var float NumberOfPlanets;
var string NameOfPawn;
var byte ShortCount;
var bool bLightIsOn;
```

These variables can all be accessed on a public basis. If you want to control access to them, then you insert an access control word, such as public or private:

```
var public float AmountOfCash;
var private int NumberOfPlanets;
var public string NameOfPawn;
local string NameOfPawn;
```

As mentioned before, if you want to make the variable appear in one of the Properties trays (or tabs), then you use the form of the var keyword that allows you to designate the Property tray you want to use:

```
var(Message) public string NameOfPawn;
var(Message) public byte ShortCount;
var(Light) public bool bLightIsOn;
```

Initialization

When you assign a value to a variable, you initialize it. As you have already seen, you use the assignment operator to assign values. To initialize a variable, you use a value that is valid for the variable. You cannot, for example, assign a word to a value of the byte type. Nor can you assign a class object of the Trigger type to a variable of a string type. Here is an example of how to declare and then initialize variables:

```
//Declare
Var int NumberOfDoors;
Local float AmountOfPower;
// Initialize
NumberOfDoors= 12;
AmountOfPower = 456467.44
```

In both instances, you first declare the variable. Then on a line that follows, you assign a value to it. You declare and then initialize the variable. Your initialization does not need to come on the line immediately following the declaration. You saw in the CommandTrigger class, for instance, that you could initialize the DefaultMessage variable inside a function placed later in body of the class.

In many instances, you might combine declaration and initialization:

```
Var int NumberOfDoors = 10;
Local float AmountOfPower = 456467.44;
```

In the programs in this book, you find a number of variations on declaration and initialization. How this activity takes place depends on the context.

Casting and Promotion

In some cases, you can assign data that appears to be of one type to a variable you have defined for another type. Consider, for example, assigning a number to an identifier you have defined for a string:

```
string ForceLevel = 23;
```

Such statements work because UnrealScript is defined so that in some cases it automatically converts one data type to another through assignment. Generally, with strings, you can almost always assign a number to the identifier. The result is that the number is converted into characters. The number 23, for example, becomes a text string consisting of the characters "2" and "3".

A concept related to automatic casting is data promotion. Generally, data types represent reserved memory spaces. A memory space is analogous to a box. The box for a byte variable is very small. The box for an int variable is larger than the box for a byte variable but smaller than the box for a float variable. Figure 5.9 illustrates how a variable of a data type can be promoted to that of another.

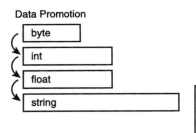

Data Promotion

byte

int

float

string

A byte variable can be assigned to an int. An int variable can be assigned to a float. A float variable can be assigned to a string.

If you reverse the process, you often get an error or a warning that you are truncating or losing data.

Figure 5.9 You can assign the values stored in variables of smaller data types to those of larger data types.

Data promotion allows you to assign values of variables you have defined using smaller data types to variables you have defined using larger data types. You can assign the value of an int variable, for example, to a variable you have defined as using a *float* variable.

The reverse is not true, however. One example of this might involve initializing an int variable with a decimal value. Here is how this might happen:

```
var int NumberOfShots;
NumberOfShots = 23.44;
```

You use a decimal value to initialize an int (integer) variable. The compiler might allow you to perform this action, but if you try to use the initialized variable later in your program, you find that the compiler has implicitly truncated your value so that you get only the integer portion of the number. In other words, 23.44 becomes 23.

Operations

Identifiers are only part of the story. A general term for an identifier or variable is *operand*. When you assign a value to an operand, you use an *operator*. The assignment operator (=) is the operand you use to accomplish this task. The primitive data types are all defined to work with a set of operators, as are the abstract data types.

Table 5.2 provides an overview of the operators UnrealScript provides. All of these work with the numeric data types. A few work with strings. A few also work with abstract data

Table 5.2 UnrealScript Operators

Operators	Discussion
=	The assignment operator. The value on the right is assigned to the variable on the left: CountOfLights = 5.
( )	Parentheses for grouping. You can use parentheses to group other operators.
- ! ~ ++ --	These are unary operators, which means that you apply them directly to a single variable: Count++.
**	Exponent operator. Raise one number to the power of another: 10**3 = 1000.
* / % = + -	Multiplication, division, modulus, assignment, addition, and subtraction operators are the primary operators you use with numbers. The % sign is called the *remainder* or *modulus* operator: 5 % 2 = 1.
< >	The operators for less than (<) and greater than (>) allow you evaluate two numbers in relation to each other: 2 < 5. Such operations return values of true or false.
<= >=	Less than or equal to (<=) and greater than or equal to (>=) allow you to include the numbers you evaluate in your control statement. The operations return values of true or false.
== !=	Equal to and not equal to serve to establish a categorical basis of evaluation. The operations return values of true or false.
~=	Approximately equal. The operator applies to both numbers and strings. For strings, it allows case-insensitive comparisons. For numbers, it allows a range of 0.0001 between the numbers. Returns true or false.
+= -= *= /=	Numeric compound assignment operators. With each of these operators, you begin with a variable on the left, perform the operation with another variable (or number) on the right, and then assign the result of the operation back to the variable on the left: NumberOfBats += 5. If NumberOfBats is 5 to start with, then the statement leaves it equal to 10.

types. Whether an operator works with a given data type (including the string data type) depends on whether the developers of UnrealScript have defined the operator in the appropriate way. In the chapters that follow, the uses of these operators are explained more extensively as you use them in different programs.

String Operators

While the operators listed in Table 5.2 are common to many primitive and abstract data types, it remains that some operators are defined to apply only to variables of the string type. Chief among these are the operators that allow you to combine the values (or text expressions) you assign to string variables with each other. Consider what happens if you begin by defining two string variables this way:

```
FirstOth = "I swear 'tis better"
SecondOthLine = " to be much abused"
```

You can combine these lines from *Othello* (Act III, line 335) so that the two lines are joined into one. To do so, you use a *concatenation* operator. UnrealScript provides several such operations. Here is a third version of the CommandTrigger class that uses concatenation.

```
//═══════════════════════════════════════════
// CommandTrigger.
// See CommandTriggerV3.txt
//═══════════════════════════════════════════
class CommandTrigger extends Trigger
    placeable;
    var (Message) public string StandUpMessage;
    var (Message) public string CommandMessage;

    var private string DefaultMessage;
    //#1
    var private string FirstOthLine;
    var private string SecondOthLine;

    function PostBeginPlay(){
      Super.PostBeginPlay();
      //#2
      //Assign initial values
      FirstOthLine = "I swear 'tis better";
      SecondOthLine = "to be much abused";

      //#3
      //Concatenate the lines
```

```
        DefaultMessage @= FirstOthLine ;
        DefaultMessage @= SecondOthLine;
        Message = DefaultMessage;
    }
```

In the lines associated with comment #1, you declare two member variables of the `string` type. These variables are private, so you must set their values and use them inside the class. At comment #2, you define the variables by assigning two parts of a line from Shakespeare's *Othello* to them. While you declare the variables at class scope, you define them in the scope of the `PostBeginPlay()` function. Within the scope of this function, in the lines associated with comment #3, you use one of the string concatenation operators to build the complete line of the play.

You use the type of concatenation operation that is known generally as a *compound operator*. The two operators that are compounded work along the lines mentioned in Table 5.2 for compound numeric operators. You start with a given value. In this case, it is the `DefaultMessage` variable with no value assigned to it. You then assign the line of text contained by the `FirstOthLine` variable to it. Then in the second use of the concatenation operator, you append the line of text stored in the `SecondOthLine` variable. You could continue to concatenate lines in this way until you had many more lines.

If you were to use the assignment operator (=) each time you assigned a value to the `DefaultMessage` variable, you would wipe out the information you have previously assigned to the variable. Concatenation allows you to continue to add new information.

Table 5.3 provides you with a summary of the operators that apply to the `string` type. Only three of these are compound operators. As the table reveals, the @= operator inserts a space between the text you concatenate. For this reason, in the CommandTriggerV3.txt example, you do not include an extra space at the beginning of the second line of quoted text.

Table 5.3 String Operators

Operator	Discussion
=	Simple assignment of one string to another.
@	Combines two strings and inserts a space between them.
$	Combines two strings with no space between them.
@=	Combines the string to the left with the string to the right and assigns the result back to the string to the left. Inserts a space between the strings.
$=	Combines the string to the left with the string to the right and assigns the result back to the string to the left. Inserts no space between the strings.
-=	Removes all occurrences of the string to the left from the string to the right.

Compiling and Testing

After all of this discussion of scope and data types, it is time to put some of the code you have developed to work. Toward this end, work in the Actor Class Browser and if you have not done so yet, type the code for the CommandTriggerV3.txt example in the code editing window for the CommandTrigger class. Click the Compile Changed Scripts icon to test and compile your code as you go.

After you have finished entering your code, scroll to the Ch04Area package and click the checkbox next to it. Select File > Save Selected Packages from the top menu. Then in the Class tree, click CommandTrigger to make it the active class.

Next, activate the Dynamic Light viewport for the Ch05Area01 level. As shown in Figure 5.10, position the cursor above the newly added jump pad. Right-click and select Add CommandTrigger Here. After you add the trigger, position it in the center of the pad and slightly above it, as you did with the StandUpTrigger object. Click the Build Changed Lighting and Build Geometry icons on the top menu to refresh your work as you go. Then left-click and open the properties dialog for the CommandTrigger object. Open the Trigger tray. Set RepeatTriggerTime to 2.0. Set ReTriggerDelay to 1.0.

Given that you have created an instance of your new trigger and placed it above the jump pad, you can then click the Play Map icon and view your work. Figure 5.11 illustrates the concatenated line from *Othello* as it appears in the message area of the player view.

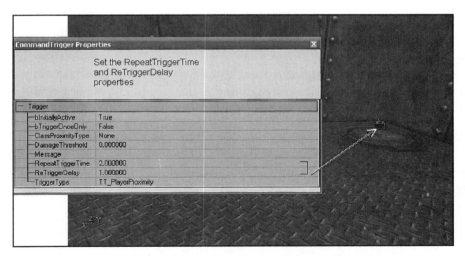

Figure 5.10 Position the CommandTrigger object and then configure its properties.

Figure 5.11 The message you see reflects the work of concatenation operators.

Constants

Before bringing this chapter to an end, one topic remains that proves important in a number of contexts. This is the concept of a *constant*. A constant is an identifier that holds a value that you cannot change. To define a constant, you use the const keyword. When you declare a constant, since its value cannot be changed during the course of your program, you must also initialize it. Here is an example of how to define an identifier as a constant:

```
const RADIUSOFSAFETY = 40;
const POWEROFSHOT = 10;
```

Constant values prove important in situations in which you want to prevent anyone from changing a given value at any point in the use or development of your program. You can define a class data member as a constant and then use it repeatedly in contexts in which you require a specific, determined value. When you learn about arrays in the next chapter, you see one important application of constants. In other respects, UnrealScript provides a few constants for you. Among these are the value of pi and the maximum value of an integer. You use the keyword (or constant name) PI to retrieve the value of pi. You use MAXINT to retrieve the maximum value of an integer. Here is how you might use PI in a statement in your program:

```
PI * (RadiusOfCircle * RadiusOfCircle);
```

Nothing more is needed than to use the constant name. Programmers usually capitalize the names of constants. This is an old programming convention used with a multitude of programming languages. It is purely a convention. A word in all caps designates an identifier to which you cannot reassign values.

Note

The PI constant is defined in a core class of the Unreal Tournament class hierarchy. This is known as the Object class. It is the class from which all other classes are derived. Much more remains to be said about the Object classes in subsequent chapters.

Conclusion

In this chapter, you have dealt extensively with review of a few things you accomplished in the last chapter and with the fundamentals of understanding how classes are laid out. Subjects such as scope and access control might seem unimportant, but as you work your way into situations involving complex class definitions, controlling the ways your classes are used and understanding, in turn, how other classes can be used depends on understanding scope and access. Additionally, learning about primitive data types and the operators that apply to them tends to be fairly slow going. Still, you can accomplish nothing without using operators. As with scope and access issues, laying out the basics at this point puts you in a position to go far in future explorations. Much remains to be done with regard to exploring basics, but with the notions you now have in place, you can begin work on such things as the built-in functions of UnrealScript control statements, and programs that involve implementing your own functions and the more complex aspects of abstract data types.

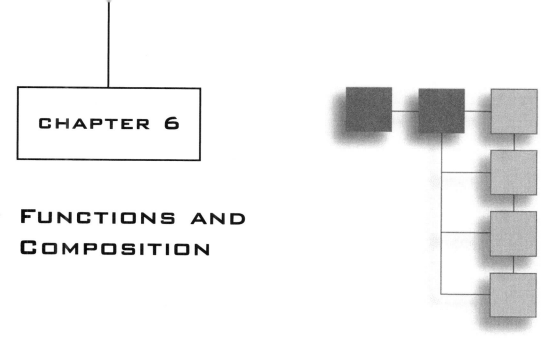

CHAPTER 6

FUNCTIONS AND COMPOSITION

In this chapter you define a class called Math that you use on the basis of composition with a new Trigger class called AddNumbersTrigger. To accomplish this task, you review how variables and functions account for the state and behavior of a class. You then explore the specifics of how to create functions. This exploration includes examining return types and argument lists, among many other things. After dealing with the basics of functions, you explore a few of the built-in functions that you get with the Unreal Tournament Object class. Among the functions you explore is the Rand() function, which generates random numbers. You then turn to developing a class from scratch. This is the Math class. After you have the Math class in place, you develop the AddNumbersTrigger. When you create this class, you work with the spawn keyword to dynamically create an instance of the Math class. In this way, you add a new dimension to your class package, one that incorporates peer classes. Among the topics included in this chapter are these:

- State and behavior for a palm tree object
- How to define the return type of a function
- Creating argument lists
- Where to find such functions as Int() an Chr()
- How to create an instance of a class dynamically
- Using cascaded function calls to optimize your code

Another Version of the Working Area

As in Chapter 5, begin by opening the map you worked on in the last chapter and save it to a new version. The version for Chapter 5 is Ch05Area01.ut2. Select File > Save As from the main menu. In the Save As dialog, enter Ch06Area01, the name of your new version. See Figure 6.1.

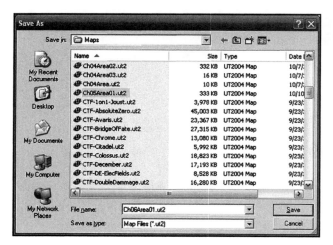

Figure 6.1 Save your previous work to a new version.

You save the work you completed in Chapter 5 to a version you can work with in this chapter because the work in this chapter builds on the functionality you have implemented to specialize the Trigger class. In this chapter, you go in several different directions, adding new jump pads and several instances of a class called AddNumbersTrigger.

After you have saved the new version of the level, click the Build Changed Lighting and Build Geometry icons on the top menu to refresh the level. Then click the Play Map icon to test run it.

Note

In this chapter, you continue to use the Ch04Area package. In the source code files for this chapter, you find a version of the Ch04Area package that includes the classes you create in this chapter. You can also find the source code in *.txt files in the Chapter 6 source code directory. Appendix A provides optional discussion of how to work with your code outside the editor.

Adding Another Pad

After you have saved and tested the Ch06Area01 map, duplicate one of the existing jump pads and place it in an open corner. As in Chapter 5, you can perform this task most readily if you work in the top viewport. Click the right mouse button and select Duplicate from the drop-down menu. Position the new jump pad as shown in Figure 6.2.

Note

In Figure 6.2, in addition to the new jump pad, you also see a new light. As you know from previous exercises, to add a Light object, you right-click and select Add Light Here.

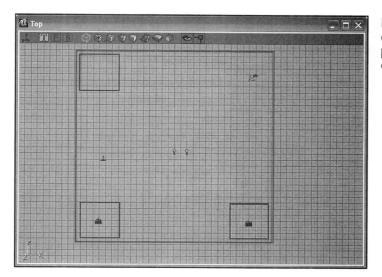

Figure 6.2 Duplicate one of the existing jump pads and place it in a corner.

After you add your new jump pad, your map allows you to move between three jump pads. Figure 6.3 illustrates the jump pads as they appear in your updated level. As in previous examples, note that the meshes and other objects are left disproportionately larger to make it easier to depict them in illustrations. You can resize your own to accord with your own sense of proportion.

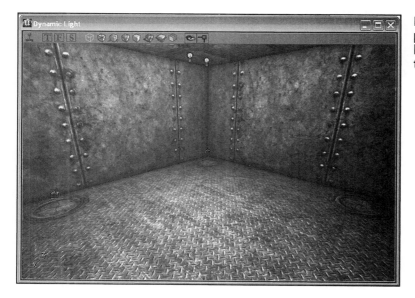

Figure 6.3 Three jump pads provide you with locations you can use to test your code.

Function Fundamentals

To create the classes in this chapter, you work extensively with functions you define on a custom basis. Functions are one of the two main elements of class definitions. Class data members are the other main element. Data members allow you to establish values that you can use in all functions of a class.

With reference to Figure 6.4, another way of expressing this is to say that a class data member establishes the *state* of a class. Functions regulate the *behavior* of a class. To understand what state and behavior involve, imagine a palm tree.

Classes are usually models of entities you find in the world or want to recognize distinctly in your game. An entity can be described according to its qualities. A palm tree, for example, has a number of palms. It has a trunk, and the trunk possesses a thickness. The palm tree has a height. It also has coconuts, and you can identify these by counting them. Finally, you can view a palm in terms of its age. Each of these qualities is an aspect of the state of a palm tree.

The state of a palm tree changes. The trunk of a palm can grow thicker. A palm tree ages. The number of coconuts can increase or decrease. The palm tree can grow in height. Such changes constitute the behavior of a palm tree.

To define a class to represent a palm tree, you can create data members to represent its state. As Figure 6.4 illustrates, NumberOfCoconuts accounts for the coconuts, and Height accounts for the height. Likewise, to cover the changing states of the palm tree, you can create functions with names like ChangeNumberOfCoconuts() or ChangeHeight(). Every class defines an entity in terms of its state and its behavior.

Functions allow you to control the behavior of a class object. In the various versions of the Trigger class you have created, when you have defined the PostBeginPlay() function, for example, you have set up a way to determine how your class object behaves. You have also

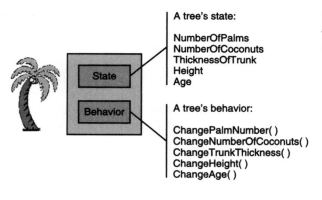

A tree's state:

NumberOfPalms
NumberOfCoconuts
ThicknessOfTrunk
Height
Age

A tree's behavior:

ChangePalmNumber( )
ChangeNumberOfCoconuts( )
ChangeTrunkThickness( )
ChangeHeight( )
ChangeAge( )

Figure 6.4 A palm tree can be described by its state and behavior.

used the `Message` property to set the message the class issues. Many other functions and variables in the base `Trigger` class might be called to attend to other aspects of the state and behavior of your class.

To the many functions and variables that you can use from base classes, you can add your own custom functions and variables. When you define a function, you add a specific type of behavior to your class. When you add a variable, you define a quality of its state.

The Math Class and Its Functions

In Chapter 5, you dealt extensively with the data members of classes. In this chapter, you continue work with data members, but you extend your work to include defining whole classes. Toward this end, you work extensively with functions.

Figure 6.5 illustrates a class named `Math`. The `Math` class contains five functions. Each function possesses a name that clearly identifies what the code it contains does. Each function likewise defines an aspect of the behavior of the class. The functions together attend to the responsibility of the class.

In this instance, the responsibilities of the `Math` class focus on basic arithmetic. The `Add()` function, for example, adds numbers. Likewise, the `Multiply()` function multiplies one number by another.

Each function has a given theme. When you define the function, you place code in it that attends to its theme in its scope. Isolating the code in this way allows you to put all the code that attends to a given task in a specific place. In each instance, the functions work in isolation from each other. The code within the scope of each function is not visible to the other functions.

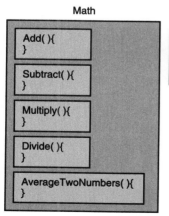

Figure 6.5 Functions provide ways to isolate and name specific activities within a class.

Here is the code for the Math class shown in Figure 6.5. You can find this class in the code in the Chapter 6 folder and the *.u file for the Ch04Area package. The Math.txt code provides the implementation of the Math class.

```
//========================================
// Math.
// See Math.txt
//========================================
class Math extends Actor;
// #1
// Takes two arguments of the type float
// and returns a value of the type float
public function float Add(float NumA, float Numb){
    return NumA + NumB;
}

public function float Subtract(float NumA, float Numb){
    return NumA - NumB;
}

public function float Multiply(float NumA, float Numb){
    return NumA * NumB;
}

public function float DivideAbyB(float NumA, float Numb){
    // #2
    // Declare a variable that is not
    // Visible to other functions
        local float Result;
    Result = 0;
    if(NumB != 0){
      Result = NumA/NumB;
    }
    return Result;
}

public function float AverageTwoNumbers(float First, float Second){
local float ResultingNumber;
    // #3
    // Call add from within the class
    // Assign the returned value of Add()
    ResultingNumber = Add(First, Second);
```

```
        // #4
        // When you assign a new value, you clear the old
        ResultingNumber = DivideAbyB(ResultingNumber, 2.0);
        return ResultingNumber;
    }
```

Table 6.1 provides specific information on the named features of the functions in the Math class. Subsequent sections discuss the code in detail.

Table 6.1 Terms for Definition of a Function

Term	Discussion
Access modifier	You have dealt with access modifiers before. The keywords most commonly used are public and private. When a function is public, you can call it from outside of your class. When a function is private, its use is restricted to the scope of the class in which you define it.
Return type	A function provides you with a value or some other item when you call it. What it provides is always data of a given type. When you define a function, then, you define its return type. This is the data type designation that starts the signature line of the function. If a function does not return a value, then you do not need to specify its return type.
Name of the function	Generally, when you name a function, capitalize it. If you use more than one word, capitalize each word. This is the case with AverageTwoNumbers(), in the Math class example.
Argument list	The argument list of a function defines the data you can submit to the function. The Add() function adds two numbers. The argument list defines the two numbers the function accepts. A function does not have to have an argument list.
Argument data type	Each identifier you include in an argument list for a function must have a data type. The data type of both of the arguments for the Add() function is float.
Argument identifier	Each argument for a function must have a name. You should identify arguments with names that help someone who is using your code understand what the arguments are for. NumA and NumB might not be the best identifier names, but the user of the code still gets the idea that two numbers are being used.
return	The return keyword makes it so that your function supplies the result of its operations to you when you call it. A function does not need to return a specific value.
Argument	To use an argument in the scope of your function, you just name it. In the Add() function, if you want to use the first number, then you type NumA. If you want to use the second number, then type NumB. You can use arguments over and over again.
Calling	When you call a function, you use it. To use a function, you name the function and supply arguments to it. To use the Add() function within your class to add two and two, you type Add(2,2);
local	You use this keyword to define the scope of variables used for specific functions. A local variable is visible only within the function in which you define it.

Figure 6.6 provides discussion of the features of the Add() function in the Math class. If you understand the Add() function, then you can understand the other functions in the class. As mentioned previously, Table 6.1 provides extended discussion of the terms used to describe the features. In essence, in addition to its name, each function is defined according to its accessibility, its arguments, and the type of its returned value. See the next few sections for specific discussion of the functions and other features of the Math class.

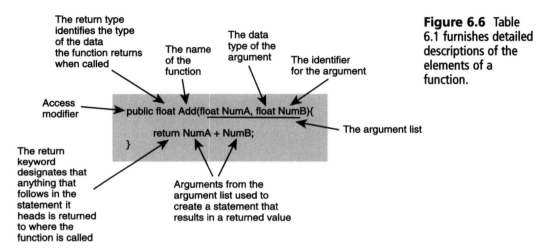

Figure 6.6 Table 6.1 furnishes detailed descriptions of the elements of a function.

Math Class Functions

In the code that follows comment #1 in the Math class, you define the Add() function. The rest of the functions are defined in roughly the same way. Each function definition begins with a statement of the access you want to allow the function. In the Math class, all of the functions are given public access. This means that when you use the class to develop another class (as happens later on in this chapter), you can access all the functions it contains.

Each function has a name, as you might expect, and following the name comes parentheses in which you define the arguments of the functions. A function can have an unlimited number of arguments, but programmers usually limit the number to only a few. Each argument is a part of the argument list for the function, and each argument in the argument list has an identifier and a data type. For the Add() function, one argument is named NumA. This argument has a data type of float.

All of the functions in the Math class return values. To return a value, you use the return keyword. You define the type of the return value in the first or signature line of the function. The keyword following the access modifier defines the return type. All returned values of the functions in the Math class are of the float type.

Local Function Scope

In the lines following comment #2 in the code sample for the Math class, you add a local variable to the definition of the DivideAbyB() function. A local variable is visible only within the function in which you define it. You define a local variable by qualifying it with the keyword local. Within the DivideAbyB() function, the local variable you define is named Result. You can use this variable only within the DivideAbyB() function.

Note

The DivideAbyB() function contains a statement that takes this form:

```
if(NumB != 0){
  Result = NumA/NumB;
}
```

This is known as a selection statement, and the syntax and uses of such statements are considered in greater detail in Chapter 7. This particular statement prevents division by 0.

If you tried to access the Result variable defined in the DivideAbyB() function within any of the other functions, the compiler would issue an error message. Figure 6.7 provides a mocked up version of the Math class in which the Result variable is defined in the DivideAbyB() function and then called in the Multiply() function. This action causes an error because the variable is not defined for use in the Multiply() function. It is defined only in the DivideAbyB() function. When used outside the scope of the function in which you define it, the compiler reports that the variable is "bad" or missing.

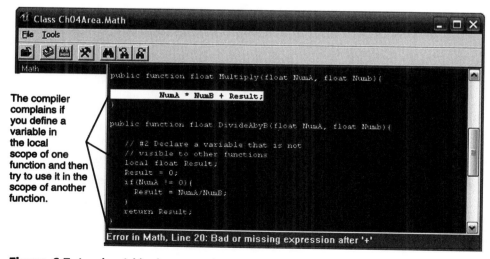

The compiler complains if you define a variable in the local scope of one function and then try to use it in the scope of another function.

Figure 6.7 Local variables have meaning only within the functions in which you define them.

To eliminate the error, you must define the Result variable in the Multiply() function. You can use approximately the same lines you see in the DivideAbyB() function definition. Here is how the corrected code might look:

```
public function float Multiply(float NumA, float NumB){
// Declare a variable that is not
// visible to other functions
   local float Result;
   Result = 1;
   return NumA * NumB + Result;
}

public function float DivideAbyB(float NumA, float NumB){
   // Declare a variable that is not
   // visible to other functions
   local float Result;
   Result = 0;
   // Lines left out
}
```

That you define two local variables with the name Return creates no problem for the compiler. The variables are not visible outside the functions in which you define them, so they exist as two separate entities.

Note

The code in this section has been created only to demonstrate the use of local variables. Do not change the definition of the Math class unless you want to test the concepts. If you change the class, you can always use the Math.txt file to retrieve the proper version of the class.

Calling Functions within a Function

When you develop classes, you often call functions within functions. In the lines following comment #3 in the definition of the Math class, you find the following line:

```
AddedNumbers = Add(First, Second);
```

You call the Add() function within the AverageTwoNumbers() function. In the lines following comment #4, you also call the DivideAbyB() function. In both cases, when you call a function defined in the class, you call it using only its name and the arguments needed for it. As a general rule, you can access any function in the class from within any function within the class.

When you call the Add() function, you supply two arguments to it. The Add() function processes the arguments and returns their sum. You assign the sum to a local variable, AddedNumbers. The return action of functions all work in a similar way. You supply arguments, the function you call processes the arguments, and then you receive the returned value by assigning it to a variable.

Assigning the returned value of a function is not the only way you can process returned values, but it is one of the easiest to understand. You use the assignment operator to assign the returned value to a variable. When you assign the returned value of the Add() function to the AddedNumbers variable, note that the data type of AddedNumbers and the return type of the Add() function are the same. Both are of the float type. The type of the variable to which you assign a returned value should be the same as the return type of the function that returns the value.

Note

The type of the variable to which you assign a returned value should be the same as the return type of the function that returns the value, but in some cases, the two types can vary. Recall the discussions of automatic data conversion in Chapter 5. Suppose a function returns a value of the int type. You assign the returned value to a variable of the float type. What happens? The returned value is likely to be automatically converted from the int to the float type. Here is an example:

```
public function int ReturnAnInt(){
    return 2;
}


public function float AverageTwoNumbers(float First, float Second){
    local float AddedNumbers;
    // The returned value differs from that of the
    // variable to which the value is assigned
    AddedNumbers = ReturnAnInt();
    // Lines left out
    return AddedNumbers;
}
```

The ReturnAnInt() function takes no arguments and always returns the same number, 2. You call it in the scope of the AverageTwoNumbers() function and assign its returned value to ResultingNumber, a local variable of the float type. The compiler does not generate an error because the int data type can be converted to the float data type.

Built-in Functions

Although you spend much time programming your own functions, UnrealScript provides you with a fairly large set of built-in functions. They are built-in functions because they are ready for you to use. You can use such functions for a variety of purposes.

Most of them are defined in the Unreal Tournament `Object` class. The `Actor` class is derived from the `Object` class. The `Object` class is the most basic of the UnrealScript classes.

The built-in functions allow you to do things like find the square root of a number or determine if a word is embedded in a given body of text. You can also call on a built-in function to generate random numbers. This you do later in this chapter.

It is beyond the scope of the current discussion to review all these functions. Table 6.2 discusses a few of the many available functions. The names of the functions in the table show the types of arguments used by the functions. Preceding the names of most of the functions is the type of the data the function returns. If the function does not return a value, then no return data type is shown.

Table 6.2 Selected Built-In Functions

Function/Constant	Discussion
`float FRand()`	This function provides you with a random number that ranges in value from 0 to 1. The numbers you see are less than 1, never equal to it. To use this function, you multiply the number it provides you by another number, such as 10. For example, it might return 0.4. If you multiply by 10, then the number you get is 4. You can shift numbers to any extent you want. If you want numbers in the range of 1000s, then you use an expression such as: `1000 * FRand()`.
`int Rand(int)`	This function provides you with random integers. To use this function, you supply it with an integer that establishes the maximum value of the range of numbers it generates. It generates numbers that start at 0 and go to one less than the value you supply. For example, if you use `Rand(10)`, then it supplies you with random numbers ranging from 0 to 9.
`float RandRange (float, float)`	This function works along the same lines as the `Rand()` and `FRand()` functions, but now you can more accurately define the numbers you want to see. You can designate the minimum and maximum values of the range of randomly generated numbers.
`float Abs(float)`	The absolute value of a number is its distance from zero in a positive or negative direction. This function returns the absolute value of any number you supply to it. The absolute value of −5 is 5, as is the absolute value of 5.
`float Sqrt(float)`	This function gives you the square root of the number you supply to it. The square root of 16 is 4.

float Square(float)	This function gives you the square of the number you supply to it. The square of 5 is 25.
float Cos(float A)	This function is one among many trigonometry functions. This one returns the cosign of an angle. You have to supply the value of the angle in radians. Discussion of what a radian is lies beyond the scope of the current discussion. Generally, however, you can convert any angle into radians. If you want to convert degrees to radians, just divide by 180.
string Chr(int)	This returns a character that represents the ASCII value you provide as an argument. ASCII means American Standard Code for Information Interchange. Letters have numeric equivalents. For capital letters, "A" is 65, "B" is 66. For lowercase letters, "a" is 90 and "b" is 91. Use of the ASCII code is somewhat antiquated because the standard has been incorporated into an international standard called Unicode, which covers the thousands upon thousands of characters used in all languages. ASCII provides you with 255 fairly useful characters. For example, for a line return, you can use Chr(10). For the letter Pi, use Chr(227). For infinity Ch(236).
int Int()	This function converts the number you are working with to an integer. Technically, when you use this function, you are casting a number to an integer. UnrealScript provides you with functions that allow you to convert other numbers in the same way: Float() and Double() are among these.
int Len(string)	This function tells you the number of letters in a line of text, including blank spaces. For example, Len("Work hard.") consists of 10 characters. The quotes only identify the characters and are not evaluated. The period and the blank space are evaluated.
ReplaceText(string, string, string)	This function is an example of one of the many built-in functions that ask you to supply more than one piece of information. It allows you to replace a portion of a source or target string with another string. It takes three arguments. The first argument is the source or target string. The second argument provides the string you want to replace in the target string. The third argument furnishes the replacement string you want to end up with.

Classes by Composition

When you create a class like the Math class, you cannot use it directly as an object in your level. Instead, you make use of it by making it part of a class that you do use in your level. In this way, you can call the functions from the Math class and use them as needed. You do have to re-create them in the class you place in your level. When you use a class in this way, one class is said to be *composed* of another. The overall relation between the two classes is called *composition*.

In all of the programming examples you have worked with so far, you have derived one class from another. When you do this, you use the extends keyword in the signature line of the class definition. To create a class called `Math` class, for example, you use this signature line:

```
class Math extends Actor;
```

Along similar lines, to derive a class called `AddNumbersTrigger` from the `Trigger` class, you use this signature:

```
class AddNumbersTrigger extends Trigger placeable;
```

In each case, you derive the class you create from a base class. The class you create is a subordinate class in a class hierarchy.

Deriving one class from another, also known as inheritance, is a key activity of programming with UnrealScript, because UnrealScript is an object-oriented programming language, and object-oriented programming involves deriving one class from another. Your derived class specializes the base class. Your derived class inherits the variables and functions from the base class. In this way, your versions of the `Trigger` class have made use of the base `Trigger` class. In this way, likewise, the `Math` class draws on the `Actor` class.

In contrast to derivation, you can use classes on the basis of composition. Composition involves creating an instance of one class inside another. You are making it so that one class is composed of one or more instances of another class.

When you define the `AddNumbersTrigger` class, you declare a member variable called `AddNumbersTrigger`. This variable is of the `Math` class type. You use this member variable to access the functions in the `Math` class. The functions in the `Math` class in this way become available to you as you develop the `AddNumbersTrigger` class. Specifically, because the `AddNumbersTrigger` class is composed of an instance of the `Math` class, you can call the `Add()` function of the `Math` class. This function helps you develop a message that includes added numbers.

Figure 6.8 provides a Unified Modeling Language (UML) class diagram that shows you how the class hierarchy you create unfolds when you include both derived and composed classes. (For further discussion of the UML, see the sidebar, "UML Views".)

The arrows with the hollow tips in Figure 6.8 show that you derive such classes as `CommandTrigger` and `AddNumbersTrigger` from the `Trigger` class. The line with the diamond tip shows a relation of composition between the `AddNumbersTrigger` class and the `Math` class. While you derive the other classes from the base class, you create an instance of the `Math` class within the `AddNumbersTrigger` class. There is no derivation involved in this relationship. Because of this, the `AddNumbersTrigger` and `Math` classes are said to be *peer* classes.

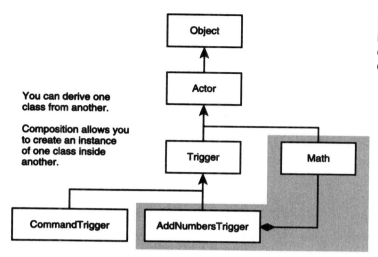

Figure 6.8 Use inheritance and composition to create events in your game.

Coding the AddNumbersTrigger Class

Here is the code that implements the AddNumbersTrigger class. Discussion of specific features of the class follows.

```
//━━━━━━━━━━━━━━━━━━━━━━━━━━━━━━━━━━━━━━━━━━━━━━━━
// AddNumbersTrigger.
// See AddNumbersTrigger.txt
//━━━━━━━━━━━━━━━━━━━━━━━━━━━━━━━━━━━━━━━━━━━━━━━━
class AddNumbersTrigger extends Trigger placeable;

    var (Message) string NumbersMessage;
    // #1
    // Data member for Math class
    var private Math NumberFromMath;
    // Data members for random numbers
    var private int RandNumberA,
                    RandNumberB;

function PostBeginPlay(){
    Super.PostBeginPlay();
    // #2
    // Set the values here rather than in the
    // the Properties dialog
    ReTriggerDelay = 1.0;
    RepeatTriggerTime = 2.5;
```

```
    // #3
    // Generate the random numbers
    // and assign them to the data members
    RandNumberA = Rand(25);
    RandNumberB = Rand(25);
    // #4
    // Pass the arguments to the function
    NumbersMessage = GetMessage(RandNumberA ,RandNumberB);
    Message = NumbersMessage;
}


public function string GetMessage(int FirstNum,
                                  int SecondNum){
    local string NumberString;
    local int SumOfNumbers;
    // #5
// Create an instance of the Math class
    NumberFromMath = spawn(class 'Math');

    // #6
    // Use the instance of the Math class to
    // call the Add() Method
    // Convert the float to an integer
    // Create a text message

    SumOfNumbers = Int(NumberFromMath.Add(FirstNum, SecondNum));
    NumberString = FirstNum @ " added to  " @ SecondNum
                         @ " is " @ SumOfNumbers ;
  return NumberString;
}
```

To create the AddNumbersTrigger class, open the Actor Class Browser and click on the Trigger class as you have when creating classes in previous chapters. Activate the Ch04Area package if it is not already active. Then add the code for the AddNumbersTrigger class to the code editor. If you want to access the text for the source code, see the AddNumbersTrigger.txt in the Chapter 6 source folder.

UML Views

The Unified Modeling Language (UML) is a formal engineering approach to planning and representing the object-oriented programs you create using UnrealScript and other object-oriented programming (or scripting) languages. Figure 6.9 illustrates two of the classes you create in this chapter, the Math and AddNumbersTrigger classes.

As Figure 6.9 shows, a UML class diagram usually consists of three compartments. In the top compartment, you name the class that the diagram represents. In the middle compartment, you list the member variables of the class. In the bottom compartment, you list the member functions of the class.

The symbols used with the class diagram allow you to know details. To indicate the access permissions you assign the variable or function, you use a plus sign (+) to show that it is public and a minus sign (–) to show that it is private. You follow the name of a variable with a colon and the keyword that identifies its data type. You follow the name of a function and a keyword that identifies the data type of its returned value. If the function does not return a value, you use the term *void*. In C++, which is the language used to create the Unreal engine, void is a keyword used to show a function does not return a value.

To accommodate the complexity of packages, the UML provides you with a package diagram. A package diagram uses a tabbed box to show the name of your package. You then use arrows with dotted lines to show the classes you have included in your package. Figure 6.10 illustrates a package diagram for the Ch04Area package.

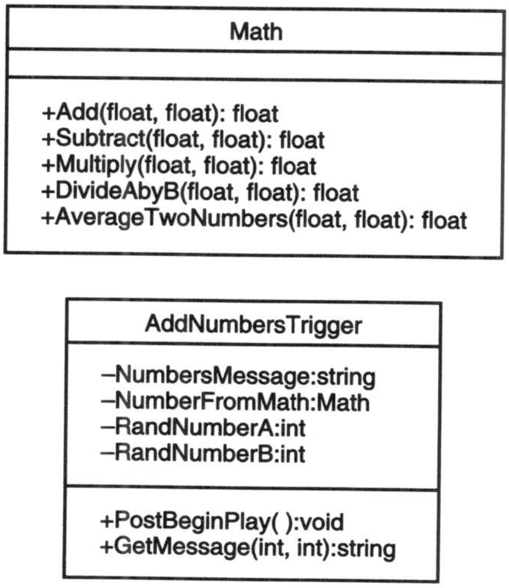

Math
+Add(float, float): float
+Subtract(float, float): float
+Multiply(float, float): float
+DivideAbyB(float, float): float
+AverageTwoNumbers(float, float): float

Figure 6.9 UML diagrams provide a quick and easy way to capture the main details of your classes.

AddNumbersTrigger
–NumbersMessage:string
–NumberFromMath:Math
–RandNumberA:int
–RandNumberB:int
+PostBeginPlay( ):void
+GetMessage(int, int):string

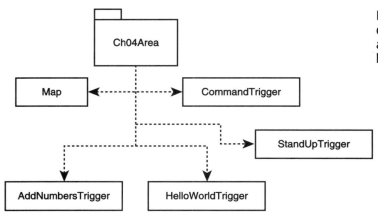

Figure 6.10 A package diagram allows you to account for the classes you have included in a package.

Creating an Instance of a Class

In the code following comment #1 in the AddNumbersTrigger class, you declare four data members for the class. As previous discussions have emphasized, declaration involves assigning a data type to an identifier. The four identifiers you define in this way employ three data types: int, string, and Math. Here are the lines that accomplish this work:

```
var (Message) string NumbersMessage;
var private Math NumberFromMath;
var private int RandNumberA,
                RandNumberB;
```

In each instance, when you declare the identifiers, you tell the compiler that you want to associate a given identifier with a given data type. You do not yet assign a value to the identifier.

Use of the Math data type introduces a new element to your activities as an UnrealScript programmer, because this is the first time you make use of a data type that you create.

The Math class furnishes you with several functions. When you call functions within a class, you need only to name the function you want to call. You observed how this worked when you called the Add() and DivideAbyB() functions within the AverageTwoNumbers() function.

When you want to use a function a given class provides within another class, more work is needed. You must create an object for the class from which you want to call functions. More specifically, you must create an *instance* of the class from which you want to call functions. In the AddNumbersTrigger class, after declaring the NumberFromMath identifier for the Math class instance at the class scope, your next stop is within the GetMessage() function. There you create an instance of the Math class to assign to the identifier. The line that accomplishes this task is associated with comment #5:

```
// #5
// Create an instance of the Math class
NumberFromMath = spawn(class 'Math');
```

To create an instance of a class, you employ the spawn keyword. The spawn keyword tells the compiler to dynamically *construct* a class object. When you dynamically construct an object, you tell the compiler to allocate memory for the object while your program is running. As an argument for the spawn keyword, in parentheses following the keyword you use the class keyword followed in single quotes by the name of the data type you want to use to create an object. In this case, the data type is Math.

Calling a Function by Using a Class Object

After you use the spawn keyword to create an instance of the Math class, you then have on hand a defined class object called NumberFromMath. Using this object, you can access all the public functions in the Math class. To access the functions, you use the Math object, the *dot operator*, and the name of the function you want to call. In this instance, you call the Add() function. You find the call in the lines associated with comment #6:

```
SumOfNumbers = Int(NumberFromMath.Add(FirstNum, SecondNum));
```

You make the call using a *cascaded* function call. A cascaded function call involves using a call to a function as the argument of another function.

To show how this works, consider first the basic function call. You use the class object, NumberFromMath, to call the Add() function:

```
NumberFromMath.Add(FirstNum, SecondNum);
```

This constitutes the basic act of calling the function from the composed class. You might assign the returned value of the function to the SumOfNumbers variable in this way:

```
SumOfNumbers = NumberFromMath.Add(FirstNum, SecondNum);
```

As you know from having implemented the Math class, the Add() function requires two arguments. These are the numbers you want to add. Here you supply values stored in two local variables, FirstNum and SecondNum. The returned value of the Add() function is the sum of the values of the two arguments you supply. As the definition of the function shows, the type of the returned value is float. That you use NumberFromMath to call the function makes no difference. The statement still returns the sum of the two numbers.

The only problem is that when you perform this operation, by default the function returns numbers that possess several places of precision, so rather than seeing 4, you see 4.0000. Such a number proves excessive for current purposes, so to get rid of the zeros you need to convert the number to a different form.

Toward this end, you embed the returned value in another function. In this case, the other function is a special type of function. This is the `Int()` function. You use it to *cast* the `float` value to an `int` value:

```
SumOfNumbers = Int(NumberFromMath.Add(FirstNum, SecondNum));
```

The final few lines in the function create the line of text you display in the game when the trigger is activated:

```
NumberString = FirstNum @ " added to  " @ SecondNum
                         @ " is " @ SumOfNumbers ;
```

When you concatenate numbers with a string, the numbers are automatically converted into string values. You repeatedly use the concatenation operator (@) to join the parts of the text message together. In this way, you create a string that tells you the two numbers you are adding and the result of the addition.

Generating Random Numbers

Creating an instance of the `Math` class and then calling the `Add()` function allows you to create a line of text that you assign to the `NumberString` variable. You declare the `NumberString` variable in the context of the `GetMessage()` message function. The `GetMessage()` function has a return type of `string`. The string returned text that might read along the following lines:

```
23 added to 23 is 46
```

To make it so that you can assign the line of text to the `Message` property and make it display as you play your level, you call the `GetMessage()` method in the scope of the `PostBeginPlay()` function. Here are the lines, associated with comment #3, that perform this work:

```
//#3
// Generate the random numbers
// and assign them to the data members
RandNumberA = Rand(25);
RandNumberB = Rand(25);
//#4
// Pass the arguments to the function
NumbersMessage = GetMessage(RandNumberA, RandNumberB );
Message = NumbersMessage;
```

To generate values that you can use to define the `RandNumberA` and `RandNumberB` variables, you call the `Rand()` function. As discussed previously, this is a built-in function defined in the `Object` class. Its argument sets the maximum number of the value you obtain from the function.

You make two calls to the `Rand()` function, and in each case you submit the returned numbers to the `GetMessage()` function. You assign the message to the `NumbersMessage` variable. You then assign the value of `NumbersMessage` to the `Message` variable. This action is performed once each time you create an instance of the `AddNumbersTrigger` class. For each instance of the class you create, the set of numbers is likely to be different, so the text you display is also likely to be different.

Optimization and Default Values

You could do things much more efficiently by rewriting the code that defines your text so that you make calls to the `Rand()` function part of a cascading statement and then assign the returned value of the `GetMessage()` function directly to the `Message` variable. However, for purposes of initial exploration, it is best to avoid such *optimized* measures. Here is the optimized version:

```
Message = GetMessage(Rand(25), Rand(25) );
```

Optimization eliminates the need for the `RandNumberA`, `RandNumberB`, and `NumbersMessage` variables. Experienced programmers do not necessarily always optimize their code. There can be much benefit from writing code that shows the general flow of activity embedded in a program. Still, excessively redundant code can slow down your programs.

Setting Defaults

In the lines associated with comment #2, you use two member variables to set properties that determine the frequency and duration of the messages your `Trigger` object displays. Here is the code:

```
// #2
// Set the values here rather than in the
// Properties dialog
ReTriggerDelay = 1.0;
RepeatTriggerTime = 2.5;
```

You have access to the `ReTriggerDelay` and `RepeatTriggerTime` member variables because they are defined in the parent `Trigger` class. If you look in the `Trigger` class definition, you find the following lines:

```
var() float RepeatTriggerTime;
// if > 0, repeat trigger message at this interval is still touching other
var() float ReTriggerDelay;
// minimum time before trigger can be triggered again
```

These variables are defined without the `public` keyword. When defined in this way, they are by default public, so you can access them directly in derived classes. As discussed previously, for each instance of the `Trigger` class you create in your level, you can set such values using the Properties dialog, as Figure 6.11 illustrates. On the other hand, you can save work if you set the values in your definition of the class.

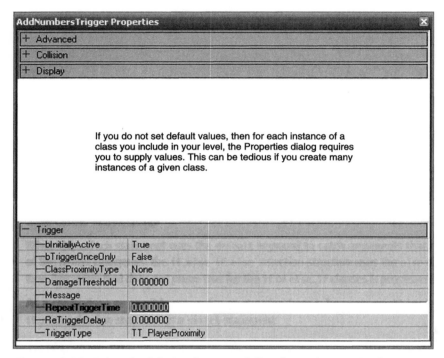

Figure 6.11 To handle default values, you define them when you implement your class.

Multiple Instances

Each time you create an instance of the AddNumbersTrigger class, you call the Rand() function to set the values of the RandNumberA and RandNumberB variables. These in turn you pass the GetMessage() function, which creates a line of text. As defined for the AddNumbersTrigger class, the Rand() function is called only when you create an instance of your class. You create an instance of the class when you compile your level.

To investigate some of the implications of this activity, delete the Trigger objects you have previously added to your Ch06Area01 map and replace them with instances of the AddNumbersTrigger class, as shown in Figure 6.12. When you finish, you should have created three instances of the class and placed each above a jump pad.

Since you have already set the ReTriggerDelay and RepeatTriggerTime values in the definition of the class, do not use the Properties dialog. Click the Build Changed Lighting and Build Geometry icons. Then click the Play Map icon.

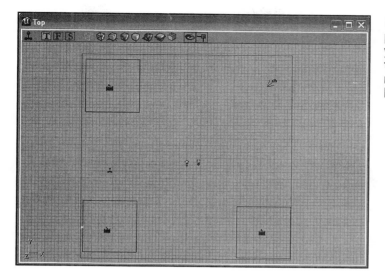

Figure 6.12 Delete previous instances of your classes and place three instances of the new class in your level.

Figure 6.13 illustrates the text generated when your player avatar encounters one of the triggers. If you go from trigger to trigger, you see the same text output, but the numbers vary according to those generated when the class object is constructed.

Figure 6.13 Each jump pad trigger generates a different set of random numbers.

Note

The jump pad has been left disproportionately large for purpose of illustration. Resize it to accord with your sense of proportion. To remove features from the display, press Alt and the minus (–) key.

In addition to the line of text, you also see an icon for each instance of the `AddNumbersTrigger` class that you put in your level. Viewed in isolation the icon appears as shown in Figure 6.14. This icon appears when you use the `spawn` keyword to create an instance of a trigger.

Figure 6.14 An icon shows that you have used the `spawn` keyword.

When you play the level, if you type the tilde to open the command area, you see a report of the messages your triggers issue. As Figure 6.15 shows, with three triggers, you generate only three sets of numbers.

As a final note, if you want to even up your text report, you can use the `Chr()` function with an argument of 9, which is the ASCII code for a tab character. You might use this statement to create the text:

```
NumberString =  FirstNum @ Chr(9) @ " added to "  @ Chr(9)
                @ SecondNum @ " is " @ Chr(9)
                @ SumOfNumbers;
```

Figure 6.16 shows you the revised output. Aligning columns can improve the appearance of any number of data displays, so such formatting functions as `Chr()` can be useful.

Figure 6.15 You get a unique set of numbers for each object you instantiate.

Figure 6.16 Tabs change the alignment of your text.

Conclusion

You have dealt with some fairly abstract notions in this chapter. At the same time, you have added a vast new dimension to your programming activities by investigating how to use composition to make use of peer classes. When you develop the Math class, you create a peer class for the AddNumbersTrigger class. At the same time, you also create a class that you can use on a composition basis with any other class you develop. Composition, like inheritance (or specialization) is one of the key activities involved in object-oriented programming.

When you developed the Math class, you had the chance to take a close look at how to define functions. Functions are important parts of classes. They tend to the behavior of classes. When you explore functions, you also extend your understanding of how important scope can be in the development and use of classes. A variable defined in the local scope of a function cannot be used in other functions.

The work you performed in this chapter sets the stage for activities in Chapter 7. Among other things, you are now ready to begin working with control structures, reference, and different uses of the Pawn class.

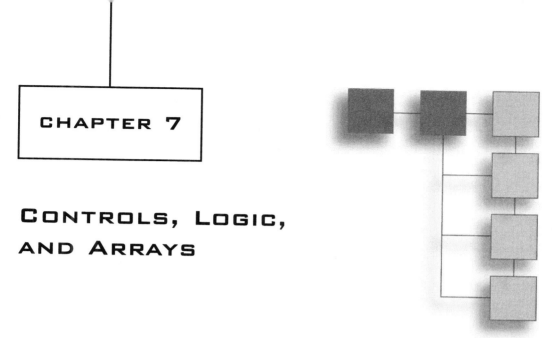

CHAPTER 7

CONTROLS, LOGIC, AND ARRAYS

I n this chapter you explore the use of control statements. Along the way, you deal with a large number of supplementary topics, such as what characterizes abstract and concrete classes, and how and why you override a function provided to you from a base class. You also begin to dig deeper into the Unreal Tournament class hierarchy, examining in detail features of the Actor, Pawn, and Trigger classes. Among these features are the IsRelevant() and Touch() functions. While pursuing these activities, you investigate the idea of program flow and see that sequence, selection, and repetition allow programmers to exercise all the actions required to create computer programs. In this chapter, the emphasis is on sequence and selection. In Chapter 8, you find extended examples of repetition. You also add to your store of tools by examining the use of Boolean logic and compound operations. To put your knowledge to work you develop several new classes, one that consists of a few hundred lines of code. These classes define the CommandTouchTrigger and CommandMessageTrigger objects. As you develop these classes, in addition to expanding your use of built-in functions, you incorporate new devices, such as enumerations and arrays. Such devices tremendously expand the complexity of the classes you create. Among specific topics are these:

- Understanding the sequential flow of programs
- How to override a function
- Using compound Boolean expressions
- Creating selection statements
- Working with enumerated values
- Using built-in expressions to create messages

125

Program Flow

When you define a class such as the CommandTrigger class in Chapter 6, you do so by adding to a fairly large program consisting of many thousands of lines of code, but the file you work in as you develop your class can also itself be viewed as a program. Regardless of the scope of programming activity you examine, both when you compile a program and when you execute it, the flow of activity that takes place generally proceeds from the start to the end of the program.

The flow of activity in a program takes place through the statements a program contains. Statements consist of combinations of operators and operands, and you usually terminate them using a semicolon. A statement is a unit of syntax the compiler recognizes as a complete unit. For this reason, when you see error messages, they usually tell you about a given statement because the compiler reads one statement after another as it makes its way through your program. When it encounters one that it cannot understand, it stops. At this point, you have written a multitude of statements.

Sequential Flow

As Figure 7.1 illustrates, if you define a variable named Counter, the line with which you define it is a statement, as is the line with which you initialize it. Following the definition of the variable, among an unlimited number of possibilities, you might write three successive statements in which you use the increment operator (++) to increase the value assigned to the variable. Each line on which you use the increment operator and that you terminate with a semicolon constitutes a statement.

As the program moves through the statements shown in Figure 7.1, it progresses *sequentially*. One statement executes and then the next. The program continues to execute until it reaches the last statement, and then it terminates. This is the default flow of all programs you write with UnrealScript. In fact, this is the default flow of computer programs generally because it reflects how the central processing unit (CPU) of your computer works. It begins a process at the first statement, proceeds to the next, and continues on until it reaches the last statement. Figure 7.1 shows but one of the many operations you can perform using the sequential flow of a program.

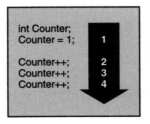

When you use an increment operator, the sequential flow of your program increases the value of Count.

With each statement, you invoke the increment operator.

Figure 7.1 The default flow of a program is sequential.

Selection and Repetition Flow

While the sequential flow of a program provides an effective way to perform a multitude of programming tasks, UnrealScript and most other programming languages also provide you with ways to alter the sequential flow of a program. One of these is called *selection*. The other is called *repetition*. Together, sequence, selection, and repetition allow you to perform all the actions required to develop any program. This generalization might sound impossible, but computer scientists over the decades have again and again confirmed it. Just three basic activities make possible the flow of all computer programs.

Saying that three basic activities make all computer programs possible overly simplifies matters, however. Selection and repetition can become extraordinarily involved activities. It remains, however, that even if they become endlessly complex, the more you explore their uses the more you find that sequence and repetition usually involve a relatively limited number of expressions. Figure 7.2 shows you some of the selection and repetition statements UnrealScript provides.

As Figure 7.3 illustrates, each of the three types of program flow has a distinct purpose. Sequence characterizes the overall flow of the program, one statement progressing to the next. Selection allows you to provide your program with alternative paths of flow. Repetition allows you to make it so that your program repeats given statements over and over again.

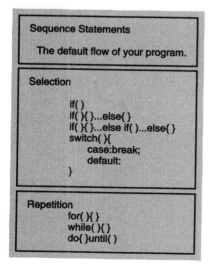

Figure 7.2 Sequence, selection, and repetition underlie all programming activity.

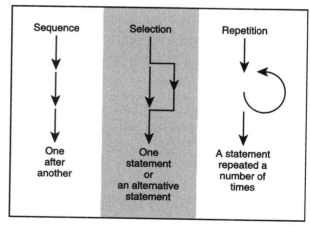

Figure 7.3 Each type of flow possesses distinctive characteristics.

The Syntax of Control Statements

Selection and repetition are made possible by specific types of statements that involve common syntactic elements. Figure 7.4 illustrates these syntactic elements. The top section of the figure displays a selection statement. In the bottom section, the figure displays a repetition statement.

Each statement involves three syntactic elements. The first is the *control* keyword. The control keyword identifies the type of action you want to perform. It is sometimes accompanied by other keywords, but it remains primary.

In close association with the control keyword is the *control expression*. You enclose the control expression in parentheses. Depending on the keyword you use, you place the control expression before or after the control keyword. For the if and while keywords, as Figure 7.4 shows, the control expression follows.

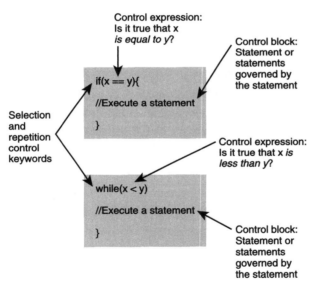

Figure 7.4 Three basic syntax features describe most control statements.

In addition to the control keyword and the control expression, you create a *control block*. The control block usually opens with an opening curly brace and closes with a closing curly brace. There are a few exceptions to this, but it is good to observe this as a general programming practice. All the statements you include in the braces are governed by the control expression. You can place as many statements in a block as you want. You can also place other control statements in the block. Such structures are called *embedded selection statements* or *embedded repetition statements*, depending on the type of control statement used.

The most complex part of a control statement is the control expression. The basic type of control expression contains a logical expression that usually takes two forms, as Figure 7.5

illustrates. The first form involves two operands and an operator. In this case, you make use of any of a number of the operators UnrealScript provides to create an expression that compares the value you have assigned to one operand to the value you have assigned to another operand.

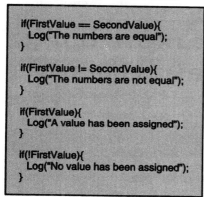

Logical Operators

==	is equal to
<	is less than
>	is greater than
=<	is less than or equal to
=>	is greater than or equal to
!=	is not equal to

Expressions

true	keyword: is always true
false	keyword: is always false
VariableName	Use the variable name alone to determine if a value has been assigned to it.
!VariableName	Use the NOT operator (!) to render a true result if no value has yet been assigned to the variable.

Figure 7.5 Control expressions involve using all the standard operators.

In the first example on the left in Figure 7.5, the equality operator allows you to compare the value assigned to FirstValue to the value assigned to SecondValue. The data types of the objects should be the same so that the equality operator can compare the values, but what matters most centrally is whether the values assigned to the operands are equal. If they are equal, then the flow of the program enters the control block, and all statements in the block are executed. If the values are not equal, then the flow of the program skips over the statements in the program.

The second example on the left in Figure 7.5 illustrates another common logical expression. In this instance, you seek to discover when one value is *not* equal to another. A typical scenario in this situation is the one you encountered in Chapter 6, in the definition of the Math class. There, a selection statement in the DivideAbyB() function evaluated the denominator of a division operation to determine if it was not equal to 0:

```
if(NumB != 0){
  Result = NumA/NumB;
}
```

To prevent division by 0, you evaluate whether the number you have supplied as the denominator is not equal to 0. Only in this instance do you allow the division to take place.

The third and fourth examples on the left in Figure 7.5 show the use of single expressions that consist of one operator and one operand. The first of the expressions tests for whether FirstValue contains any value greater than 0. If you assign 0 to a variable, the variable evaluates to false. This expression, then, tests to determine whether the value is greater than zero.

When you deal with primitive data types, if no value has been assigned to a variable, then the variable usually contains by default a value of zero. If the data type of the variable is bool, then the value of a variable you have not initialized is false. If the data type is of an abstract type, then it holds a null or none value, which for practical purposes is the same as 0. A selection or repetition statement evaluates null, 0, and false as false.

Flags

In the last of the examples in Figure 7.5, you use the negation operator to qualify the FirstValue operand. In this case, the expression evaluates true if FirstValue is 0, null, or false. As an example, consider a situation in which you create a variable of the bool type called FirstValue. The variable allows you to control how many times you are going to perform a given action. In this case, the action involves creating an Actor object. Here is a bit of code that might perform such an operation:

```
Var bool FirstVar;
// Later in your program
FirstVar = false;
// Still later in your program,
// in a function that repeatedly executes
// The negation of false is true
if(!FirstVar){
   //Create the Actor object
   FirstVar = true;
}
```

You want to create the Actor object only once. You use FirstValue as a *flag*. When your program starts, you set the value of FirstValue to 0 or false. You then embed the code that creates the Actor object in the if selection statement. When the selection statement evaluates the variable, it finds that the negative of false is true, so the flow of your program enters the control block and creates the Actor object.

After you perform the statement, within the control block you set the FirstValue variable to true. Following this action, the flow of your program exits the block but cannot again enter it, because when the selection expression evaluates the FirstValue variable, it finds it set to true, and the negative of true is false.

When you use a variable in this way, you use it as a *flag*. The selection statement in which you use it is called a *toggle*. As you see in the code that defines the CommandTouchTrigger class, many functions return bool values that allow you to control the activities of your program on this basis.

Tip

Initially setting a flag to false is not the only way to create a toggle. You can just as easily set the flag to true. In this case, the logic follows the same course. You set the flag to false after you perform the operation you want to toggle.

Return Values' Control Values

In addition to expressions that consist of operands and operators, you can also use the values functions return to control selection and repetition statements. You see such actions frequently used in most of the classes in the Unreal Tournament hierarchy. Here is an example of a typical situation:

```
var int FirstVar;
FirstVar = 12;
if( IsThisValid(FirstVar) ){
    // Perform an action
}
// The definition of the function used in the selection statement
function bool IsThisValid(int Value){
    local bool Evaluation = false;
    if( Value > 10){
        Evaluation = true;
    }
    return Evaluation;
}
```

The IsThisValid() function checks any integer value you provide to it as an argument and determines if the value is greater than 10. The return type of the function is bool. If the value is greater than 10, the function returns true. If the value is 10 or less than 10, the function returns false. You use a call to the function to control the selection statement. You call it in place of using an explicitly stated control expression.

The CommandTouchTrigger Class

The CommandTouchTrigger class allows you to create a trigger that differs from those you have viewed in previous chapters. You can program a trigger so that it responds to the *state* of another object. In this instance, the object to which it responds is a Pawn. Pawn objects, like Trigger objects, are specialized versions of the Actor class. Pawn objects provide a way to add animated character meshes to your levels. One important Pawn object is the one associated with the player, which you see when you activate a level and press F4.

The state and behavior of the object that provides the player Pawn objects are fairly complex, but in this chapter, you concentrate on only its position and whether it is standing or crouching. By assessing the value of the member variable that stores the crouching status of the Pawn object, you can control the actions your trigger performs.

To implement the CommandTouchTrigger class, begin as in previous chapters by creating a new version of your level. Begin in this case with the Ch06Area01.ut2 map. Save this as Ch07Area01.ut2. After you have saved the level, Click the Build Changed Lighting and Build Geometry icons. Then click the Play Map icon to test it. Press the tilde key and type EXIT to return to the editor.

Having completed a sanity check, delete the three icons for the existing Trigger objects, so that your level contains only the three jump pads. This now puts you in a position to add three instances of the CommandTouchTrigger class after you have implemented the code for it.

Implementing the CommandTouchTrigger Class

To implement the code for the CommandTouchTrigger class, open the Actor Class Browser. In the lower of the fields, click to activate the Ch04Area package. In the top field, navigate to the Trigger class, right-click, and select New. In the dialog, type Ch04Area for the package name and CommandTouchTrigger for the class name. Click OK to generate the class signature line and open the code editor.

To implement the class, type or copy the CommandTouchTrigger.txt listing into the code editor. The CommandTouchTrigger.txt file is located in the Chapter 7 code folder. Here is the code for the class. Extensive review of its specific features follows.

```
//════════════════════════════════
// CommandTouchTrigger
// See CommandTouchTrigger.txt
//════════════════════════════════
class CommandTouchTrigger extends Trigger placeable;
    // #1
    // data members for messages and random numbers
    var private string FirstMessage;
```

```
    var private string SecondMessage;
    var private int RandomNumber;

function PostBeginPlay()
{
    // #2
    // Call PostBeginPlay() in the parent class (Trigger)
    Super.PostBeginPlay();
    Message = FirstMessage;
}// end PostBeginPlay()


// #3
// As defined in the parent class,
// Touch() is called when an actor touches the trigger.
function Touch( actor Other )
{
    // #4
    // Can the touching Actor object affect this Trigger object
    if (IsRelevant( Other ) )
    {
        // #5
        // Cast the Other reference and determine
        // if the pawn is crouching
        if (Pawn(Other).bIsCrouched){
            // #6 Generate a random number and display a message
            // relevant to crouching pawns
            RandomNumber = Rand(10);
            SecondMessage = "Get up!" @ RandomNumber;
            Message= SecondMessage;
        }// end if
        else{
            // #7 The actor's pawn is not crouching
            RandomNumber = Rand(10);
            FirstMessage = "Get down!" @ RandomNumber;
            Message = FirstMessage;
        }// end else
        // #8 Call the parent class version of Touch()
        super.Touch(Other);
    }// end outer if
}// end Touch()
```

Data Members

The `CommandTouchTrigger` class becomes visible in your level primarily as a message that reports the state of your player `Pawn` object. Two of the three data members, `FirstMessage` and `SecondMessage`, attend to messages. You declare these data members in the code following comment #1. They are both of the `string` data type. You define both as private, meaning that they cannot be accessed directly from outside the class.

In addition to the two data members that attend to the messages the class issues, you declare a data member of the `int` type (`RandomNumber`) to accommodate values you generate using the `Rand()` function. Initially, this activity is trivial. You merely append the value assigned to the `RandomNumber` variable to the end of the text you issue for a message. In subsequent iterations of the `CommandTouchTrigger` class in this chapter, however, you use the `RandomNumber` variable to arrive at more interesting results.

Abstract Classes and Functions

The `CommandTouchTrigger` class contains two functions. These are the `PostBeginPlay()` and the `Touch()` functions. Before discussing the specific features of these functions, it is in many ways helpful to discuss their origins in the Unreal Tournament hierarchy and how it is that you use them in the implementation of the `CommandTouchTrigger` class.

Key concepts in this regard are *abstract classes*, *concrete classes*, and *function overriding*. As Figure 7.6 illustrates, both the `Actor` and the `Trigger` classes are abstract classes. The formal definition of an abstract class is a class that contains an abstract function.

An abstract function is a function that you declare without defining it, much as you declare a member variable without defining it. Here are how the `PostBeginPlay()` and `Touch()` functions are declared abstractly in the `Actor` class.

```
// As defined in the Actor class
event PostBeginPlay();
event Touch( Actor Other );
```

The keyword `event` is in some ways the equivalent of the keyword `function`, but it designates in this instance functions that are abstract. Declared in this way, these functions make the class in which they are declared abstract.

From a formal point of view, when you derive a class from an abstract class, the derived class remains abstract unless you define all the abstract functions the derived class inherits from the abstract class. As Figure 7.6 shows, the `Triggers` class is derived from the `Actor` class. It does not define any functions. It remains abstract. The `Trigger` class is derived from the `Triggers` class. It defines functions and it is not abstract. Here are partial signature lines of the three classes:

```
class Actor extends Object abstract  /*code left out */;
class Triggers extends Actor abstract  /*code left out */;
class Trigger extends Triggers /*code left out */;
```

As the signature lines show, to declare a class abstract, you use the abstract keyword. While the signature lines of the Actor and Triggers classes contain the abstract keyword, the signature line of the Trigger class does not. Likewise, the signature line of the CommandTouchTrigger class also lacks the abstract keyword:

```
class CommandTouchTrigger extends Trigger;
```

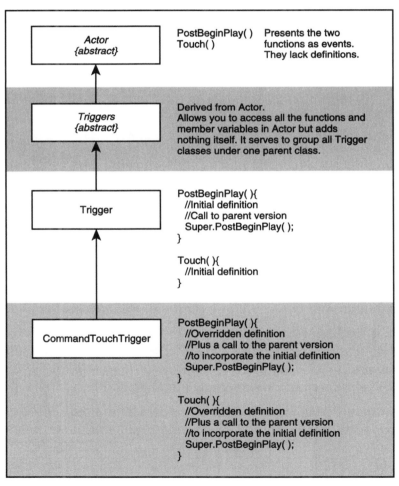

Figure 7.6 When you override a function, you write a new version, but you can use the super keyword to bring forward the old version to include it in your new version.

The `Trigger` and `CommandTouchTrigger` classes are referred to as *concrete classes*. They are concrete because you can create instances of them. This is not the case with abstract classes. You do not use abstract classes directly; instead, you derive classes from them. In the classes you derive from them, you define the abstract functions the abstract classes contain.

When programmers create abstract classes or functions, they do so because they seek to create patterns for derived classes. This is evident with the `Triggers` class. It brings forward all the functions of the `Actor` class and presents them as a pattern for all the classes you create to specialize the `Trigger` class. The functions it brings forward become fundamental features of the concrete classes derived from the `Trigger` type.

Member Functions and Overriding

As the discussion of abstract and concrete classes indicates, abstract classes invite you to define certain functions. This is what happens in the creation of the `Trigger` class. To make this a concrete class, all the functions declared abstractly in the `Actor` class are defined. The `PostBeginPlay()` and the `Touch()` functions fall into this category.

As it stands, however, when you get to your class, the `CommandTouchTrigger` class, you inherit defined versions of these functions. The class that provides them to you is not abstract, so you can use the defined versions as is or create your own versions of them. When you create your own versions, you *override* them.

As Figure 7.6 illustrates, when you override a function, you remake it in a specific class context. It already exists in a concrete, defined form in a parent class. Instead of initially defining the function, your use of it involves redefining it for a specific purpose.

When you override a function, you use the exact signature line of the function you find in the parent line and create a new set of statements for the function. Your actions instruct the compiler to replace the previous version of the function with your new version.

In the implementation of the `CommandTouchTrigger` class, you override two functions. The `PostBeginPlay()` function is necessary as a starting point for the activities of `Trigger` objects. It attends to the initialization of the `Trigger` objects. Among other things, it assigns values to the `Message` property. You have seen this many times at this point.

The `Touch()` function attends to detecting activities in other objects in your program. Since this is the first time you have sought information about an object with which your `Trigger` object might have contact, you have not before had need of it.

The Super Keyword

When you override a function from a parent class, you wipe the slate clean for the function and start over. Associated with comment #2 in the CommandTouchTrigger class, you see these lines:

```
function PostBeginPlay(){
   // #2
   super.PostBeginPlay();
   Message = FirstMessage;
}
```

Associated with comment #8, you see this line:

```
      Super.Touch(Other)
```

When you define the PostBeginPlay() and Touch() functions in the CommandTouchTrigger class, your code declares to the compiler that you want to erase the previous versions of the functions as defined in the Trigger class and replace them with your own.

With respect to the PostBeginPlay() function, your definition involves two lines of code. It remains, however, that there are many statements in the version of the PostBeginPlay() function in the Trigger class that you still want to use. To see how this is so, here is the code for the function as defined in the Trigger class:

```
// As defined in the Trigger class
function PostBeginPlay(){
   if( !bInitiallyActive ){
      FindTriggerActor();
   }
   if( TriggerType == TT_Shoot ){
      bHidden = false;
      bProjTarget = true;
      SetDrawType(DT_None);
   }
   bSavedInitialActive = bInitiallyActive;
   bSavedInitialCollision = bCollideActors;
   // Lines left out
}
```

What these lines accomplish need not be explained in detail at this point in the discussion, but the general story is that they attend to initializing data members of the Trigger object. In the class you derive from the Trigger class, you still use these data members, and it remains necessary to continue to initialize them. To make it so that you can initialize them without having to rewrite the code, do so in your own definition of the `PostBeginPlay()` function, you include the following line:

```
super.PostBeginPlay();
```

As Figure 7.7 illustrates, the `super` keyword calls to the version of the `PostBeginPlay()` function defined in the `Trigger` class. Calling the parent version in the definition of the `PostBeginPlay()` function you implement in the `CommandTouchTrigger` class pulls all the functionality implemented in the function as defined in the parent class into the function as defined in the derived class. You can use the `super` keyword in this way to access any public, defined function in the parent class.

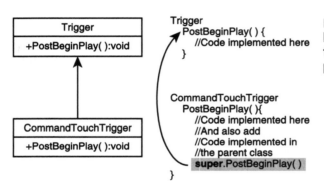

Figure 7.7 The `super` keyword allows you to call functions defined in the parent class.

Note

Although not shown in the current code samples, in addition to `public` and `private`, UnrealScript provides a third access modifier keyword. This is the `protected` keyword. A protected member function or data member can be accessed by a derived class but not by a peer class. In the examples given in Chapter 5, you could not access a function in the `Math` class defined with the `protected` access modifier. To access such a function or data member, you must extend the `Math` class.

Detecting Touching

You also override the `Touch()` function in the definition of the `CommandTouchTrigger` class. The definition of the `Touch()` function in the `Trigger` class is much more extensive than the definition of the `PostBeginPlay()` function. To include this functionality from the parent class, as with the `PostBeginPlay()` method, you use the `super` keyword. The call using the `super` keyword occurs in association with comment #8.

Since the `Touch()` function is an overridden function, the signature line of the `Touch()` function in the `CommandTouchTrigger` class precisely conforms to the signature line of the `Touch()`

function as defined in the parent class. You see this signature line in the code following comment #3:

```
function Touch( Actor Other){
```

The argument of the function is of the Actor type. The Touch() function is called when an Actor object in your level collides with your CommandTouchTrigger object. In the broadest terms, one object collides with another when the two objects simultaneously occupy the same virtual space. The Touch() function detects when other objects collide with a Trigger object. It can detect objects selectively or generally. In this context, you can designate that it should detect all Actor objects in your level by setting the bCollideActors property to true.

Detecting a State Using Selection

In the lines associated with comment #4 of the CommandTouchTrigger class definition, you call the IsRelevant() function. The IsRelevant() function is defined to return a bool value. Its argument is of the Actor type. It takes as its argument the Other object you have passed to the Touch() function. The Other object is any object of the Actor type that collides with your Trigger object.

Not all Actor objects are suitable as objects to activate your trigger. You determine the Actor objects that are suitable by setting the TriggerType property of your Trigger object. The IsRelevant() function determines if the Actor is allowed by TriggerType setting. If it is suitable, then the IsRelevant() function returns true.

You use an if statement to evaluate the value the IsRelevant() function returns. This form of selection statement is known as a *single selection statement*. If the expression is true, then the flow of your program enters the block for the statement. If the expression is not true, then the single selection statement tells the flow of your program to skip its block and go to the closing bracket, which in this instance is commented with the expression end outer if. Selection statements of this type provide a specific set of actions that execute only if the control expression is true. They do not designate specific actions to be performed if the control expression is false. Here is the code:

```
// #4
if (IsRelevant( Other ) ){
    // #5
    // Cast the Other reference and determine
    // if the pawn is crouching
    if (Pawn(Other).bIsCrouched){
        // #6 Generate a random number and display a message
        // relevant to crouching pawns
        Message= SecondMessage;
    }// End inner if
```

```
    else{
        // #7 The actor's pawn is not crouching
        Message = FirstMessage;
    }//end else
}// End outer if
```

As you see in the lines following comment #5, within the outer if block is an if…else selection statement. Such a statement extends the logic of the if selection statement, because with this type of selection, you can cover both true and false outcomes of a control expression.

The if…else statement consists of two parts. The first part, an if selection statement, evaluates the Other object to determine if a value of true has been assigned to the bIsCrouched data member. If this is so, then the flow of the program enters the block associated with the if statement, and the text defined for SecondMessage ("Get up!") is assigned to the Message property (see comment #6).

If a value of false is assigned to the bIsCrouched data member, then the flow of the program passes to the else block, and the text defined for the FirstMessage data member ("Get down!") is assigned to the Message property (see comment #7).

Unlike the single selection statement, the if…else statement enables you to cover the paths that correspond to the two possible states of the bIsCrouched data member. Either the Actor object is crouched (the Shift key is down and the value of bIsCrouched is true) or the Actor object is standing (the Shift key is not down and the value of bIsCrouched is false). Your program uses the selection statement to ensure that your Trigger object issues messages to cover both states.

Casting a Class Object Down to a Subclass Object

The argument to the Touch() and IsRelevant() functions is of the Actor type. In the Trigger class, you find the functions defined in this way:

```
function Touch(Actor Other)
function IsRelevant(Actor Other)
```

When you test the value of the bIsCrouched data member following comment #5, however, you test an object of the Pawn type. You do so because the bIsCrouched data member is of the Pawn class, not the Actor class. The Pawn class is derived from the Actor class. Here is the line that performs this action:

```
if (Pawn(Other).bIsCrouched){
```

When you define an argument for a function using a parent data type, then any variable of a data type derived from the parent data type can also be used as an argument to the function. This makes sense with the Touch() and IsRelevant() functions, because you want to work with all the classes derived from the Actor class. In many cases, however, when you pass an argument in this way, the object you pass might have data members or member functions not found in the parent class. When you try to access these data members or member functions using the parent class object, an error results.

Casting the argument *down* to the type of the derived object becomes necessary. When you cast a type down, you cast it from the parent to the derived type. Casting a parent object to the type of a derived object restores the definition of the derived object so that specialized data members and member functions can be accessed.

To cast a parent object down to the type of a derived object, you use a special type of function. The name of this function is identical to its data type. The casting function for the Pawn class is Pawn(). The casting function takes the parent object as its argument, and it returns an object of the derived type. Here is the isolated cast you find in the code following comment #5:

```
Pawn(Other);
```

The statement returns an object of the Pawn type. You might rewrite this expression in this way:

```
Pawn MyPawn;
MyPawn = Pawn(Other);
```

The Pawn class gives you access to the bIsCrouched data member. Since this data member is defined as public in the Pawn class, you can access it with the dot operator, just as you would a function. If you had on hand the MyPawn object, then you might write this code:

```
Pawn MyPawn;
MyPawn = Pawn(Other);
if(MyPawn.bIsCrouched){
    // Lines execute
}
```

To use fewer lines, you combine the cast with the dot operator and the name of the accessed data member:

```
if(Pawn(Other).bIsCrouched){
    // Lines executed
}
```

Note

To review a little, the Pawn class is a specialized version of the Actor class that is usually employed to represent a player or characters. Pawn objects are almost always associated with meshes. The Pawn class proves important and complex because it is the primary way that you interact with the game. Working with objects of the Pawn class involves experimenting with meshes, collision dynamics, and assets such as sounds, weapons, and the game inventory. It is also the case that you deal with specialized states, such as crouching.

Enumerations and Values for TriggerType

As mentioned previously, the IsRelevant() function evaluates objects based on the TriggerType property. If you access the Actor Class Brower and click on the Trigger listing in the class list, the code editor opens with the code for the Trigger class definition. At the top of definition, the TriggerType property is defined using an *enumeration*. The keyword used to designate enumerations is enum. An enumeration is an abstract data type that allows you to define three things: a data type, an identifier of the enumeration type, and a set of values you can use for the data type. In the first few lines of the Trigger class, you find this code:

```
var() enum ETriggerType
{
    TT_PlayerProximity,
    TT_PawnProximity,
    TT_ClassProximity,
    TT_AnyProximity,
    TT_Shoot,
    TT_HumanPlayerProximity,
    TT_LivePlayerProximity
} TriggerType;
```

The data type is named ETriggerType. The name of the instance of this data type you create is TriggerType. The values you can assign to the TriggerType variable are prefixed with TT_. Given the var keyword, the property these lines add to the Trigger class is TriggerType, which you find in the Trigger Properties tray.

When you define an enumeration, the items in the comma-delimited list are called *elements*. You can add as many elements as you want. By default, the first element possesses a numerical value of 0. Each time you add an element, the value of the added element is one greater than the previous value.

The enumeration provides, then, a way to escape having to use numbers to set properties. As Figure 7.8 illustrates, the integer value of TT_PlayerProximity or the other values you assign to the TriggerType property are not important. You select only the name of the element. The value of TT_LivePlayerProximity is 6.

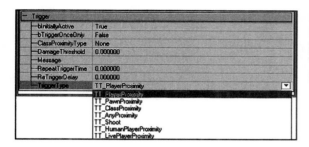

Figure 7.8
Enumerated values provide you with values for the TriggerType property.

Selection Using a Case Statement

In addition to if and if…else statements, you can use an extended form of selection that involves several keywords. This is known as the *switch structure*. A representative use of a switch structure can be found in the definition of the IsRelevant() function in the Trigger class. (To find it, you use the Find utility of the code editor.) This function determines whether the Actor object your Trigger object has encountered should elicit a response from your Trigger object. To set your Trigger object so that it knows which Actor objects fall into this category, you assign one or another of the enumerated values to the TriggerType property, as was discussed in the previous section.

When you call the IsRelevant() function, the function evaluates the value set for the TriggerType property against the possible types and determines on this basis whether your trigger object should interact with it. To view the specifics of this activity, here is the code for the IsRelevant() function in the Trigger class. It has been truncated and rewritten in this context so that it conforms to the standard syntax definition given for the switch selection statement for UnrealScript:

```
// This is a modified version of what you find in the class
// Trigger::IsRelevant()
// See IsRelevantSelection.txt
function bool IsRelevant( actor Other ){
   local bool Relevance;
   // Lines left out
   // class data member defined by Properties
   switch( TriggerType )
   {
```

```
    case TT_HumanPlayerProximity:
       Relevance = ( Pawn(Other) != None)
                      && Pawn(Other).IsHumanControlled();
   break;
   case TT_PlayerProximity:
       Relevance = ( Pawn(Other) != None)
                      && ( Pawn(Other).IsPlayerPawn()
                      || Pawn(Other).WasPlayerPawn() );
   break;
   case TT_LivePlayerProximity:
       Relevance = ( Pawn(Other) != None)
                      && Pawn(Other).IsPlayerPawn();
   break;
   // Lines left out
   case TT_AnyProximity:
       Relevance = true;
   break;
   case TT_Shoot:
       Relevance = ( (Projectile(Other) != None)
                      && (Projectile(Other).Damage >= DamageThreshold) );
   break;
   default:
       // No relevancy found
       Relevance = false;
   }// End switch structure
   return Relevance;
 }// End IsRelevant()
```

Following the switch keyword, in parentheses you provide the argument you want to evaluate. In this instance, the argument is the TriggerType property you define using the enumeration. As discussed in the previous section, you then assign one of the enumerated
values to it in the properties dialog. Since the TriggerType data member is defined at class
scope, it can be accessed in the scope of the IsRelevant() function. When the IsRelevant()
function is called, it uses this property to evaluate which flavor of Actor is relevant to your
Trigger object.

In the structure of the switch statement, you include case statements. Each case statement
consists of the case keyword followed by the term you want to compare to the switch argument. After this comes a colon. The colon defines the beginning of the block for the case.
Within the block you place all of the statements you want to associate with the case. To
close the block, you use the break keyword.

The flow of your program enters the switch structure through the argument you provide following the switch keyword. It continues to the case that satisfies the argument you provide. It skips all cases that do not satisfy your argument. If you have set the TriggerType property to TT_PlayerProximity, then it skips the block for the first case (TT_HumanPlayerProximity) and goes into the block for the second case. After executing the statements for this block, when it reaches the break keyword, it skips to the end of the case structure.

In the event that the argument supplied to the switch argument satisfies none of the cases, you can set up a default clause. In this case, if something has gone wrong, so that the value assigned to TriggerType corresponds to no defined case, then the default clause handles the situation.

In each instance, the case statements shown for the IsRelevant() function makes use of the Relevance variable, which is of the bool type and is defined locally. The flow of the program passes to a given case, and expressions evaluate characteristics of the Actor object you pass to the IsRelevant() function. The result is then assigned to the Relevance variable. At the end of the function, the value stored in the Relevance variable is returned.

Compounded Boolean Expressions

The case statements in the IsRelevantSelection.txt example provide a number of expressions that fall into the category of *compound Boolean expressions*. In a previous section, you dealt with relational operators and their use with operands in single expressions. Here you see how single expressions can be combined into more complex expressions. Consider the case for the TT_PlayerProximity value:

```
Relevance = (Pawn(Other) != None)
            && ( Pawn(Other).IsPlayerPawn()
            || Pawn(Other).WasPlayerPawn() );
```

This compound expression uses one relational operator (!=) and two Boolean compound operators. (&&, ||). Figure 7.9 provides a summary of how these compound operators work.

The AND operator (&&) joins two expressions. Each of the joined expressions is enclosed in parentheses. The first of these expressions determines whether a Pawn object has been created:

```
(Pawn(Other) != None)
```

If the Pawn object is not equal to the value assigned to the None keyword, then the Pawn object exists and the result returned by the not-equal-to expression is true. This is the first term or condition of the compound expression.

The second term is itself a compound expression. This expression uses the OR compound operator (||). The OR operator returns a true result if either of the terms it joins is true. In other words, if one is false and one is true, it returns true. Likewise, if both are true, it also returns true. Only if both are false does it return false.

The OR operator compounds the returned values of the IsPlayerPawn() and WasPlayerPawn() functions of the Pawn class. Either or both of these can be true, and if so, then the compounded statement returns true.

This leaves the AND operator. The AND operator returns true only if both of the expressions it compounds are true. Given this situation, for a true value to be assigned to the Relevance variable, these conditions must be met:

```
(The Pawn object is not equal to None)
AND
(The IsPlayerPawn() returns true OR  The WasPlayerPawn() returns true)
```

Compounded Boolean expressions are evaluated from left to right, so when the compiler reads this statement, if it finds that the Pawn != None expression is false, it reads no more and assigns false to the Relevance variable.

AND &&			
T	T	Two true statements are true.	T
T	F	A true statement and a false statement are false.	F
F	F	A false statement and a false statement are false.	F
OR ||			
T	T	Two true statements are true.	T
T	F	A true statement and a false statement are true.	T
F	F	Two false statements are false.	F

Figure 7.9 Boolean operators allow you to create compound expressions.

Testing the CommandTouchTrigger Object

To test your class, create instances of the CommandTouchTrigger and place them in the Ch07Area01 level. When you place the CommandTouchTrigger objects in the level, because you are not using the spawn keyword as a part of the class, you no longer see the gargoyle icon. As Figure 7.10 illustrates, when you activate the trigger, you see "Get down!" or "Get up!"

Figure 7.10 Each time the `Pawn` touches the trigger, a unique message is generated.

messages followed by a randomly generated number. The "Get up!" message appears when you hold down the Shift key.

The difference between this specialization of the `Trigger` class and those you have dealt with previously is that you can now generate unique events every time the player `Pawn` object encounters a `CommandTouchTrigger` object. Before, you saw the same message over and over again. The new version of the `Trigger` class responds differently, according to whether the player `Pawn` object is crouching or standing, and for each interaction between the player `Pawn` object and the `CommandTouchTrigger` object, you see a newly generated random number.

Refactoring to Create Random Messages

Refactoring is a term used to describe the activity of revising your code. It refers to a fairly formal process that several excellent books on software engineering describe in detail. Generally, however, you can say that refactoring involves changing your code to improve its performance or make it easier to understand.

Refactoring can involve almost anything you do to a program. You can divide functions that perform several actions so that you end up with two or more functions that perform single actions. If a group of functions in a given class attends to actions that you can more clearly understand and use if you view them in isolation, then you can create a second class and put them in it. You then call the functions from this class using an object of the refactored class, much as you did the functions in the Math class.

One of the most frequent activities grouped under the heading of refactoring involves inspecting your classes for redundant code and finding ways to create functions that can be called in place of the redundant code. To accomplish this task, you examine the redundant code to find out what it does. You create a function or functions to attend to this activity. In place of the redundant code, you then use function calls.

To refactor the code for the CommandTouchTrigger class, you begin with the code you have worked with in the previous sections of this chapter and save it as a new class. This class is titled CommandMessageTrigger. This class also goes in the Ch04Area package. In this version of the code, you remove code from the Touch() function that creates the message and place it in a function called MakeMessage(). You then call the MakeMessage() function in the Touch() function to provide text for the Message property.

To supplement the MakeMessage() function, you create a second function, GetMessageText(). In the second function, you work with an array. Arrays can contain several objects, primitive or abstract. In this context, you work with the string data type, creating an array that holds a variety of messages from which you select for the Message value when your Trigger objects encounter the player Pawn object. Here's the code.

```
//============================================================
// CommandMessageTrigger
// See CommandMessageTrigger.txt
//============================================================
class CommandMessageTrigger extends Trigger placeable;
    // #1
    // Data members for messages and random numbers
    var private string FirstMessage;
    const NUMOFMESSAGES = 6;
    // Define an enumeration
    enum PState{
            UP,
            DOWN
    };

function PostBeginPlay()
{
    FirstMessage = "Go!";
    Super.PostBeginPlay();
    Message = FirstMessage;
}// End PostBeginPlay()
```

```
function Touch( actor Other )
{
    if (IsRelevant( Other ) )
    {
        // #2
        if (Pawn(Other).bIsCrouched){ // down state
            Message= MakeMessage(PState.DOWN);
        }// End if
        else{ // up state
            Message= MakeMessage(PState.UP);
        }// end else
        super.Touch(Other);
    }// End outer if
}// end Touch()

private function string MakeMessage(PState state){
    // #3
    local int RandomNumber;
    local string ActionMessage;
    RandomNumber = Rand(NUMOFMESSAGES);
    // #4
    // Build messages on the basis of up or down state
    if( state == PState.UP ){
        ActionMessage @= "Get down!";
        ActionMessage @= GetMessageText(RandomNumber);
    }
    else if( state == PState.DOWN ){
        ActionMessage @= "Get up!";
        ActionMessage @= GetMessageText(RandomNumber);
    }
    else {
        ActionMessage = "Okay.";
    }
        return ActionMessage;
}

private function string GetMessageText(int index){
    // #5
    // Define a static array of the string type
    local string PawnMessages[NUMOFMESSAGES];
    local string TMessage;
```

```
    // #6
    // Assign text values to elements
    PawnMessages[0]= "Watch out behind you!";
    PawnMessages[1]= "Turn to your left!";
    PawnMessages[2]= "Get ready to go!";
    PawnMessages[3]= "Did you see the danger?";
    PawnMessages[4]= "Can we move again?";
    PawnMessages[5]= "How many did you see?";
    // #7
    // Retrieve an element from the array
    if(index < NUMOFMESSAGES && index >= 0){
        TMessage = PawnMessages[index];
    }
    return TMessage;
}
```

You can represent the CommandMessageTrigger using a UML diagram. The diagram reduces the features of the class to their essential aspects. As Figure 7.11 shows, the definition of the class consists of three data members and four member functions. Since this class specializes the Trigger class, to glimpse the full features of the class, it would be necessary to see a UML diagram of the Trigger class. Still, in the current context, the diagram serves to show you the relevant features of the class you are dealing with.

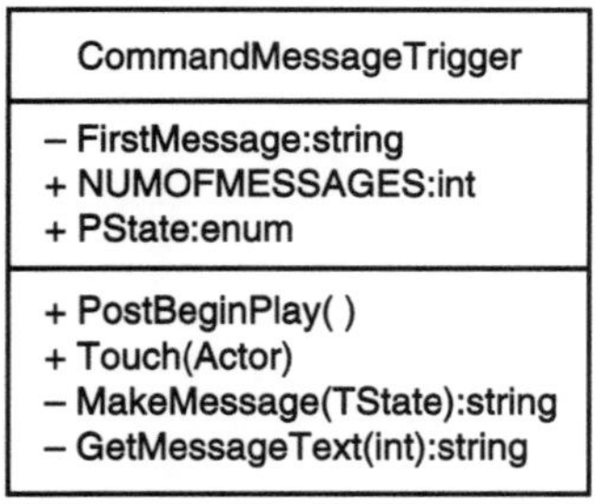

CommandMessageTrigger
- FirstMessage:string + NUMOFMESSAGES:int + PState:enum
+ PostBeginPlay( ) + Touch(Actor) - MakeMessage(TState):string - GetMessageText(int):string

Figure 7.11 A UML diagram of the CommandMessageTrigger class shows the essentials.

Data Members

In the line associated with comment #1 in the CommandMessageTrigger class definition, you create a data member of the string type, FirstMessage. You no longer need more than one data member to handle text messages. After declaring the FirstMessage data member, you create an enumeration. The definition of this enumeration differs from the definition you worked with in the Trigger class, because in this case you define the enumeration so that it does not have a corresponding property identifier. Instead, you use it in a fixed way. As you see later on, if you want to use the values of the enumeration, you type PState.UP or

PState.DOWN. Even if this seems odd, it is still much more convenient than trying to remember number values to designate when a Pawn object is in a standing or crouching position. A third data member is the NUMOFMESSAGES constant. Constants are by default of the int type. This constant serves in several places to allow you to know the number of messages you create for the CommandMessageTrigger objects to issue as it interacts with the player Pawn object.

Member Functions

As the UML diagram in Figure 7.11 shows, you implement four functions in the CommandMessageTrigger class. You have dealt with the PostBeginPlay() and Touch() functions before. These are both overridden functions from the Trigger() class. While you add functionality to these functions, you also use the super keyword to access the functionality defined in the parent versions.

Of the two functions you define from scratch, the MakeMessage() function creates a message based on its evaluation of whether the player Pawn object is crouching or standing. To accomplish this, it makes use of the Rand() function to generate a random number each time you call it. When you use the random number in the call to the GetMessageText() function, you generate a different text message for each random number.

To trace the flow of activity in the class, you can start at comment #2, in the overridden definition of the Touch() function. There you make calls to the MakeMessage() function. The argument to the MakeMessage() function is of the PState type. As mentioned previously, this data type allows two arguments, PState.UP and PState.DOWN. When the player Pawn object is crouching, you submit the PState.DOWN value to the MakeMessage() function. When it is standing, you submit PState.UP. The value tells the MakeMessage() function what kind of message to create.

The definition of the MakeMessage() function occurs in the lines accompanying comment #3. Within this function, you declare two local variables, RandomNumber and ActionMessage. RandomNumber is a local version of the variable you defined in the previous version of the class at the class scope. Now you move it to the scope of the MakeMessage() function. To initialize the RandomNumber variable each time the MakeMessage() function is called, you use the NUMOFMESSAGES constant as an argument to the Rand() function.

The ActionMessage variable is of the string type. It serves to allow you to build messages. To build the messages, you use actions you have seen before. You use the concatenation operator to append text through repeated statements. In this instance, the statements take several forms. In addition to "Get up!" and "Get down!" you include messages you get from an array in the GetMessageText() function.

Using if...else if...else

The MakeMessage() function uses a form of a selection statement that extends those discussed earlier. This is the if...else if...else selection structure, which appears in association with comment #4. The structure of this selection statement works like that of the switch statement, but rather than using such terms as switch, case, and break, it extends the use of the if statement to else if. You can add as many else if refrains as you want. You commonly see this pattern:

```
if(condition){
}else if(condition){
}else if(condition){
}else{
}
```

Selection Variations

While the switch statement uses the default keyword to catch arguments that do not fit into any of the tested categories, the if...else if...else selection structure uses the else clause of the structure. Any value that does not prove true for the if or else...if clauses is processed by the else block.

As a comparison or possible source for an exercise, here is how you might implement the if...else if...else selection structure as a switch statement:

```
switch(state){
   case PState.UP:
      ActionMessage @= "Get down!";
      ActionMessage @= GetMessageText(RandomNumber);
   break;
   case PState.DOWN:
      ActionMessage @= "Get up!";
      ActionMessage @= GetMessageText(RandomNumber);
   break;
   default:
   ActionMessage = "Okay.";
}// End switch
```

For practical purposes, the if...else if...else and switch selection structures accomplish the same task. The switch statement is preferable in situations that are seeking to increase the performance of your code. In the CommandMessageTrigger.txt file, you find both forms of selection. One form is commented out. You can test the concept by changing the commenting and recompiling.

In the MakeMessage() function, the structure opens with an if statement that tests whether the value assigned to the state argument is equal to the PState.UP. If this is true, then you create a text message that consists of "Get down!" concatenated with text provided by the GetMessageText() function.

If the if statement does not evaluate to true, the flow of the program passes to the else if refrain of the structure. The else if refrain tests the value assigned to the state argument to determine if it is equal to PState.DOWN. If this is true, then you create a text message that consists of "Get up!" concatenated with the text the GetMessageText() function provides.

If you had other options, as you did in the IsRelevant() function, you might continue to add many more else if statements. At the end of the structure, you could then use an else refrain to provide a default block. This works just like the default element of the switch statement. If the value assigned to state is not equal to any of the values given by the if and else if conditions, then the statement assigns "Okay" to the ActionMessage variable.

Working with Arrays

In the code associated with comment #5 of the definition of the CommandMessageTrigger class, you declare an array. As mentioned previously, the primary responsibility of the GetMessageText() function is to provide you with a set of text messages that your CommandMessageTrigger object can issue when the player Pawn object encounters it. The array makes this possible.

An array is a set of variables of a specific type that you can access using a single identifier. In this case, the type is the string type. The identifier is PawnMessages. When you declare an array, you must indicate right at the start how many elements you want to be able to access using the identifier. For PawnMessages array, you use the NUMOFMESSAGES constant. In the code associated with comment #1, you define this constant with a value of 6. You then use it in the declaration of the PawnMessages array in this way:

```
local string PawnMessages[NUMBEROFMESSAGES];
```

Declaration of an array involves using the name of the array followed by square brackets. In the brackets you indicate the number of items you want to store in the array.

Figure 7.12 illustrates the basic concept of an array. You can view the PawnMessages identifier as designating the starting point of the storage activity. The staring point is 0. You store the first value in association with 0. The next you associate with 1. Each variable value is associated with a memory address. The addresses are designated by *indexes*.

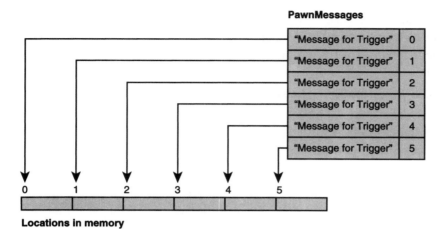

Figure 7.12 The indexes of arrays designate the locations of individual array elements.

In the context the array provides, the variable is called an *element*. Each element is characterized by the size of the data type used to define it. Since the index values of the elements begin with 0, you can view the indexes as numbers that multiply the size of the element. To find the location of the first element, the complier multiplies by 0. To find the location of the second element, the compiler multiplies by 1. Such a way of determining the locations of the elements means that the highest index value is one less than the number of elements you define for the array.

The number of elements you can store in an array turns out to be an important concern. Since only so many places are allocated for storage of elements when you define an array, if you use an index that is larger than the number of memory spaces you have designated, you get a compiler error. The error indicates that you have *exceeded the bounds* of the array. In other words, you have gone outside the bounds of the memory reserved for the array.

As the lines following comment #6 show, to assign a value to an element, you use brackets at the end of the name of the array. Within the brackets you use an index number to indicate the element to which you want to assign a value. To access a value you have assigned to an element, you use the same approach.

In the lines associated with comment #7, you employ a compound Boolean expression to verify that the value of the index argument is equal to or greater than 0 *and* less than the value of NUMBEROFMESSAGES. Since NUMBEROFMESSAGES has been assigned a value of 6, the less than operator (<) restricts the size of index numbers to the range extending only to 5. This operation ensures that the number you use for the index is not outside the bounds of the array.

If the value of the index number is within bounds, then you use it to access one of the values stored in the array and assign it to the local TMessage variable. In the last statement in the GetMessageText() function, a copy of this variable is returned by the function.

Testing the CommandMessageTrigger Objects

To test the CommandMessageTrigger class, open the Ch07Area01 level. Save it as Ch07Area02. Delete one of the existing Trigger objects and put a CommandMessageTrigger object in its place. Figure 7.13 illustrates the messages the CommandMessageTrigger object generates. Now you see that the messages change each time the player Pawn object encounters a CommandMessageTrigger object. You also are able to see that the message starts with "Get up!" if the player Pawn object is crouching. It starts with "Get down!" if the player Pawn object is standing.

Figure 7.13 The CommandMessageTrigger objects generate changing text messages selected randomly from an array.

Conclusion

This chapter has involved you with a set of programming tasks that have led to the creation of the most involved classes yet. The emphasis has remained on using UnrealScript to develop the logic of programs, but in the process, with the exploration of control structures, you have entered a realm in which you can now implement any number of classes that carry out complex chores. The knowledge you acquire through exploration of this chapter provides a basis for investigating a number of scenarios that involve more extended, graphically oriented events. Text messages can provide an excellent way to learn about programming, but it remains that a key objective is to create visual and sound effects that make greater use of the powers of the Unreal Tournament class hierarchy.

Chapter 8 continues to develop the themes you encounter in this chapter. The `CommandTouchTrigger` and `CommandCodeTrigger` classes allow you to explore topics, such as enumeration, that you can put to work as you take much of this functionality of these classes through another iteration that leaves you with a system of classes and many fairly complex operations that illustrate the uses of selection combined with repetition. Given that grounding, it is possible to then proceed into programs that are less involved and yet make more use of the Unreal Tournament hierarchy and the graphical and other features of the Unreal Tournament development environment.

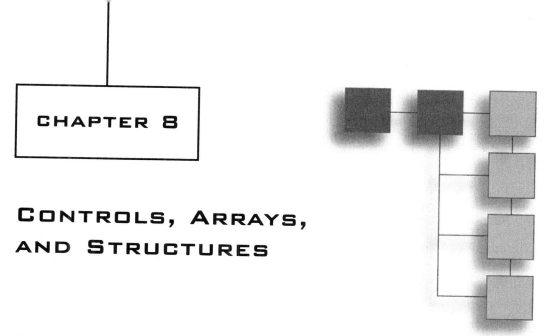

CHAPTER 8

CONTROLS, ARRAYS, AND STRUCTURES

I n this chapter you create a fairly complex set of classes that brings forward code from Chapter 7. Your explorations include use of logic, selection, and repetition. To start with, you expand on the work you have done on the CommandMessageTrigger. In this iteration, you add several functions that create a "code" that can become the basis of a game the player Pawn engages in as it goes from location to location and encounters events. The class you develop to implement this functionality is called CommandCodeTrigger. The code for this class serves as the basis of a project that involves refactoring its functions into a package consisting of three peer classes. Toward this end, you create the CommandGoalTrigger, CodePlay, and Story classes. By placing the functionality in separate classes, you are able to reduce the complexity of your project while extensively increasing the range of actions available to you as you develop your level. In addition to the work of creating a system of classes, you also explore the use of another way to create abstract data types. This approach involves the struct keyword. You create a data type called CodeStatus that allows you to trace the process of discovering a code. You also revisit arrays, this time to implement a dynamic array. The array you develop allows the player Pawn object to hear a story told as it visits the different event points in the level. Among the topics in this chapter are the following:

- Generating codes
- Using repetition statements
- Refactoring classes to create systems of classes
- Creating customized data types using structures
- Creating dynamic arrays
- Making further use of built-in functions

Preparations for the Work Ahead

As mentioned in the introduction, you develop a total of five abstract data types in this chapter. You write hundreds of lines of code to do so, and you create a new package to hold your work. The project you undertake consists of two phases. In the first phase, you develop a "bloated" class called `CommandCodeTrigger`. This class contains functions that generate random messages as the player `Pawn` objects interact with it, and it adds to this the generation of codes (or ciphers) that the player `Pawn` can try to discover as it moves from event to event.

Bloated classes characterize almost all programming efforts. You begin working on a given programming project. You add features to the class you work on. Soon the class consists of hundreds of lines of code and possibly several different types of responsibilities. In this chapter, you see the `CommandCodeTrigger` incorporates both the generation of random messages and the creation of codes for the player `Pawn` object to try to discover.

After a time, bloated classes tend to become extremely difficult to work with. When something goes wrong with them, you can find it almost impossible to fix them. The compilation of the classes requires more time. It becomes easier to add code to them that causes them to malfunction. When they malfunction, if you have all of the functionality of your level tied up in them, then the play comes to an abrupt halt.

You have seen refactoring at work in previous chapters. You have also explored the notion of a set of peer classes used on a composition basis. Now you put this knowledge to work to refactor a bloated class and refactor its responsibilities into peer classes. The two peer classes allow you to exert greater control over your programming and increase the scope and sophistication of the events in your level. Figure 8.1 shows you the general scheme of activities. You start by developing one "large" class. You end with three smaller classes in a new package.

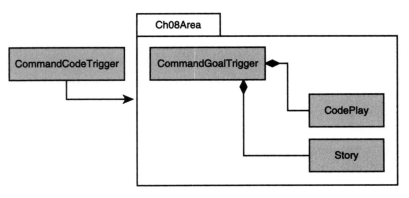

Figure 8.1 You start with a bloated class and end with three smaller ones in a new package.

The folder the arrow points at in Figure 8.1 represents another Unified Modeling Language (UML) representation of your work. The diamonds at the ends of the lines show that the `CommandGoalTrigger` class is composed of instances of the `CodePlay` and `Story` classes. The enclosing tab folder shows you that the three classes are part of a single package, `Ch08Area`.

Adding to the Map

First open Ch07Area01 map and save it as `Ch08Area101`. Build the lighting and geometry and then click the Play Map icon and test play the map.

Although it has been the assumption all along that you have been adding details to your maps as you go, at this point it might be helpful to in some way enhance your level so that one event position is more visible than others. This can augment your testing efforts.

Figure 8.2 illustrates a map with a few wall panels that isolate one of the jump pads. The panels you see are duplicates of the `AlleriaHardware jWallC01AL` static mesh. They have been sized to be tall and thin. On top of the wall panels is the `AlleriaHardware jCeilingB01AL` mesh. Also, the level contains four lights. The map contains four jump pads and four triggers. The Trigger icons shown are of the `CommandMessageTrigger` type or the `CommandTouchTrigger` type, but for starters, you can choose from any objects in the `Ch04Area` package. The chamber contains one jump pad and one `Trigger` object.

Figure 8.2 Enhance our level so that you isolate a jump pad and one of the `Trigger` objects.

Adding a New Package

After you have in some way enhanced your map to isolate one of the Trigger objects, access the Actor Class Browser. Navigate to the Trigger class listing under Triggers. Right-click and select New. Type Ch08Area for the package name. Type CommandCodeTrigger for the class name. Click OK. Compile the class file with only the signature line and opening commentary as a sanity check. Click the Ch08Area package, and select Save Selected Packages.

The CommandCodeTrigger Class

As mentioned in Chapter 7, repetition control statements allow you to use control expressions to repeatedly execute a set of statements. The for and while statements fall into this category. In the CommandCodeTrigger class, you use such statements in the ReportCodeFound() and MakeCode() functions.

You can find the code for this new iteration of your specialization of the Trigger class in the CommandCodeTrigger.txt file in the Chapter 8 code folder. As you can see from a cursory glance at the code, the definition includes the functionality you have previously developed but adds several new elements. In addition to the use of repetition statements, it incorporates a number of selection statements and several built-in functions, such as InStr(), Rand(), RandRange(), Int(), and Chr(). Here is the code for the class. Subsequent sections discuss it in detail.

```
//==========================================
// CommandCodeTrigger
// See CommandCodeTrigger.txt
//==========================================
class CommandCodeTrigger extends Trigger placeable;

    // data members for messages and random numbers
    var private string FirstMessage;
    // #1
    var private string CodeForSearch;
    const NUMOFMESSAGES = 6;
    enum PState{
            UP,
            DOWN
    };
    const CODELENGTH = 8;
    const NUMOFTRIES = 20;
    const LOWASCII = 97;
    const HIGHASCII = 122;
```

```
function PostBeginPlay()
{
    FirstMessage = "Go!";
    Super.PostBeginPlay();
    Message = FirstMessage;
    // #2
    CodeForSearch = MakeCode(CODELENGTH);
}// end PostBeginPlay()

function Touch( actor Other )
{
    if (IsRelevant( Other ) )
    {
        if (Pawn(Other).bIsCrouched){ // down state
            Message= MakeMessage(PState.DOWN);
        }// end if
        else{ // up state
            Message= MakeMessage(PState.UP);
        }// end else

        Super.Touch(Other);
    }// end outer if
}// end Touch()

private function string MakeMessage(PState state){
    local int RandomNumber;
    local string ActionMessage;
    RandomNumber = Rand(NUMOFMESSAGES);

    // Build messages on the basis of up or down state

    if( state == PState.UP ){
      ActionMessage @= "Get down! ";

      // #3
      // Reveal the code
      ActionMessage @= "Here is the code: ";
      ActionMessage @=  GetCodeForSearch();
    }
```

```
            else if( state — PState.DOWN ){
               ActionMessage @— "Get up! - ";
               //Convey a message
               ActionMessage @— GetMessageText(RandomNumber);
               //find a letter of the code
               // #4
               ActionMessage @—  ReportCodeFound( CodeForSearch  );
            }
            else {
               ActionMessage — "Okay.";
            }
            return ActionMessage;
      }


      private function string GetMessageText(int index){
         // Define a static array of the string type
         local string PawnMessages[NUMOFMESSAGES];
         local string TMessage;
         // Assign text values to elements
         PawnMessages[0]— "Watch out behind you!";
         PawnMessages[1]— "Turn to your left!";
         PawnMessages[2]— "Get ready to go!";
         PawnMessages[3]— "Did you see the danger?";
         PawnMessages[4]— "Can we move again?";
         PawnMessages[5]— "How many did you see?";
         // Retrieve an element from the array
         if(index < NUMOFMESSAGES && index >— 0){
            TMessage — PawnMessages[index];
         }
         return TMessage;
      }


      private function string MakeCode(int limit){
          local int Ctr;
          local string Code;
         //Control for the while statement
         Ctr — 0;
         // #5
         while(Ctr < limit){
            // Build a string using random numbers
            // Convert the numbers to letters
            Code $— Chr(GenerateRandom());
```

```
        // Increment the count
        Ctr++;
    }// end while
    return Code;
}


// #6
private function int GenerateRandom(){
    local float high, low;
    Low = LOWASCII;
    High = HIGHASCII;
    // Return an integer in a range
    return Int( RandRange( Low , High ));
  }


// #7
private function string GetCodeForSearch(){
    return CodeForSearch;
}


private function string ReportCodeFound(string Code){
    local string SelectedLetter, Report;
    local int Ctr;

    // #8
    for(Ctr = 0; Ctr < NUMOFTRIES; Ctr++){
        // Cast numbers to a string
        SelectedLetter = Chr(GenerateRandom());
        // See if it is in the string
        //# 9
        // Use compound Boolean to determine if
        // the letter is in the code range
        if( InStr(Code, SelectedLetter) >= 0
            && InStr(Code, SelectedLetter) <= CODELENGTH){
          Report @= "Okay, you have found part of the code: ";
          // Add the letter to the report
          Report @= SelectedLetter;
          break;
        }// End if
      }// End for
    return Report;
}
```

As with the definition of the CommandMessageTrigger class in Chapter 7, a UML diagram can provide a convenient summary of the features of the CommandCodeTrigger class. As Figure 8.3 illustrates, you define eight data members and eight functions for the class. The PostBeginPlay() and Touch() methods are overridden. The six others are custom. The MakeMessage() and GetMessageText() are changed little from the previous version. The MakeCode(), ReportCodeFound(), GenerateRandom(), and GetCodeForSearch() functions are new. The functions are divided into two main groups, those that provide an interface and those that support the interface. The interface functions are public; the others are private.

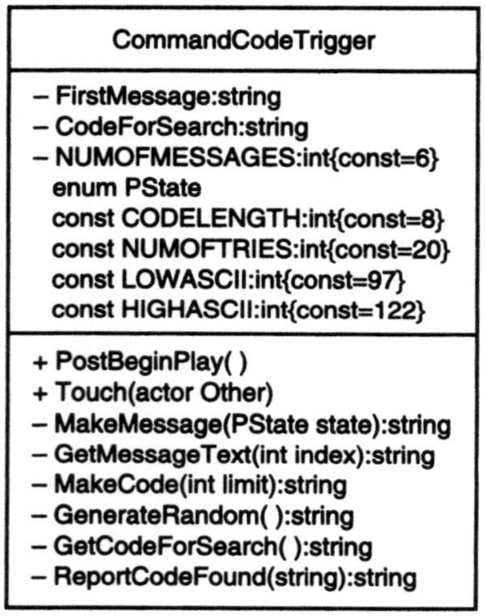

```
┌─────────────────────────────────────┐
│           CommandCodeTrigger         │
├─────────────────────────────────────┤
│  – FirstMessage:string               │
│  – CodeForSearch:string              │
│  – NUMOFMESSAGES:int{const=6}        │
│    enum PState                       │
│    const CODELENGTH:int{const=8}     │
│    const NUMOFTRIES:int{const=20}    │
│    const LOWASCII:int{const=97}      │
│    const HIGHASCII:int{const=122}    │
├─────────────────────────────────────┤
│  + PostBeginPlay( )                  │
│  + Touch(actor Other)                │
│  – MakeMessage(PState state):string  │
│  – GetMessageText(int index):string  │
│  – MakeCode(int limit):string        │
│  – GenerateRandom( ):string          │
│  – GetCodeForSearch( ):string        │
│  – ReportCodeFound(string):string    │
└─────────────────────────────────────┘
```

Figure 8.3 You define four new functions in the CommandCodeTrigger class.

The MakeCode() function includes a while repetition statement that creates a unique "code" that your player Pawn object can discover as it encounters CommandCodeTrigger objects. The ReportCodeFound() function uses a for repetition statement to examine the code to simulate the activity of discovery. Both of these functions are called from the MakeMessage() function. The GenerateRandom() function *wraps* the RandRange() function, allowing you to conveniently convert the values returned to integers. The GetCodeForSearch() function is an example of an *accessor* function. As for the new data members of the class, you add four. One regulates the difficulty of code discovery. The others allow you to create code messages.

Data Members

The CommandCodeTrigger class includes eight data members. As you can see in the lines associated with comment #1, you add a CodeForSearch data member. This allows you to track the code the player avatar searches for. The type of the data member is string. You also add the

CODELENGTH data member to set the length in characters of the code. A code consists of a set of randomly generated letters. You can vary the length by changing the value you assign to CODELENGTH, but for starters, you assign 8 to this data member.

You use a NUMOFTRIES data member to set the "difficulty" of the discovery process. Discovery involves using a randomly generated letter to "guess" one of the letters that constitutes the code. The higher this number, the easier it is to make a correct guess. You assign 20 to this data member. This means that each time the player Pawn object encounters a CommandCodeTrigger object, up to 20 randomly generated letters might be used to make a guess. If you want to make the guess harder, lower the value you assign to NUMOFTRIES.

Two further data members are LOWASCII and HIGHASCII. These values establish a range of numbers that you can use with the RandRange() function to generate letters to make up a code. In the ASCII code, lowercase "a" possesses a value of 97. Lowercase "z" possesses a value of 122. The numbers from 97 to 122 account for all the lowercase letters. (If you want uppercase letters, then you can use values from 65 through 90.)

Code Creation

The most important function call for creating code occurs in the PostBeginPlay() function. In the lines trailing comment #2, you call the MakeCode() function. When you call the MakeCode() function, the argument you provide to it is CODELENGTH. As mentioned previously, the value of this data member is set to 8.

The MakeCode() function is defined in the lines associated with comment #5. In this function, you use a while repetition statement. To control this statement, you create a local variable named Ctr. You initialize it with a value of 0. In the control expression of the while statement, you test to discover whether the value of Ctr is less than the value assigned to limit. The argument to the function sets the value of limit, and it is equal to CODELENGTH (8).

The while statement repeats 8 times and with each repetition calls the GenerateRandom() function. It repeats only 8 times because with each repetition the value of Ctr is incremented by 1. When this value grows to be equal to 8, the control expression evaluates as false, and the flow of the program exits the while block.

As the while block repeats, the GenerateRandom() function returns int values in the range extending from 97 through 122. You call the Chr() function to convert these numbers into letters. You then use the concatenate operator to successively assign the letters without spaces to the Code variable. In this way, you form a string of 8 randomly generated characters that serves as your code.

Message Making

In the lines trailing comment #3, you add a call within the `MakeMessage()` function. This call is to the `GetCodeForSearch()` function. You can find the definition of the `GetCodeForSearch()` function in the lines accompanying comment #7. It provides an example of an *accessor* function. An accessor function is a function that does one thing. It returns the value stored in a given data member of a class.

An accessor function serves in many contexts as the only way that users of a class can gain access to the value stored in a data member of a class. The reason for this is that if the data member is defined as private, then it is not possible to access the data member directly outside the class. Defining data members as private is generally considered good object-oriented practice. The practice is known as *data hiding*. Data hiding stipulates that the data member names a class contains should remain hidden from the user of the class. If users of the class want to access the values the data members hold, they should have to use accessor functions.

UnrealScript is set up so that in addition to using accessor functions, you use properties. The properties you see displayed in the Properties dialog are a form of accessor. You can assign values to the data members of a class without seeing them directly. This works for the variables you qualify using the `var` keyword followed by parentheses. For other types of `var` variables, you might want to hide them. If so, then you can use accessor functions. To create such a function, you declare the data member as private and the accessor function as public. The accessor function returns the value assigned to the data member it represents. The `GetCodeForSearch()` function returns the value stored in the `CodeForSearch` data member. Prefixing the word "Get" to the name of the represented data member is a common way of naming accessor functions.

Within the `CommandCodeTrigger` class, you can access several of the data members directly. Those you can access directly are constants or enumerated values. Such values cannot be changed and so are left public.

Within the `MakeMessage()` function (see comment #3), you assign the value returned by the `GetCodeForSearch()` function to the `ActionMessage` variable. This gives you a way to see the entire code when the player `Pawn` object in the non-crouching state encounters the `CommandCodeTrigger` object.

Reporting Clues Found

At comment #4 in the `MakeMessage()` function, you call the `ReportCodeFound()` function. The argument for this function is the `CodeForSearch` data member. You might just as easily call the `GetCodeForSearch()` function, but in this case the more direct approach is used since the accessor function is designed to be a part of the interface of the class. Functions in the class can access the data member directly.

N o t e

You directly access the value assigned to CodeForSearch. Within your class, accessing the values of data members using accessor functions is often the best approach. Function calls require more processing than directly accessing data members. Within a class, if you access a data member by name you maintain the practice of data hiding. Outside the class, as mentioned previously, directly accessing non-constant data members violates the practice of data hiding.

The ReportCodeFound() function returns a single letter representing one of the 8 letters in the code string. Reporting the finding of a single letter is a way to make the player Pawn object's actions more interesting. It also opens the door to the possibility of extending the actions of the level so that after the player finds all the letters, a goal event is initiated. At this stage of development, you see only the reported find of a letter.

The ReportCodeFound() function is defined in the code associated with comment #8. In this function, you make use of a for repetition statement. The for repetition statement is one of the most fundamental statements in programming. As Figure 8.4 illustrates, you use three expressions to control its actions. You begin by declaring a control variable, such as Ctr. Then, in the first term of the control expression, you assign a starting value to this variable. It is common to use 0.

In the second term, you include an expression that can be evaluated to limit the action of the for statement. For this value, you use the NUMOFTRIES data member. You allow the for block to repeat until Ctr increases to a value of NUMOFTRIES. At this point, it is no longer less than NUMOFTRIES, and the flow of the program does not again enter the block.

For the third term, you provide a way to increase the value of the control variable. In this case, you use Ctr++, again a common approach to incrementing the value of a control. You can use any of the increment operators. For example, to increase the value in steps of 2, you might use Ctr += 2 rather than Ctr++.

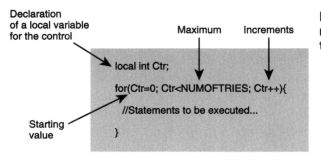

Figure 8.4 The for repetition statement has three terms of control.

As the for block repeats, you call the GenerateRandom() function. As mentioned previously, this function generates random integer values. By making the returned value of the function an argument to the Chr() function, you convert it into a letter. The value the GenerateRandom() function returns is in the range from 97 to 122, so you potentially get all the letters of the alphabet. As it is, given the assigned value of NUMOFTIMES, only 20 letters can be generated with each call of the function. These letters you assign to the SelectedLetter variable, which is defined locally and of the string type.

Then comes a selection statement. This statement uses a compound Boolean expression to accomplish two tasks. The first task involves calling the InStr() function. This is one of the built-in functions for the string data type. It takes two arguments. The first argument is text you want to search for a given character or set of characters. The second argument is the character or set of characters you want to find. The InStr() function returns the starting position in the string of the character or character set you are looking for.

If the InStr() function finds that any letter assigned to the SelectedLetter variable is anywhere in the eight-letter string assigned to the Code variable, it reports the starting position of the letter. As a safety measure, the selection statement verifies that the starting position is greater than or equal to 0 (which is the first "position" in any string) and less than or equal to the length of the string (CODELENGTH). After verifying this is true, the selection statement then creates a report.

The report consists of the text, "Okay, you have found part of the code:" concatenated with the character found. The report is assigned to the Report variable, which like the SelectedLetter variable is defined locally and of the string type. The function then returns a copy of this variable.

Note the use of the break statement at the end of the selection block. The use of break makes it so that the for repetition terminates as soon as a letter in the code is identified. In this way, even if it might be possible for the for block to repeat 20 times, if a letter in the code is generated before that point, the break keyword causes the flow of the program to immediately exit the for block and the return action of the function to immediately return the found letter.

Refactoring Random Number Generation

As mentioned previously, the `GenerateRandom()` function is a *wrapper* for the built-in `RandRange()` function. A wrapper function is a function that you create that makes it easier than it would be otherwise to use a built-in function (or any function obtained from a class or group of classes you incorporate into your program).

The `RandRange()` function creates a problem because it uses two arguments of the `float` type to set a range for the random values it generates. It generates values of the `float` type. To establish the range for random numbers in the `CommandCodeTrigger` class, however, you create the `LOWASCII` and `HIGHASCII` data members. Both of these are defined as constants, and constants are of the type integer (`int`). They do not work as valid arguments for the `RandRange()` function. Add to this that the `Chr()` function, which converts ASCII numbers into letters, requires `int` values. Since the `RandRange()` function returns a `float` value, it creates a problem here, too.

You address such problems by creating a wrapper function. As you can see in the code associated with comment #6, to overcome the problem of using the `LOWASCII` and `HIGHASCII` data members as arguments, you declare and define local variables of the `float` type named `Low` and `High`. You assign the values of the `LOWASCII` and `HIGHASCII` data members to these variables and implicitly promote them to the `float` type.

On the other side, you use the `Int()` function to convert the returned value of the `RandRange()` function into an `int` value. This becomes the returned value of the `GenerateRandom()` function. In this way, in different contexts in the `CommandCodeTrigger` class, when you need random numbers of the `int` type to generate letter values using the `Chr()` function, you can easily do so.

Testing the CommandCodeTrigger Object

To test the `CommandCodeTrigger` class, replace an instance of one of the classes you developed earlier and replace it with an instance of the `CommandCodeTrigger` class. To reduce the number of text messages you see, in the Properties dialog, set the `RepeatTriggerTime` and `ReTriggerDelay` properties to 5 each.

When you play the map, periodically press the Shift key to make the Player pawn crouch. After you have activated the `CommandCodeTrigger` object a few times, you are likely to see a message that part of the code has been discovered. Figure 8.5 illustrates the message that results from the action of the `CommandCodeTrigger` object.

Figure 8.5 Add a CommandCodeTrigger object to your level and test it.

Revision

The CommandCodeTrigger class provides a few variations of behavior based on the stand and crouch actions of the player Pawn object. As Figure 8.6 shows, addition of two forms of behavior to the class makes it more interesting, but at the same time, the code for the class becomes harder to understand and maintain. Although the CommandCodeTrigger class remains relatively small, consisting of roughly 150 lines of code, it sets a pattern that characterizes the development of many classes. Adding functionality to a class both increases its size and tends to blur its responsibilities.

Addition of functionality bloats the class and makes it more difficult to know the primary responsibility of the class.

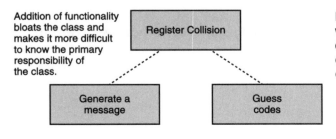

Figure 8.6 Asking what a bloated class does introduces opportunities for creating new classes.

Generally, a class should have one responsibility. All the functions in it should attend to this one responsibility. When you find that a class is doing different things, such as both providing the player with a game that involves simulating guessing and creating random messages, then it is time to begin assessing how the class can be refactored. Refactoring in this case involves creating two new classes, as was discussed earlier in this chapter.

Detecting Messages

The first responsibility that might be considered in the CommandCodeTrigger class involves the activity of guessing about the ciphers or codes that the class automatically generates. A Trigger object is concerned with detecting collisions. Generating ciphers and simulating guessing activities do not fall under this heading.

The solution to the problem lies in taking all the activity involving generating ciphers and guessing the letters they contain and placing it in another class. When any class derived from the Trigger class needs to include ciphers and guessing, it can then use an object of this class and with a few statements access the needed functions.

Toward this end, you begin by developing the CommandGoalTrigger class, which is the CommandCodeTrigger class without the extra functions.. This class lacks the functions that generate messages and simulate a cipher guessing game. It attends primarily to detecting whether a player Pawn object is standing or crouching. On the basis of this activity, it then calls two other classes to retrieve messages or invoke actions relative to a guessing game. The other classes are called CodePlay and Story and receive close attention in the sections to come. Here is the code for the CommandGoalTrigger class. Discussion of specific features in the code follows.

```
//==========================================
// CommandGoalTrigger.
// See CommandGoalTrigger.txt
//==========================================
class CommandGoalTrigger extends Trigger
   placeable;
    var private string FirstMessage;
   // #1
   // var private CodePlay Score;
   // var private Story StoryToTell;

   enum PState{
         UP,
         DOWN
    };
```

```
function PostBeginPlay()
{
    // #2
    // Score = spawn(class'CodePlay');
    // Score.MakeCode();

    // StoryToTell = spawn(class'Story');
    // StoryToTell.MakeStory();

    FirstMessage = "Go!";
    Super.PostBeginPlay();
    Message = FirstMessage;
}// end PostBeginPlay()

function Touch( actor Other )
{
    if (IsRelevant( Other ) )
    {
        if (Pawn(Other).bIsCrouched){ //down
            Message = MakeMessage(PState.DOWN);
        }// end if
        else{ // up state
            Message = MakeMessage(PState.UP);
        }// end else
        Super.Touch(Other);
    }// end outer if
}

private function string MakeMessage(PState state){
    local string ActionMessage;
    if( state == PState.UP ){
        // #3
        ActionMessage @= "Goal - Get down! ";
        // ActionMessage @= Score.ProvideCodeMessage();
    }
    else if( state == PState.DOWN ){
        // #4
        ActionMessage @= "Goal - Get up! - ";
        // ActionMessage @= StoryToTell.TellStory();
    }
```

```
    else {
        ActionMessage = "Okay.";
    }
    return ActionMessage;
}
```

Type the code for the `CommandGoalTrigger` and compile it. Note that eight lines have been commented out. Leave these lines commented out for now. Their use depends on the implementation of the `CodePlay` and `Story` classes, so if you do not comment them out, your compiler issues errors. For now, you do not yet need the class to interact with the other two classes. Place an object of this class in your `Ch08Area01` map and verify that it issues the "Goal – Get up!" and "Goal – Get down!" messages.

As far as the other classes go, you see them first mentioned in the lines associated with comment #1. There, you declare two data members. One of the data types is `CodePlay`. The other is `Score`. After declaring identifiers for these two new data types, within the `PostBeginPlay()` function following comment #2 you use the `spawn` keyword to create instances of the classes and assign them to the identifiers.

After you create instances of the classes, you call the `MakeCode()` and `MakeStory()` functions. For the `CodePlay` class, the `MakeCode()` function generates a code that becomes the object of a game of discovery. For the `Story` class, the `MakeStory()` function creates a story and makes it available for display, a line at a time, as you play your level.

In the lines associated with comment #3, you use the instances of the two classes to call the `ProvideCodeMessage()` and `TellStory()` functions. These functions are called over and over again, depending on whether the player `Pawn` object is crouching or standing, and the messages vary according to actions attended to in the `Story` and `CodePlay` classes. The `MakeMessage()` function does nothing more than call two functions, but even with this brief interaction, the class accesses many more actions than those you implemented in dozens of lines in the `CommandCodeTrigger` class. This is the goal of refactoring.

Deriving a Class from Actor

Providing ciphers and guessing activities is the primary responsibility of the `CodePlay` class. To create this class, access the Actor Class Browser. Right-click the `Actor` class. In the New Class dialog, type `Ch08Area` for the package name and `CodePlay` for the class name. After you generate the shell of the class, click the Compile Changed Scripts icon on the code editor. Then click the `Ch08Area` package check box and select File > Save Selected Packages. You can now begin developing the code for the `CodePlay` class.

The code for the class follows, but before you start typing, read the section that follows titled "Dependencies." This discussion both reviews features of the class and provides you a strategy for entering the code so that you can build the class a step at a time.

```
//========================================
// CodePlay.
// CodePlay.txt
//========================================
class CodePlay extends Actor placeable;
  // #1 Data Members
      // Create a structure with three members
      struct CodeStatus{
         var string Letter;
         var bool Found;
         var int Times;
      };
      // These are public because constant
      const CODELENGTH = 8;
      const LOWASCII = 97;
      const HIGHASCII = 122;
      const NUMOFTRIES = 50;


      // #2 Use the struct type to declare an array
      var private CodeStatus AttemptedFinds[CODELENGTH];
      var private string CodeForSearch;
      var private string MessageAboutCode;
      var private string Report;

  // The interface consists of a few public functions
  // ======== Interface of Code Class ========
  // Create the code (use in PostBeginPlay())
      function public MakeCode(){
         local int Ctr;
         while (Ctr < CODELENGTH){
           CodeForSearch $= Chr(GenerateRandom());
           Ctr++;
         }
      }
  // #3
  // Provide messages for Message property
      function public string ProvideCodeMessage(){
         RunCodeFinder();
```

```
            return CodeForSearch $ MessageAboutCode $ Report;
        }
// Accessor for the text of the code
    function private string ShowCode(){
            return CodeForSearch;
        }
// Most functions cannot be accessed outside the class
// ======= Functions the Interface uses =============
function private int GenerateRandom(){
        local float High, Low;
        Low = LOWASCII;
        High = HIGHASCII;
        return Int(RandRange(Low, High));
    }
// #4
// Wrap calls to the private functions of the class
    function private RunCodeFinder(){
      SetGoals();
      DetectLetter();
      CheckForCompleteCode();
      CreateReport();
    }


// #5
// Use Right() and Left() built-in functions
// to sequentially retrieve letters and place
// them in the Letter member of the array elements.
// Initialize all Founds with false.
// Initialize all Times to 0.
    function private SetGoals(){
        local int Ctr;
        Ctr = 0;
        while(Ctr < CODELENGTH){
          AttemptedFinds[Ctr].Letter
                    = Right( Left(CodeForSearch, Ctr+1), 1);
          AttemptedFinds[Ctr].Found = false;
          AttemptedFinds[Ctr].Times = 0;
          Ctr++;
        }
    }
```

```
// #6
// Gather the information on the status of each
// attempted discovery and assign it to Report
   function private CreateReport(){
      local int Ctr;
      Report="";
      while(Ctr < CODELENGTH){
         Report $= AttemptedFinds[Ctr].Letter
               $ AttemptedFinds[Ctr].Found
               $ AttemptedFinds[Ctr].Times;
         Ctr++;
      }
   }


// #7 Embedded while statements with a selection statement
   //    While the number of tries allowed
   //    While each letter in the code string
   //       Compare a randomly generated letter
   //       with the letter in the Letter member
   //     If the letters match
   //       set Found to True
   //       increment Times
      function private DetectLetter(){
        local int Ctr, Itr;
        Ctr =0;
        while(Ctr < NUMOFTRIES){
           Itr = 0;
           while(Itr < CODELENGTH){
              if( AttemptedFinds[Itr].Letter == Chr(GenerateRandom() ) ){
                 AttemptedFinds[Itr].Found = true;
                 AttemptedFinds[Itr].Times++;
               }// end if
             Itr++;
           }// end inner while
           Ctr++;
        }// end outer while
      }// end Detect
```

```
//#8  For the length of the code string
//        Find all the letters that have been found
//        If all letters have been found, show code complete
//        If all letters have not been found, say keep looking
    function private CheckForCompleteCode(){
        local int Itr, Goal;
        Itr - 0;
        Goal - 0;
        while(Itr < CODELENGTH){
          if(AttemptedFinds[Itr].Found - true){
            Goal++;
            if(Goal - CODELENGTH){
              MessageAboutCode - "Great! You found the complete code!" ;
              CodeForSearch="";
              MakeCode();
              SetGoals();
              break;;
            }else{
              MessageAboutCode - "Still incomplete. Keep looking." ;
            }// end inner if else
          }// end outer if
          Itr++;
        }// end while
    }// end Check
```

Figure 8.7 illustrates the contents of the CodePlay class. The two UML diagrams show essential views of the data members and the functions. On the right, you see a UML representation of a structure. The CodePlay class contains the definition of the structure, CodeStatus. How you work with structures receives detailed discussion later on in this chapter.

The CodePlay class possesses several of the same features you saw in the CommandCodeTrigger class. The difference here is that the functionality of the class focuses only on creating codes, assessing the codes a letter at a time when prompted to do so by events of the game, and reporting whether or not the code has been found.

Figure 8.7 represents the functions of the class in two categories. In the upper part of the lower (functions) division, three of the functions constitute the interface of the class. These are public functions. They are the only functions you call from the *client class*. The client class in this instance is the CommandGoalTrigger class. You saw in the discussion of the code for the CommandGoalTrigger class how two of the interface functions are called.

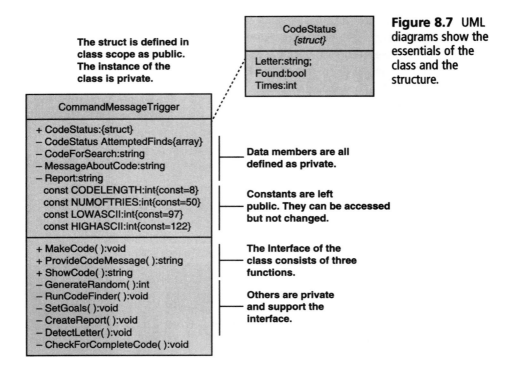

Figure 8.7 UML diagrams show the essentials of the class and the structure.

The only function of the interface not called is the ShowCode() function. This function does exactly what it says it does. It provides a message that reveals the whole cipher or code to you. While it is not included in the calls of functions in the version of the CommandGoalTrigger class shown previously, you can easily change the situation by including another line of code in the MakeMessage() function and assigning the returned code to the ActionMessage variable.

The private functions of the class are all designed to support the interface of the class. No reason exists for the client class to access them. They attend to creating a cipher and the actions related to playing a game in association with the cipher. The ProvideCodeMessage() serves to channel all of this activity to the client class with a single function call.

Dependencies

The CommandGoalTrigger class is fairly small when you compare it with many of the classes in the Unreal Tournament hierarchy. If you are relatively new to programming with UnrealScript, however, it can present several challenges if you enter the code line by line from scratch.

Developing a class that attends to multiple, complex tasks involves considering from the first the order of dependencies. Figure 8.8 summarizes the order in which you need to implement the code for the CodePlay class.

	Order of Development	Desc	Called In			Call order
1	CodeStatus	Struct	*			
2	GenerateRandom( )	Private	MakeCode( ) DetectLetter( )			
3	MakeCode( )	Interface	Client			
4	ShowCode( )	Interface	Client			
5	SetGoals( )	Private	RunCodeFinder( )		1	SetGoals( )
6	CreateReport( )	Private	RunCodeFinder( )		2	DetectLetter( )
7	DetectLetter( )	Private	RunCodeFinder( )		3	CheckForCompleteCode( )
8	CheckForCompleteCode( )	Private	RunCodeFinder( ) MakeCode( ) SetGoals( )		4	CreateReport( )
10	RunCodeFinder( )	Private	ProvideCodeMessage( )			
11	ProvideCodeMessage( )	Interface	Client			

Figure 8.8 Attention to the order of dependency make implementation in steps possible.

UnrealEd Strategies

Here are a couple of steps you can use as you implement a class like CodePlay.

1. After you have used the Actor Class Browser to create the class, you can uncomment the code associated with comment #1 in the CommandGoalTrigger class. This allows you to see if the CommandGoalTrigger class recognizes the class.

2. Attend to declaring the CodeStatus structure and all the other data members of the CommandGoalTrigger class.

3. Then implement the GenerateRandom() and MakeCode() functions. You create the GenerateRandom() function first and then MakeCode() function. You can then uncomment the code associated with comment #2 in the CommandGoalTrigger class.

If you want to see the code, then you can implement the ShowCode() function and call it in the MakeMessage() function in the CommandGoalTrigger class. Here is an example of how you can accomplish this.

```
if( state == PState.UP ){
    ActionMessage @= "Goal - Get down! ";
    // Temporary test code
    ActionMessage @= Score.ShowCode();
}
else if( state == PState.DOWN ){
// lines left out
```

You see an eight-character code displayed whenever the player Pawn object is in a standing position.

As you know, you must compile the CodePlay object before you can use it. As for the CommandGoalTrigger class, you have options. You can recompile it after changing the CodePlay class to incorporate the functionality of the CodePlay class. Until you want to do that, you do not need to worry about the CommandGoalTrigger class. The CommandGoalTrigger class calls whatever version of the CodePlay class you have available.

Subsequent sections of this chapter discuss the CodePlay code in detail. You can develop SetGoals(), CreateReport(), DetectLetter(), and CheckForCompleteCode() functions in isolation from each other. Other functions cannot be developed in isolation. Previous chapters have offered a number of opportunities to develop such functions. In this case, you need only to apply a little more planning to your work. When you finish the four primary functions, you include calls to these functions in the RunCodeFinder() function. This function groups the flow of the activity of the class in one place. You make this function private to conceal it from user classes. You then provide the user access to it through the ProvideCodeMessage() function, which is public.

Working with Structures

In the lines following comment #1, you create an abstract data type known as a *structure*. The keyword associated with structures is *struct*. To declare a structure, you employ the keyword struct followed by the name of the data type you are creating. A structure, like a class, is a type of data. After you define it, you can use it over and over to create variables, just as you do any other abstract data type.

When you create a structure, you include one or more *members*. To define a member, you use the *var* keyword, the data type of the member, and then the name of the member. The members can be of any data type you choose. After you define a member, you access it using the dot operator. For each instance of a structure you create, the members possess unique values.

A structure is a way of conveniently grouping a set of data members together. In this case, the structure contains three members. One is of the string type, Letter; one is of the bool type, Found; and one is of the int type, Times. The name of the data type is CodeStatus, and you use it to track the status of each letter of the eight-letter ciphers you work with when in the CodePlay class. If you have a cipher that reads "mudrsizo", each letter can be tracked according to its identity, the number of times it has been detected, and whether or not it has not been detected. (The goal of the game is to guess all the letters at least once.)

To create an instance of a structure, you proceed in the same way you proceed with the creation of an instance of any other data type. The only difference is that you cannot assign values directly to the identifiers you create. Instead, you use the dot operator to access the structure member. Then you assign the values. Here is an example of declaring and defining an instance of the CodeStatus data type:

```
// Declare it
CodeStatus FirstLetter;
// Assign values to the members
FirstLetter.Letter = "m";
FirstLetter.Found = false;
FirstLetter.Times = 1;
```

As you see in the code for the CodePlay class, you can treat the member of a structure like any other variable as long as you continue to reference it using the name of the structure identifier that it is associated with. Here are a few examples:

```
// Concatenate two letters and assign them to a third string
SummaryString.Letter = FirstLetter.Letter @ SecondLetter.Letter;
// Add two Times and assign the sum to a third
SummaryString.Times = FirstLetter.Times + SecondLetter.Times;
// Evaluate the value and then assign a new value to it
if( SecondLetter.Found == true){
    SecondLetter.Found = false;
}
```

As you might expect, if you can use data types you create using a structure just as you use any other type of data, then you can also use it to create an array. In the declaration associated with comment #2, you define an array in this way:

```
var private CodeStatus AttemptedFinds[CODELENGTH];
```

This declaration creates a set of eight `CodeStatus` elements in an array called `AttemptedFinds`. You can then use the array to call the members of the `CodeStatus` elements as the name of the identifier for the elements. You use an index within square braces to indicate the element you want to access, just as you do with other arrays. Here are some examples:

```
//Add 1 to the Times member of the third element of the array
AttemptedFinds[2].Times  += 1;
//Set the Found member of the second element of the array to true
AttemptedFinds[1].Found = true;
```

Making a Code

The `MakeCode()` and `GenerateRandom()` functions work together. You have already seen how to implement the `GenerateRandom()` function. The `MakeCode()` function is implemented in the lines preceding comment #3. Implementation involves the use of a `while` repetition statement. The `while` statement works along predictable lines. The flow of the program reaches the control expression. If the value assigned to `Ctr` is less than the value assigned to `CODE-LENGTH`, then the flow of the program enters the `while` block. Within the block, it repeats eight times, calling the `GenerateRandom()` function. With each call of this function, an integer ranging in value from 97 through 122 is returned. You call the `Chr()` function to convert it into a letter and then employ the concatenation operator to create a string of eight letters. To control the `while` statement, you increment `Ctr` once each time the block repeats.

The cipher or code itself is assigned to a data member of the class. This is the `CodeForSearch` data member. Given that you assign the code to this data member, you can then implement the `ShowCode()` function. This accessor function exists solely for the purpose of returning the value of this data member, and as mentioned earlier, it provides a convenient tool for testing.

In the lines following comment #3, you define the `ProvideCodeMessage()` method. Notice that this function calls the `RunCodeFinder()` function. If you comment out the call to the `RunCodeFinder()` function, you can begin testing this function right away in the `CommandGoalTrigger` class, right along with the `ShowCode()` function. Here is the commented form:

```
function public string ProvideCodeMessage(){
    // Comment out while developing your class
    // RunCodeFinder();
    return CodeForSearch $ MessageAboutCode $ Report;
}
```

You can leave the `return` statement because it uses only the data members of the class. Given that you comment out the call to `RunCodeFinder()`, then you can work from the `ShowCode()`

function alone, without the `RunCodeFinder()` function. If you go this route, remember to remove your comments when you have satisfied dependencies. Here is how your test session might look in the `CommandGoalTrigger` class given the use of comments in the `ProvideCodeMessage()` function:

```
if( state == PState.UP ){
    // #3
    ActionMessage @= "Goal - Get down! ";
    ActionMessage @= "Goal - Get down! ";
    // Lines commented out within ProvideCodeMessage()
    // You call the function, but get only a limited response
    ActionMessage @= Score.ProvideCodeMessage();
    // Call the accessor function, temporarily, to see the code
    ActionMessage @= Score.ShowCode();
}
else if( state == PState.DOWN ){
// Lines left out
```

Assembling Everything

In the lines accompanying comment #4, you define the `RunCodeFinder()` function. Due to its dependencies, this is the last function you can develop, so the most you can do early on is type its signature line and opening and closing braces. Comment out the four function calls within it. This function serves to organize and group the activities of the class so that they can be seen in one place. You make the function private so that users of the class cannot see the inner workings of the class. To have public access to services the function provides, the users call the `ProvideCodeMessage()` function, which as you have already seen is part of the interface of the class.

Visiting Individual Letters and Getting Status

In the lines following comment #5, the `SetGoals()` function attends to setting up the values for each letter in the eight-letter cipher. To attend to this task, you use another `while` repetition statement. The `while` control allows the block to repeat eight times. Its action is controlled by the value of `CODELENTH`. The `Ctr` variable is incremented by 1 each time the flow of the program enters or reenters the control block.

To visit each letter in the cipher string, you use a combination of the `Right()` and `Left()` functions. These are built-in functions that you obtain from the `Object` class of the Unreal Tournament class hierarchy. The functions work in the same general manner. The `Right()` function extracts a designated number of letters from the end of a string. Of its two arguments, the first designates the string. The second designates the number of letters.

The `Left()` function works in the same way, except that it extracts a designated number of letters from the front of a string. To make it so that you can go through the letters of the cipher, from beginning to end, and successively assign them to the elements of the `AttemptedFinds` array, you use the returned value of the `Left()` function as the first argument of the `Right()` function. When the flow of the program enters the `while` block the first time, the `Left()` function extracts a string from the start of the series of eight letters. The length of this string increases by one letter with each iteration of the `while` block. On the other hand, the `Right()` function simply takes the last letter of the string.

The first time through, you get the first letter and the `Right()` function returns it. The second time through, you get two letters, and the `Right()` function returns the second letter. The third time, you get the third letter. In this way, you get one letter each with each repeat of the block and assign it to the element the `Ctr` variable designates. In the end, each `Letter` member of each of the `CodeStatus` elements in the `AttemptedFinds` array contains one letter.

As for the other `CodeStatus` members, `Times` and `Found`, you set them to default values. So far the search for the letter in the cipher has not started, so the letters have been found 0 times. Likewise, you assign `false` to the `Found` member. This member remains `false` until the letter is found the first time and remains `true` after that.

In the lines associated with comment #6, you once again use a `while` control statement to access the elements in the `AttemptedFinds` array. This time around, the purpose for accessing the elements is to merely extract information about them. The `CreateReport()` function is a reporting function. It takes information from the three members of each of the `CodeStatus` elements in the array and concatenates it into a long string that tells you the identify of the letter, whether its `Found` status is `True` or `False`, and how many times each letter has been found. The string is pretty ugly but serves to add to the excitement of the search. The result is assigned to the `Report` data member, which the `ProvideCodeMessage()` function uses as part of its output. Here is an example of the information assigned to the `Report` data member:

        `aTrue2uTrue2sTrue1sTrue1kTrue2gFalse0oTrue4dTrue2`

Each letter appears first, following by the bool value reporting its `Found` status. Then you see the number of times it has been found. Only the "g" at this point remains unfound.

Finding Letters in Ciphers

The implementation of the `DetectLetter()` function occurs in association with comment #7. This function guesses the identity of letters. The game of guessing or finding letters in the codes or ciphers involves using the `GenerateRandom()` function. This function makes the guesses. In this implementation of the `CodePlay` class, you make it so that guessing a letter in a cipher is not hard. Each time the player `Pawn` object approaches a `CommandGoalTrigger` while standing, the `DetectLetter()` method iterates through the eight letters 50 times.

Making the guess involves two while statements and an embedded selection statement. The pseudocode in the comments preceding the function review the flow of the function specifically. The outer while block repeats NUMOFTRIES times (50). The inner while block traverses all the letters in the cipher. For each letter, the GenerateRandom() function provides an integer value in the ASCII lowercase letter range, which the Chr() function converts into a letter. The if selection statement tests whether the character assigned to the Letter member of the CodeStatus element equals this letter. If so, then a true value is assigned to the Found member associated with the letter, and the Time attribute is incremented by 1. In this way, all finds are recorded.

The Whole Code

In the lines associated with comment #8, the CheckForCompleteCode() function examines the Found member of each of the elements of the AttemptedFinds array to see if it is set to true. If all the elements are set to true, then the code has been solved, and the player can see a message of congratulations for having guessed all the letters in the code. If a guess is made, however, and not all the Found members for the letters yet report true, then another message is generated. This reads, "Sill incomplete. Keep looking."

Checking for completeness involves a while repetition statement with embedded selection statements. The while statement iterates through the letters of the cipher. The first of the selection statements checks the Found member of each of the letters to see if its status has been set to true. If this is so, then the Goal variable for the string is incremented by 1. The Goal variable is defined locally.

In an embedded if...else statement, the value of Goal is checked against the value assigned to CODELENGTH. This value is 8, as you know well by now. When an expression for the if statement renders true, then the message of congratulations is issued. If the cipher has been solved, then it is also time to create a new cipher, so the MakeCode() function is called, along with the SetGoals() function. You also assign an empty string to the CodeForSearch data member. The use of the break keyword in the first if statement causes the while loop to terminate.

Note

This is probably an opportunity for the addition to the class of a new function called Reset(). Any takers?

The CheckForCompleteCode() function updates the MessageAboutCode data member. The value stored in this data member, along with those of the Report and CodeForSearch data members, allows the player of the level to see statements about the status of the guessing activity. The message you see in Figure 8.9 shows the information these three data members convey when the detection process is still incomplete. With the NUMBEROFTRIES data member

Figure 8.9 When you stand, you hear whether you have found the complete code (see the note).

value set to 50, the player Pawn object usually encounters the CommandGoalTrigger object five or six times before a message indicating success is issued.

Note

In Figure 8.9, note that quite a bit of jargon follows the basic message. This is more or less an activity of showing your progress so far. If you look closely, you see, for the first two letters in the cipher the following information:

LFALSEORTRUE2

If you add spaces, the message is a little easier to read:

L FALSE 0 R TRUE 2

You see information that tells you L is still false, that it is in position 0 in the cipher and R has been found and is in position 2 in the cipher. You can exclude such information from the report by commenting out the call to the CreateReport() function in the RunCodeFinder() function (following comment #4).

If you want to change the message so that the information is less garbled, then in the definition of the CreateReport() function following comment #6, change the concatenation operators so that $= becomes @= and $ becomes @. This places spaces between the characters. If you then view the log (using ~), you can see the complete messages, which take two or more lines due to the additional spaces.

Figure 8.10 provides a view of logged messages. If you inspect the messages through several cycles of play, you can see that each time the cipher is solved, CodePlay class generates a new code. The game goes on.

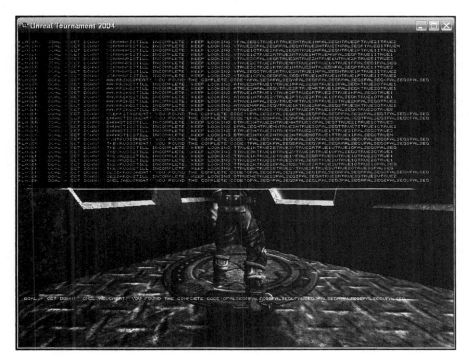

Figure 8.10 The log allows you to see the guessing game unfold an event at a time.

If You're Down, Listen to a Story

The use of random messages has provided a means of diversion, but a more interesting approach to life in a given level involves displaying messages that tell a part of a story with each new event. To make this possible, you create the Story class. The Story class contains a story that you store, line by line, in an array. The array this time around differs from those you have seen before. It is a *dynamic array*. This array allows you to add items as you go.

To create the Story class, open the Actor Class Browser. Right-click on the Actor class and select New. In the New Class dialog, type Ch08Area for the package name and Story for the class name. When the code editor opens, click the Compile Changed Scripts icon. Then click to activate the Ch08Area package and select File > Save Selected Packages. You are then ready to go.

As soon as you have compiled the signature line of the class, you can uncomment the declaration and definition lines for the Story class in the CommandGoalTrigger class. Type and test all the rest of the class before removing the comments from the line containing StoryToTell.TellStory(). Here is the code for the class:

```
//═══════════════════════════════════════════════
// Story.
// See Story.txt
//═══════════════════════════════════════════════
class Story extends Actor placeable;
    var private string ActionMessage;
    var private int Next;
    // #1
    // Dynamic array
    var private Array<string> Story;

    // Goes in MakeMessage
    public function string TellStory(){
        local string StoryLine;
        StoryLine = GetLineOfStory();
        return StoryLine;
    }

    // Goes PostBeginPlay
    public function MakeStory(){
        CreateStory();
    }
    #2
    private function CreateStory(){
        // Assign text values to elements
        Story[0]= "In a village";
        Story[1]= "Once there lived a holy man";
        Story[2]= "He was poor";
        Story[3]= "His house had a dirt floor";
        Story[4]= "His house had a stove";
        Story[5]= "This man had a dream";
        Story[6]= "Three times he had the dream";
        Story[7]= "And so he thought it from God";
        Story[8]= "Of going to a city";
        Story[9]= "And a palace in the city";
        Story[10]= "Where he, poor man";
        Story[11]= "Would find a treasure";
        Story[12]= "He went to the city";
```

```
      Story[13]= "It was far away";
      Story[14]= "And in the city he found the palace";
      Story[15]= "It was well guarded";
      Story[16]= "And a guard stopped him ";
      Story[17]= "\"What are you doing here?\" the guard demanded ";
      Story[18]= "\"I had a dream to come here, to this palace";
      Story[19]= "\"Do not be foolish, said the guard";
      Story[20]= "\"I once had a dream that a poor holy man would come here";
      Story[21]= "\"And I would follow him home, to a village far away";
      Story[22]= "\"And behind his stove would in his wretched home ";
      Story[23]= "\"A treasure would be buried ";
      Story[24]= "\"Go home, old one, and do not believe foolish dreams.\"";
      Story[25]= "So the holy man thanked the guard.";
      Story[26]= "After many days, he arrived home.";
      Story[27]= "Behind his stove he started digging.";
      Story[28]= "Soon he found the buried treasure.";
   }
   // #3
   private function string GetLineOfStory(){
      local string TMessage;
     // Retrieve an element from the array
      if(Next < Story.Length){
         TMessage = Story[Next];
         Next++;
      }else{
         Next = 0;
      }
      return TMessage;
   }
```

To define the Story class, you first create the data members of the class. As you can see in the lines associated with comment #1, declaration of a dynamic array involves using a *template*. A template is characterized most by the name of the template data type followed by a set of angle braces (<>). In this case, the data type is Array. Within the angle braces, you follow Array with a specification of the type of data you want to store in the array. In this case, it is data of the string type. You then furnish the name of the array. In this case, the name of the array is Story.

To add elements to a dynamic array, you can proceed in the same way that you proceeded when you added elements to a static array. In this instance, however, you do not need to worry about the length of the array. As the term *dynamic* implies, the array automatically expands every time you increase the value of the index you use to designate the position of the element you want to add.

After declaring the data array, you can proceed to implement the CreateStory() function. This activity occurs in association with comment #2. This function serves to add a narrative of 29 lines to the Story array. To add the lines, you assign the line, in quotes, to the index with which you want to associate it. This is a familiar routine by now. The only feature that might seem a little strange is the use of a slash within some of the quotes. A slash is used to indicate an escape character. An escape character tells the compiler to view a given character (such as opening or closing quotation marks) as literal, so it is not read as part of the syntax of the programming language. To create words in quotations, then, you use \" to make the quotation marks appear as part of the string.

Following comment #3, you can then write the code for the GetLineOfStory() function. This function uses the data member Next to traverse the array, retrieving its elements, start to end, and returning the line retrieved through the TMessage variable. When you have called the function a number of times equal to the length of the array, then the value of Next is set back to 0, and the telling of the story begins again.

One new item is the Length property of the Array class. You access it using the dot operator. Story.Length returns the number of items in the array. This property tells you the number of items in the array. It is important to remember this. The number of items is 29, not 28. The Length property does not track index values. It tracks the number of elements.

The TellStory() function provides one of the two interface functions for the class. It calls the private GetLineOfStory() function and assigns the returned line to the StoryLine data member. It then returns the value assigned to StoryLine.

Like the CodePlay class, the Story class includes an interface function that initializes the information it provides to its client class. This is the MakeStory() function. It calls the CreateStory() function. As with the CodePlay class, a public function wraps a private function to keep the inner workings of the class from being exposed in the client class.

You call the MakeStory() function in the PostBeginPlay() method of the CommandGoalTrigger class. You then call the TellStory() function in the DOWN selection block of the MakeMessage() function.

Place an instance of the CommandGoalTrigger in the level. Figure 8.11 shows the event as triggered in association with a jump pad placed in the chamber discussed previously. To make it so that the story unfolds at a leisurely pace, set the RepeatTriggerTime and ReTriggerDelay properties of the object to 5 each. Position the player Pawn object in proximity to the jump pad and hold down the Shift key. The story unfolds a line at a time. If you let up and attend to other actions, have no fears. When you return, the story remains where you left off.

Figure 8.11 When you stoop now, the gargoyle tells you a story.

Conclusion

If you examine the classes in this chapter, you can probably find several ways to improve on the "game" of discovering a "code". As it is, when the various functions report codes or discovered pieces of a code, the game is not yet real. At best, the messages you see have the appearance of a game.

Still, the purpose of the CommandCodeTrigger class is to illustrate several practical programming activities that involve UnrealScript and the Unreal Tournament class hierarchy. By implementing the functions in this chapter, you broaden your understanding of control structures, Actor classes, and other features of UnrealScript and in this way make progress toward larger programming problems.

The CommandGoalTrigger class allowed you to develop a set of classes that made interaction with your level a bit more interesting. Granted, text messages leave a great deal to be desired, but it still stands that given the use of such things as structures, built-in functions, enumerations, compound logical operations, arrays, and selection and control statements, the classes you end up with contain many potentials for subsequent development efforts.

Can you now implement a class that provides a random message service? Define it as you do in the CommandGoalTrigger class as a data member. Initialize it in the PostBeginPlay() method. Then call it in the MakeMessage() function. How can you make it so that you can use a third type of message? Or how about adding a feature to the CodePlay class that makes a player a winner only after solving five ciphers? Or suppose you have your own stories, such as those from *Aesop's Fables*. Suppose you want to hear half a dozen stories rather than just one. What would you do to make this possible? And don't forget that pesky matter of the Reset() function in CodePlay.

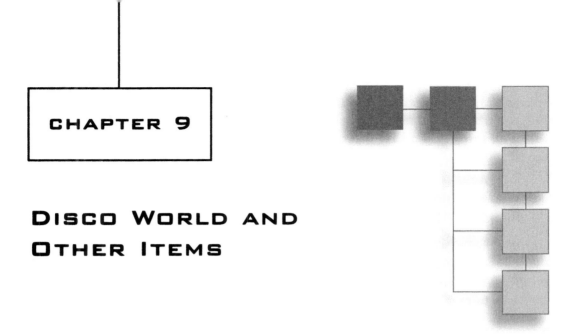

CHAPTER 9

DISCO WORLD AND OTHER ITEMS

n this chapter, you work with a class derived from the KActor class and a static mesh object that you create using the sphere brush. You make it so that the static mesh can be moved around your level. To manipulate the object, you use values you assign to a Vector object and then pass an argument to the Velocity property of the KActor class. You learn about a few more built-in functions. One in particular is the vect() function, which is defined to create Vector objects. You also review the SetTimer() function, which enables you to control the rate at which a KActor object can move the static mesh associated with it. Among the topics in this chapter are the following:

- Creating a static mesh object
- Creating a KActor class
- The Vector class as a data type
- Functions to use with Vector objects
- Code for controlling events
- Placing a KActor object in your level

Getting Started with Disco World

In this chapter, you develop a class you derive from the KActor class. The KActor class is often identified as a key physics class in the Unreal Tournament class hierarchy. Among many other things, you can associate a static mesh with a KActor class. When you do this, you then have on hand a static mesh object that you can move around your level.

Throughout this book, the work involved in creating maps has been reduced to a minimum with the assumption that this is something you want to pursue on your own. Although that practice remains in place in this chapter, as a starter map, if you want to work from absolute zero, so to speak, you can access the Ch09Disco00.ut2 file in the Maps directory for Chapter 9. This map provides a cube with textures, nothing more. This map is a remake of the previous cube level. Here are the textures applied:

- Walls—AlleriaTerrain.Wal23AL
- Floor—AlleriaTerrain.Flr04AL
- Ceiling—Cel04AL

Figure 9.1 gives you a view of the map. A feature missing at this point is a static mesh representing a large ball of ice. You create this static mesh. You then associate it with a class you derive from the KActor class.

Figure 9.1 The AlleriaTerrain texture package provides assets you can use as a starting point.

Preliminaries

In this chapter, you perform operations that require the Unreal Engine to be able to process the details of maps on an extremely refined basis. For this reason, the setting of your display must be set as shown in Figure 9.2. To adjust your settings, the best approach is to exit UnrealEd and open Unreal Tournament. Wait a few seconds for the introductory screens to display and then press the Esc key. Click the Settings option. Click the Display tab. On the right side of the window under Options, set all options to High or Highest. Then click Back and exit the game. The Display options are saved so that they become the default values for UnrealEd.

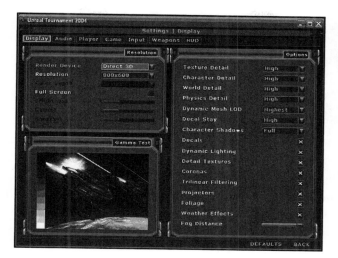

Figure 9.2 Developing KActor objects requires that you set your Display options to the highest level.

Adding a Tetrahedron

The first order of business is to create an object that you can move around your level using the KActor object. You can use classes you derive from the KActor class to control any number of objects, but as a starter project, creating a static mesh representing a large ice ball keeps things simple.

Your objective is to create a tetrahedral brush object. In less cumbersome language, you create a sphere. You change this object into a static mesh. The name you assign to the ice ball is DiscoBall. The name you assign to the KActor object you associate with the ice ball is also DiscoBall. One item is a static mesh file. The other is a code file. That they possess the same name makes it easier to remember them in association with each other.

First, to create the spherical object that you transform into a static mesh, begin work with the Texture Browser. Open the Texture Browser before you start on any other work. You should select the texture to use for the surface of the ice ball prior to using the tetrahedron brush to create the ball.

As shown in Figure 9.3, select File > Open from the Texture Browser to access the AlleriaTerrain.utc texture package. After you open the package, select the AlleriaTerrain *ground* option and the ice01AL texture. Click the texture to make it active.

Now right-click on the tetrahedron (or sphere) builder brush. The icon for the brush is located in the brush primitive area at the bottom of the palette, as Figure 9.4 shows.

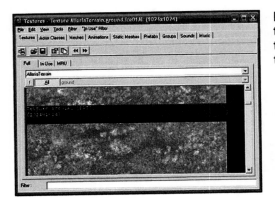

Figure 9.3 Select the texture before you use the brush to create the tetrahedral object.

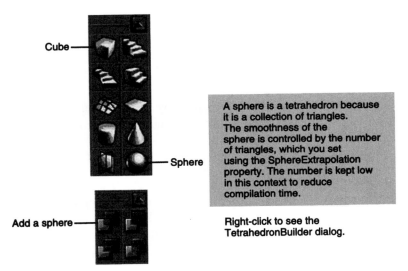

Cube

Sphere

A sphere is a tetrahedron because it is a collection of triangles. The smoothness of the sphere is controlled by the number of triangles, which you set using the SphereExtrapolation property. The number is kept low in this context to reduce compilation time.

Add a sphere

Right-click to see the TetrahedronBuilder dialog.

Figure 9.4 Setting the SphereExtrapolation property to 3 reduces the compilation time but results in a fairly crude object.

In the TetrahedronBuilder dialog, set the Radius property to 120. Assign 3 to the SphereExtrapolation property. The value of SphereExtrapolation establishes the number of vertices on the sphere. The higher the number, the more it looks like a sphere. Click Build at this point. See Figure 9.5.

Now move to the Add icon in the CSG Operations area (see Figure 9.4). Click the Add icon on the top left. The brush appears in the viewports. Work with the sphere object as it appears in the Top 2D viewport.

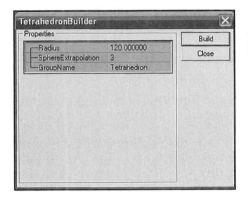

Figure 9.5 Click Build after you set the properties.

If you have not done so, click Build in the TetrahedronBuilder dialog. Then Press Shift and left-click to move the red brush object away and expose the newly created tetrahedron object. Position the ice ball at the top, in the middle, and toward the back of the cube. Figure 9.6 shows the front view. Adjust the lighting or add more lights.

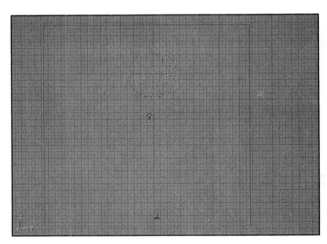

Figure 9.6 The Top viewport shows the object toward the back.

Click the Build Geometry and Build Lighting icons. You should immediately see an ice ball in the Dynamic Light viewport. If you do not, delete your work, go to the Texture Browser, and select the texture. Then use the Add icon to add another sphere and click Build in the TetrahedronBuilder dialog. Save your level when you are done. Keep in mind that this is just a temporary object. You will shortly delete it and replace it with another object.

Saving the Object as a Static Mesh

You save the primitive object as a static mesh so that you can more readily associate it with the class you derive from the KActor class. The object you create with a brush is not technically a static mesh. You can apply physics to a static mesh fairly easily.

To convert the brush object to a static mesh, work in the Top 2D view and right-click on the brush object. Select Convert > To Static Mesh.

As Figure 9.7 illustrates, you see a New Static mesh dialog that displays three properties. Name the Package Ch09Disco. Name the Group Disco. In the field corresponding to the Name property, type DiscoBall. Click OK.

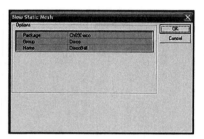

Figure 9.7 The static mesh is identified by its package, its group, and its name.

The actions you perform in the New Static Mesh dialog generate a static mesh that remains in a provisional state until you save it. To save the static mesh, activate the Static Mesh Browser, as shown in Figure 9.8. Select Ch09Disco as the static mesh package. Locate the DiscoBall item in the lower list. Then from the menu of the Static Meshes dialog, select File > Save.

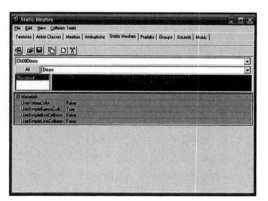

Figure 9.8 Save your created static mesh.

Note that in the Save Static Mesh Package dialog, the name of the package is Ch09Disco.utx. Static meshes are automatically saved to the StaticMeshes directory, as Figure 9.9 shows. All static meshes have the same file type and are placed in the same location. After you click Save to save the new static mesh package, leave the Static Mesh browser open. Then from the UnrealEd top menu, select File > Save to save your level.

Figure 9.9 Save the static mesh package.

Replacing the Preliminary Object

You can now replace the temporary brush with a static mesh. To accomplish this, in the 2D Top viewport, locate the sphere you previously created and delete it. After you have deleted the temporary object, click the Build Geometry icon to refresh the geometry of your level. If an image of the tetrahedron object remains in the Dynamic Light viewport, this action should clear it away.

If the Static Mesh Browser is not still active, activate it. Right-click the DiscoBall static mesh to select it. It resides, of course, in the Ch09Disco package in the Disco group.

Then move to the Dynamic Light viewport and right-click above the light, in the position previously occupied by the temporary object. As shown in Figure 9.10, select Add Static Mesh: 'Ch09Disco.Disco.Discoball'.

You then immediately see the DiscoBall static mesh. Work in all the viewports to adjust its position to accord with Figure 9.11. Select File > Save from the top menu and save your level.

Figure 9.10 Select Add Static Mesh.

Figure 9.11 The DiscoBall static mesh object occupies the position previously occupied by the temporary object.

Extending the KActor Class

As Figure 9.12 illustrates, your next step is to permanently associate a class you derive from the KActor class with the DiscoBall static mesh. KActor is a class that is convenient for performing actions involving physics. You permanently associate the DiscoBall static mesh with the DiscoBall class. Then, you create an instance of the DiscoBall class; in addition, you automatically create an instance of the DiscoBall static mesh.

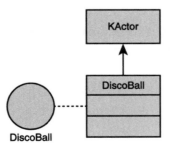

Figure 9.12 You can specialize the KActor class and then permanently associate the specialized class with a static mesh object.

First, you specialize the KActor class. Toward this end, open the Actor Class Browser and navigate to the KActor listing. Right-click and select New. As shown in Figure 9.13, in the New Class dialog, enter Ch09Disco as the name of the package and DiscoBall as the name of the class. Click OK.

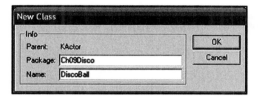

Figure 9.13 Create the DiscoBall class.

You see the signature of the class in the code editor, as usual. To save this first version, click the Save Change Script icon. You see the newly specialized version of the KActor class in the Actor Class Browser, as shown in Figure 9.14. To save your work, activate the Ch09Disco package and select Save Selected Packages from the top Actor Classes Browser.

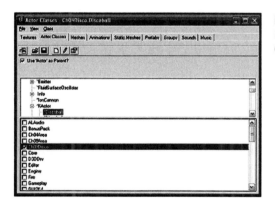

Figure 9.14 Save your KActor object to the Ch09Disco package.

Writing the Code

The code you write for the DiscoBall class accomplishes three tasks. It adjusts a few variables before the level begins to execute. It sets the duration of an event timer as the class is instantiated. It then regulates the motions of its associated object as it executes. The code for the first version of the class is given in the DiscoBall.txt listing in the code folder for Chapter 9. After you enter the code, activate the Ch09Disco package and select Save Selected Packages. Here's the code:

```
//===============================================
// DiscoBall.
// See DiscoBall.txt
//===============================================
```

```
class DiscoBall extends KActor placeable;
// This function gets called before anything happens to the object.
// It is called to set up all the objects
// with relation to the actions for the level generally
function PreBeginPlay() {
    // # 1
    // Sets the timer to go off every 9 seconds
    // The 'true' argument means call the Timer
    SetTimer(9.0, true);
}
function PostBeginPlay() {
    // # 2
    // Sets the initial velocity vector to point down
    // The speed of movement is 90 units
    // The arguments defined x, y, and z coordinates
     Velocity = vect(0, 0, -90);
}
function Timer() {
    // # 3
    // Flip the velocity vector around
    Velocity = (-1) * Velocity;
}
```

The SetTimer() Function

In the lines following comment #1, you call the PreBeginPlay() function. As the name implies, this function allows you to set parameters concurrent with the initialization of the KActor object. The utility of this function becomes evident if you consider that it is useful to be able to set parameters that define the starting condition of your object. In this function, you call the SetTimer() function. This function defines the units that govern the duration of a timer pulse relative to the object being created.

When you provide an argument of 9.0 to the SetTimer() function, you tell the timer to allow 9 units of duration to elapse between changes. The argument of true tells the SetTimer() function to audit each pulse the game engine provides.

Values for Vectors

In the code associated with comment #2, you define a familiar function—the PostBeginPlay() play function. Within this function, you call the vect() function, which defines a vector. A vector is basically an arrow (ray) that has *direction* and *magnitude*. Direction is described by the x, y, and z coordinates of the world space. Magnitude is described by the number of UT space units an object moves in a given period of time.

The vect() function formats the data you provide it as a structure (an object of the Vector data type) and then assigns this value to the Velocity property. The Velocity property is also of a structure (Vector) data type. This property tells the object how many units and in what direction to move each time the SetTimer() function allows the game engine to prompt it to move. If you consider each impulse to be a second, then every 9 seconds the game allows the object to move 90 units.

As Figure 9.15 illustrates, when you use a vector, you designate movement and direction, so by combining x, y, and z values, you can move your object in any direction relative to its position in the world space of the level.

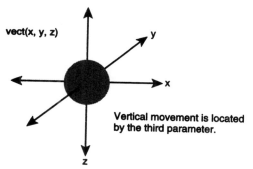

Figure 9.15 The vect() function allows you to designate directions of movement.

In the lines associated with comment #3, you multiply the current value of the Velocity property by −1 to reverse the movement of the object. When you multiply the Vector data type by −1, the multiplication operator is defined so that it acts on all three members of the vector. Vector math stipulates that when you multiply a vector in this way, each of the members of the vector is multiplied by the same number.

The Built-in Vector Data Type

The Vector structure is defined along with the built-in functions in the Object class of the class hierarchy. You use the Vector data type to manipulate 2D and 3D objects. As with any other data type, you can use the Vector data type to declare variables in local or class scope.

As the discussion in Chapter 8 revealed, when you define a structure, you define data members for it, much as you do a class. In Chapter 8, you worked with a structure in some ways analogous to a 2D vector. When you work with the Vector data type, you work with a 3D data type. Here is how these two structures can be defined:

```
//3D vector - defined in this way as a built-in data type
struct Vector{
  var float    x;
  var float    y;
  var float    z;
};
//2D vector
struct Vector{
    var float x;
    var float y;
};
```

The data members of the built-in data type are defined as float values. As the example shows, they are identified simply as x, y, and z.

In addition to the Vector type itself, the Object class provides definitions of overloaded operators. How to define overloaded operators lies beyond the scope of his book, but the purpose of such activities is to make it so that you can use standard math (and other) operators with objects of an abstract class in the same way that you use them with variables of the primitive data types.

For the Vector class, you find such operators as *,*=,+,-,-=,/,/=, and ━. To consider the implications of overloaded operators, suppose you define two Vector objects in this way:

```
local Vector VectorA, VectorB;
// Assign values
VectorA = vect(2,3,4);
VectorB = vect(3,4,5);
```

As mentioned previously, the vect() function defines values to the Vector objects. How this happens becomes evident momentarily. As it is, however, if you want to add these two

Vector objects using standard operators, you must access the value assigned to each member of each vector. The procedure might proceed as follows:

```
// Define a vector to hold the sum
local Vector VectorC;
VectorC.x = VectorA.x + VectorB.x;
VectorC.y = VectorA.y + VectorB.y;
VectorC.z = VectorA.z + VectorB.z;
```

This activity tends to be fairly cumbersome. If you have to add several such Vector objects, you would soon refactor your code to crate a function. One recourse in this respect might be a function you name AddVectors(). You might define it in this way:

```
function Vector AddVectors(Vector VectA, Vector VectB){
    local Vector VectorC;
    Vect.x = VectA.x + VectB.x;
    Vect.y = VectA.y + VectB.y;
    Vect.z = VectA.z + VectB.z;
    Return VectC;
}
```

You could then proceed as follows:

```
VectorC = AddVectors(VectorA + VectorB);
```

UnrealScript defines a math operator that you use in place of the AddVectors() function. You can then carry out the operation in this way using the overloaded addition operator:

```
VectorC = VectorA + VectorB;
```

You can also carry out operations of this type:

```
VectorC = 2 * VectorB;
```

When you use the multiplication operator in this way, you multiply each of the values assigned to the members of the Vector object by 2.

In addition to overloaded operators, the Vector class provides built-in functions. Among these you find the VRand() function, which generates a vector that contains random values. The values the VRand() function supplies to the Vector object it generates all lie between 0 and 1, so the function works along the line of the FRand() function. It supplies three random values rather than one. It also works along the same lines as the Vect() function, for it processes all the values in the vector.

If you write your own vect() function, it unfolds along the following lines:

```
function Vector vect(float x, float y, float z){
    Vector Vect;
    Vect.x = x;
    Vect.y = y;
    Vect.z = z;
    Return Vect;
}
```

Associating Your Static Mesh with a KActor Object

You can associate physics properties with a static mesh. To accomplish this, you work with both the Actor Class Browser and the Static Mesh Browser. You toggle between them as you work.

First select the DiscoBall listing in the Static Mesh Browser, as Figure 9.16 shows. If you have closed out of your session since the last section, access this static mesh in the Ch09Disco static mesh (*.usx) package. After you click on the DiscoBall listing, the name of the static mesh resides in the UnrealEd buffer.

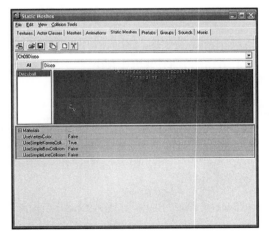

Figure 9.16 Select the DiscoBall static mesh.

Then right-click on the DiscoBall class in the Actor Class Browser and select Default Properties, as shown in Figure 9.17. The Default Properties dialog applies to all objects of a class, not just specific instances. You want all objects of the DiscoBall class to be associated with a DiscoBall static mesh.

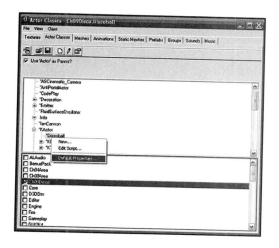

Figure 9.17 Select Default Properties from the menu.

You see the Default Properties dialog for the `DiscoBall` object. Click the Display tray, as shown in Figure 9.18. Find the `StaticMesh` property and click the adjacent field. Then click the Use button. The name of the static mesh object stored in the buffer immediately fills the field. The static mesh object is now associated with the `DiscoBall` object. Close the Default Properties dialog.

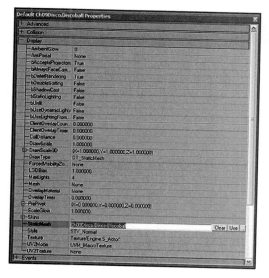

Figure 9.18 In the Display tray find the StaticMesh field.

Save your work. To accomplish this, select the `DiscoBall` class in the Actor Class Browser. Confirm that you have the checkbox activated for the `Ch09Disco` package, and select File > Save Selected Packages.

Replace the Old Mesh

If you have not done so already, access the Dynamic Light viewport. Delete the static mesh you created as a placeholder. Open the Actor Class Browser. Access the DiscoBall class in the KActor class tree and click to activate it. Then right-click in the Dynamic Light viewport and select Add DiscoBall Here.

Figure 9.19 illustrates that the new object closely resembles the old. The differences are concealed, but if you click the object, the Properties dialog informs you that it possesses properties related to physics. The next section deals with these properties in greater detail.

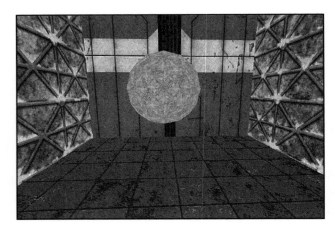

Figure 9.19 The KActor object replaces the static mesh.

Setting DiscoBall Object Properties

In the previous section, you employed the Default Properties dialog to associate the DiscoBall static mesh with the DiscoBall class. This created an object that you can instantiate at any time to create a dynamic ice ball.

Even if all DiscoBall objects are associated with the DiscoBall static mesh, each DiscoBall object possesses its own set of properties. For the current scenario, it is necessary to set a few of these.

To set the properties, refer to Figure 9.20 and right-click the DiscoBall object you have placed in your level and open the Properties dialog. Open the KParams tray and access the KarmaParams.myLevel tree item. Then under this access the KarmaParams branch. Find the KStartEnabled property and set it to True.

Next move to the Movement tray. In this tray, find the Physics property. Select the PHYS_Projectile item from the list. This enumerated value allows the object to move in a path that is characterized by a straight line. Be sure to save your work.

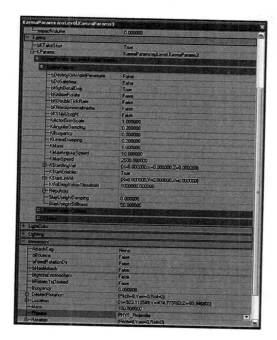

Testing Your Object and Its Code

When you test your level, you might need to make some adjustments to eliminate errors. One error you are likely to encounter occurs when the path you have set for your `DiscoBall` objects takes the object outside the bounds of the cube that defines your level. This situation is illustrated in Figure 9.21. You probably will not have the chance to fully anticipate this problem prior to running your level, so do not be surprised if the ball proceeds along its trajectory, passes into the wall of the cube, and then freezes.

Exit play and access the 2D Side viewport. Press the Control key and the left mouse button to reposition the `DiscoBall` object so that it is fairly high in the cube. The timer action, combined with the number of units you assign to the `vect()` arguments determines the distance the cube travels. If the `DiscoBall` object passes into the wall of the cube, then it freezes. Run the level and adjust the position of the ball until it goes up and down on a continuous basis.

Figure 9.22 illustrates the player `Pawn` object in the foreground. When the `Vector z` member value is set to `-90` and the `x` and `y` values are set to `0`, then the ball proceeds upward to nearly touch the ceiling. At that point, it descends until it nearly touches the floor.

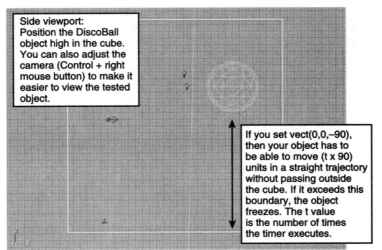

Side viewport:
Position the DiscoBall object high in the cube. You can also adjust the camera (Control + right mouse button) to make it easier to view the tested object.

If you set vect(0,0,–90), then your object has to be able to move (t x 90) units in a straight trajectory without passing outside the cube. If it exceeds this boundary, the object freezes. The t value is the number of times the timer executes.

Figure 9.21 Testing allows you to adjust the starting position of the DiscoBall object so it remains free of the boundaries of your cube.

Figure 9.22 The initial version of the DiscoBall class provides an object that proceeds along a vertical path extending from ceiling to floor.

Revising the DiscoBall Class

You can revise the DiscoBall class to turn it into something resembling a moving target for the player Pawn object to practice shooting at. In this implementation of the class, you add code that creates a square path for the ball. To revise the class, repeat the procedure that you followed in the first part of this chapter to derive a class from the KActor class. Start by saving the Ch09Disco00.ut2 file to Ch09Disco01.ut2.

You can reuse the DiscoBall static mesh. You need only to add it to another class. To create the new class, here is the procedure:

1. Open the Static Mesh Browser. Access the Ch09Disco package. Then access the DiscoBall static mesh. Click on it to store its name in the buffer.

2. Click the Actor Class Browser tab. Activate the Ch09Disco package. Access the KActor class in the class tree. Right-click and select New. In the New Class dialog, type Ch09Disco for the package name and DiscoBallB for the class name. Click OK.

3. After you see the signature line for the class in the code editor, click the Compile Changed Scripts icon. Then in the Actor Class Browser select File > Save Selected Packages.

4. Now locate the DiscoBallB class in the KActor class tree. Right-click to view the Default Properties dialog. Click the Display tray and find the StaticMesh property. Click to activate the StaticMesh field and click the Use button.

5. Now save your class once again.

6. In the Dynamic Light viewport, right-click and select Add DiscoBallB here. At this point, you see the ball of ice, as before.

7. Save your level.

8. Click the DiscoBallB object and open the Properties window. Click the Karma tray. Click the KParams tray. Click the KarmaParams tray. For the KStartEnabled property, select True.

9. Click the Movement tray and set the Physics property to PHYS_Projectile. Close the properties window and save your level.

These steps leave you with a DiscoBallB object in your level. But it helps if you position the ice ball object and adjust the camera and other features of the level to make testing your code easier. Refer to Figure 9.23 for approximate settings.

Note

Although it is difficult to tell from Figure 9.23, the size of the DiscoBallB object has been reduced. As a reminder, to scale objects, you click the Actor Scaling icon, hold down the Control key, and press the right or left mouse buttons.

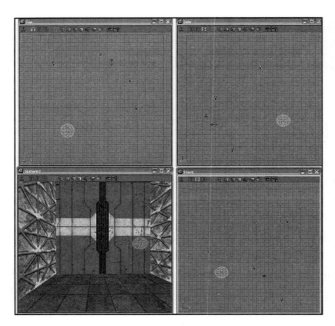

Figure 9.23 Positioning the DiscoBallB object so that it can complete its course.

Programming the DiscoBallB Class

The objective in defining the DiscoBallB class involves making it so that the ice ball follows a simple path described by changing vector coordinates. This path is a square, as shown in Figure 9.24. The ball continues to travel in this pattern for as long as the level remains active. The course followed begins on the x axis, moving in a positive direction. It then turns and moves downward on the z axis. It then completes its course by returning on the x axis in a negative direction and then climbing along the z axis to return to its starting point.

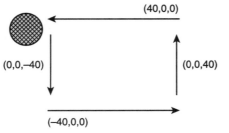

Figure 9.24 The ball of ice travels in a square.

The code for the DiscoBallB class is given in the DiscoBallB.txt code sample in the folder for Chapter 9. Here is the code for the class:

```
//================================================
// DiscoBallB
// DiscoBallB.txt
//================================================
// #1
class DiscoBallB extends KActor placeable;
var private int Next;
var private float TimerD;
enum SIDES{
        TOP,
        LEFT,
        BOTTOM,
        RIGHT
};
const PATHS = 4;
var Vector Square[PATHS];

// #2
function PreBeginPlay() {
    // Called once to set initial values
    SetTimeD(9.0);
    // From the KActor class
    SetTimer(TimerD, true);
    // Set for this class
    Next = 0;
}

// #3
private function CreatePaths(){
    Square[SIDES.TOP]    =    vect(40.0 ,0,       0);
    Square[SIDES.LEFT]   =    vect(0,    0,  -40.0);
    Square[SIDES.BOTTOM] = vect(-40.0 ,0,       0);
    Square[SIDES.RIGHT]  =    vect(0,    0,   40.0);
}

// Accessor for the array
private function Vector GetPath(SIDES path){
  return Square[path];
}
```

```
function PostBeginPlay() {
    Velocity = vect(0 , 0, 0);
     CreatePaths();
}


// #4
function Timer() {
    ChangePath();
}


// #5
// Sets initial values for the time durations
// Call once to set the initial state of the class
private function SetTimeD(float dur){
      if(dur < 0){
         dur = 0;
      }
      TimerD = dur;
}


// #6
// Creates a "square" path for the object
private function ChangePath(){
 if(Next == SIDES.TOP){
      // positive x direction
      Velocity = GetPath(SIDES.TOP);
      Next++;
    }else if(Next == SIDES.LEFT){
      // negative z direction
      Velocity = GetPath(SIDES.LEFT);
      Next++;
      }else if(Next == SIDES.BOTTOM){
      // negative x direction
      Velocity = GetPath(SIDES.BOTTOM);
      Next++;
    }else if (Next == SIDES.RIGHT){
      // positive z direction
      Velocity = GetPath(SIDES.RIGHT);
      Next = SIDES.TOP;
    }else{
      Next = SIDES.TOP;
    }
}
```

Data Members

In the code that follows comment #1, you set up several data members to take care of the actions of the DiscoBallB class. The Next data member allows you to control which side of a square you want the ball to follow. You create the SIDES enumeration to furnish values you can use in a number of ways. For one thing, you compare the values with the Next data member to control the path of a moving object. You also use this enumeration to identify Vector references that you store in the Square array. The TOP, LEFT, BOTTOM, and RIGHT members of the SIDES enumeration provide you with values ranging from 0 to 3. As mentioned in previous chapters, when you create an enumeration, you no longer have to worry about specific numerical values. Instead, the names of the members of the enumeration serve in place of confusing number values. In this respect, TOP allows you to select the top of a square path. The other members designate the other three sides. You finish off the data member declarations by creating a static array of the Vector type. This array contains the vector values that guide your moving object. To define this array so that you can store all the vector values in it needed to navigate a square route, you define the PATHS constant, which is set at 4.

Initial Conditions

Inside the PreBeginPlay() function, in the lines trailing comment #2, you call the SetTimerD() function. Such a function is known technically as a *mutator* function. A mutator function sets the value of a data member. It is the obverse of an accessor function. The SetTimerD() mutator function allows you to set values for the TimerD data member. Use of the prefix of "Set" for mutator function is a common programming practice.

You defined the SetTimerD() function in the lines affiliated with comment #5. The function performs a common task among mutator functions. It uses an if selection statement to check for an acceptable argument for the TimerD attribute. If you supply a value less than 0, then the function resets your value to 0.

Continuing with the lines following comment #2, after the call to the SetTimerD() function, you call the SetTimer() function that you inherit from the base class. As arguments for this function, you employ the TimerD data member and the true keyword. After this function call, you then initialize the Next data member to 0. This sets the first control value you use in the ChangePath() method to access vector values to guide the ball in its movement along the first side of the square.

The next section deals with the code accompanying comment #3. In the lines accompanying comment #4, you define the Timer() function. The Timer() function remains the primary function of the class, for in this function you introduce the changes you want to make in your KActor object with each pulse of the timer. In other words, you issue instructions that move the ball around the square. The Timer() function in this version of the class controls only one object. You might easily change things to make it control many more. To make it so that the Timer() function is not cluttered up with confusing code, you refactor your code and create the ChangePath() function. This function is explained in the next section, along with the CreatePaths() function.

Vector Use

As mentioned previously, you create the Square array to store values of the Vector type. By storing Vector values in this array, you make them available for controlling how you move the KActor object around the level. To set the values for this array and then to access the values to change the position of the KActor object, you implement two functions. These are the CreatePaths() and ChangePath() functions.

As defined in the lines following comment #3, the CreatePaths() function employs the vect() function four times in succession to assign Vector references defining the path the DiscoBall object is to follow. To designate the indexes of the Square array for the assignments, you use the members of the SIDES enumeration. Figure 9.24 illustrates the values you use to create the vectors.

Immediately after the definition of the CreatePaths() function, you see the definition of the GetPath() function. The GetPath() function is an accessor function for elements from the Square array. Notice that the argument type for the function is defined using the SIDES data type. Use of this data type helps ensure that legitimate values are used for the function.

The code for the ChangePath() function trails comment #6. This function consists of an if…else if…else selection structure that makes repeated use of the calls to the GetPath() function. Each stanza of the control structure checks the value of Next against one of the enumerated values. The first time the ChangePath() function is called in the Timer() function, the value of Next is 0, which corresponds to the SIDES.TOP value. The flow of the program enters this block and sets the Velocity data member by retrieving the SIDES.TOP Vector values from the Square array. To retrieve the values, a call is made to the GetPath() function. After assigning the value, the GetPath() function returns a value to the Velocity data member; then you increment the value of Next by 1. Use of the enumerated values makes it possible to easily understand and control the flow of activities.

Each time the Timer() function is called, it in turn calls the ChangePath() function, and with each call of the ChangePath() function, the value of Next is incremented and another set of Vector values is retrieved using the GetPath() function. In this way, four sets of Vector values are retrieved from the Square array, and four different definitions of vectors are assigned to the Velocity data member. The value of Next starts at SIDES.TOP. When it reaches SIDES.RIGHT, it is reset to SIDES.TOP.

Figure 9.25 illustrates the DiscoBallB object as it moves within the map. To shoot at the ball, it is best to leave the player Pawn unseen.

Figure 9.25 The DiscoBallB object moves in a square pattern and offers the player Pawn an opportunity to melt the ice with a little target practice.

Conclusion

In this chapter, you have developed a class that allows you to put the physics of the game engine to work to create an object that moves around your level. Working with such objects allows you to apply structures and control statements in new ways. They also expose a number of opportunities for adding animated items to your levels that you can create on a wholly customized basis. The process remains the same for all such objects. You use the brushes to create graphical primitives. You convert these into static meshes. You then associate the meshes with a class you derive from the KActor class. In the end, you can refine your techniques for controlling the object by customizing the code you write for the class or by setting the properties of the object to achieve built-in effects.

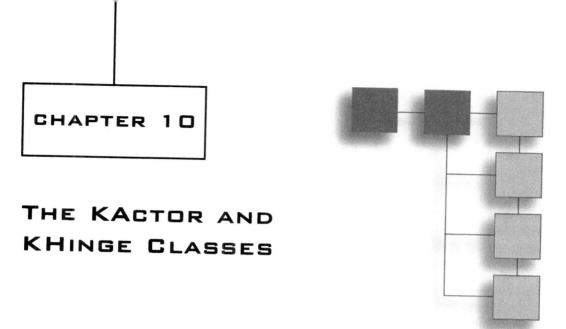

CHAPTER 10

THE KACTOR AND KHINGE CLASSES

I n this chapter you continue with the work you performed in the previous chapter. In addition to working with the KActor class, you examine the use of the TriggerLight and KHinge classes and explore how to develop another specialized version of the Trigger class. In this instance, you develop a class that employs a foreach() control to iterate through the Actor objects in your level to change their properties dynamically. You also explore a few supplementary topics, such as how to work with sound. This chapter is the last in this book. The projects you pursue represent a few among many that you might engage in using the skills you have gained through this book. This and the other work you have performed represent a beginning. At the same time, such work reveals that the Unreal Tournament class hierarchy provides you with possibilities that extend in many directions and far beyond the scope of this book. With the projects this book offers, it is hoped that you have been able to make a good start on what turns out to be an endlessly satisfying exploration of the Unreal Engine and the activities of programming and developing levels. Among the topics in this chapter are the following:

- Developing a TriggerLight class
- Working with Light objects
- How to iterate through objects of a given type
- Creating the DiscoTriggerLight class
- Creating messages from Groucho Marx
- Rotating a KActor and adding sound

Preparing for Work

As in previous chapters, begin your work by saving the previous work you have performed to a new version. In this case, access the Ch09Disco01.ut2 map and save it as Ch10Disco01.ut2. In this chapter, you do not create a new package. You use the Ch09Disco package.

In this version of the map, perform some preliminary work at this point to make things a little easier as you go. First, save your map to a new version, as mentioned above. Then, with the new map open, replace the DiscoBallB object with the DiscoBall object. For review, to accomplish this, open the Actor Class Browser. Access the Ch09Disco package. Navigate to the KActor listing in the class list. Click the DiscoBall class to make it active.

Then, in the Dynamic Light viewport, click to activate the DiscoBallB object and delete it. In its place, right-click and select Add DiscoBall Here. After you add the DiscoBall object, access the KarmaParams tree in the Karma tray and set the KStartEnabled property to True. Then in the Movement tray, set the Physics property to PHYS_Projectile. You can now test your map. The ice ball moves up and down. Adjust its position as needed until it moves through its complete cycle of motion without running into the floor or ceiling. If this happens, as you know, the ball can freeze. (See Chapter 9 for review of the DiscoBall object. Also, see Figure 10.1.)

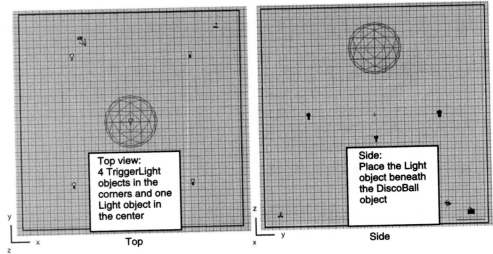

Figure 10.1 Position the TriggerLight objects in the corners and the Light object in the middle beneath the DiscoBall object.

TriggerLight Objects

The TriggerLight class is a specialized version of the Light class. One of the leading characteristics of the TriggerLight class is that it provides you with a number of enumerated values under the InitialState property, as Figure 10.2 illustrates. The initial state of a TriggerLight object characterizes how it behaves after you trigger it. In this case, you set the light so that you can change its initial state so that in some cases when you trigger it, it is turned off.

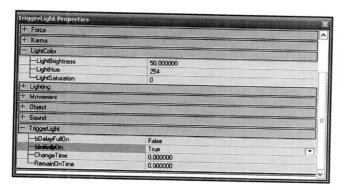

Figure 10.2 Set the bInitiallyOn property to True in the TriggerLight Properties dialog.

You already have at least one Light object in your level. Refer to Figure 10.1 as you go. Place the existing Light object in your level directly beneath the DiscoBall object. Place the four TriggerLight objects in the corners. To find the TriggerLight class, look in the Actor Class Browser under the Light class.

As Figure 10.2 illustrates, for each of the lights, temporarily access the LightColor tray of the Properties dialog and set the LightBrightness attribute for each light, center and corners, to 50. Additionally, access the TriggerLight tray and set the bInitiallyOn property to True.

Adding a Jump Pad

In previous chapters, you have set up a jump pad to identify the position of the trigger. At this point, add a jump pad for the Trigger object you develop later in the chapter. Position the jump pad in a corner to make it convenient to find. Figure 10.3 shows you the Top viewport with the jump pad positioned in the corner. See Chapter 4 for a discussion of how to create a jump pad.

After creating the jump pad and setting the position and properties of the DiscoBall, Light, and TriggerLight objects, test your level. As Figure 10.4 illustrates, the ice ball should move from the top to the bottom of the level.

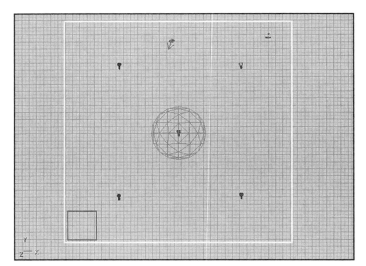

Figure 10.3 Position a jump pad in the corner.

Figure 10.4 The ice ball moves from the top to the bottom of the level, and five lights are in place.

Another Version of the DiscoBall Class

Now that you have the basic level in place, you can modify its features in a deeper way. The first change is to create a new version of the DiscoBall class. To accomplish this task, open the Actor Class Browser and access the KActor and Ch09Disco package. Create a new class that extends the KActor class. Call it DiscoBallC. Include it in the Ch09Disco package. Save the package and the class. Here is the code for the class.

```
//════════════════════════════════════════
// DiscoBallC.
// See DiscoBallC.txt
//════════════════════════════════════════
class DiscoBallC extends KActor placeable;
// #1
// Adjust the time to 6
function PreBeginPlay() {
   // # 1
    SetTimer(6.0, true);
}
function PostBeginPlay() {
    // # 2
    // Sets the initial velocity vector to point down
    // The speed of movement is 60 units
    // The arguments defined x y and z coordinates
    Velocity = vect(0, 0, -60);
}
function Timer() {
    // # 3
    // Flip the velocity vector around
    Velocity = (-1) * Velocity;
}
```

To create this class, you can copy the code from the DiscoBall class. (Control + A selects code, and Control + V pastes it.) The only changes you make to the original, aside from the comments, are the name of the class, the time setting for the StartTimer() function, and the unit you assign to the z coordinate in the vect() function (–60).

After you make these changes, here is a review of how you associate the DiscoBall class with the DiscoBall static mesh.

You can reuse the `DiscoBall` static mesh. You need only to add it to another class. To create the new class, here is the procedure:

1. Open the Static Mesh Browser. Access the `Ch09Disco` package. Then access the `DiscoBall` static mesh. Click on it to store its name in the buffer.

2. Click the Actor Class tab. Activate `DiscoBallC` class.

3 Now locate the `DiscoBallC` class in the `KActor` class tree. Right-click to view the Default Properties dialog. Click the `Display` tray and find the `StaticMesh` property. Click to activate the `StaticMesh` field and click the Use button.

4. Now save your class once again.

5. Delete the old `DiscoBall` object and then, in the Dynamic Light viewport, right-click and select Add DiscoBallC here. At this point, you see the ball of ice, as before. Save your level.

6. Set properties. To accomplish this, click the `DiscoBallC` object to open the Properties dialog. Click the `KParams` tray. Click the `KarmaParams` tray. For the `KStartEnabled` property, select `True`. Then click the `Movement` tray and set the `Physics` property to `PHYS_Projectile`. Close the properties window and save your level.

After you complete these steps, test your level with the `DiscoBallC` object. If necessary, adjust the position of the `Light`, `TriggerLight`, and `DiscoBall` objects so that as the `DiscoBall` object descends, it does not become completely black.

Setting the Light Colors and Styles

You have now placed and positioned five lights in your level. You now can add some color to this lighting by the properties of the `Light` and `TriggerLight` objects. To set the properties, click the respective light properties. As Figure 10.5 illustrates, access the `Events`, `LightColor`, and `Lighting` trays for each of the objects. Refer to Table 10.1 as you go.

With respect to the "Light" column in Table 10.1, these designations are purely arbitrary. There is no "Light" property. The important point is to work around the perimeter of the chamber from light to light and assign values to the five properties shown. Then go to the center and assign values to the center light. Save your work when you finish.

The setting for the `LightEffect` property of the light in the center of your level is `LE_Disco`. This setting creates an effect that resembles that of the mirrored balls typical of discotheques.

As you set the light values, periodically click the Build Changed Lighting icon. Although Figure 10.6 shows shades of gray, in the Dynamic Light viewport, you see the lights change to accord with the colors you have assigned to them.

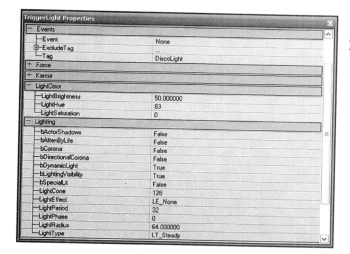

Figure 10.5
Add some color to the lights.

Table 10.1 Settings for the Light and TriggerLight Objects

Light	Brightness	Hue	Saturation	LightEffect	Tag
TriggerLight1	50	197	0	LE_None	DiscoLight
TriggerLight2	50	83	0	LE_None	DiscoLight
TriggerLight3	50	173	0	LE_None	DiscoLight
TriggerLight4	50	254	0	LE_None	DiscoLight
Center	100	43	0	LE_Disco	Light

Figure 10.6 Lights change colors as you assign hues to them.

Testing Your Lights

As Figure 10.7 reveals, when you run the program, you see the lights change as the ball moves. The ball displays red, green, purple and blue, and yellow lights, reflecting the hue values you have set for the lights. Notice that the yellow light displays spots of yellow light, simulating a discoteque ball.

Figure 10.7 The effect of setting the center light to Disco.

Iterating through Objects

When you program events for a level, you can use a control that allows you to pass through all the objects you have placed on a level and identify them on a selective basis to change them. The control that allows you to accomplish this work is the foreach() control. The foreach() control works like the for and while repetition statements, but its control mechanism is not a control variable that you declare and set. Instead, as Figure 10.8 illustrates, it uses a background array that stores the identities of all the Actor objects in your level. When you call the foreach() control, it traverses or iterates through this array and allows you to visit each object on your level.

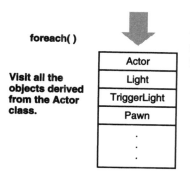

Figure 10.8 The `foreach()` control iterates through objects of the types you designate.

If a control is designed to iterate through objects of a base class, such as the `Actor` class, then among the objects it detects are all classes derived from the base class. As Figure 10.9 illustrates, as the `foreach()` control iterates through the different objects of the level, it can access properties in those cases that are defined in the base class. In this way, the control allows you to change those properties.

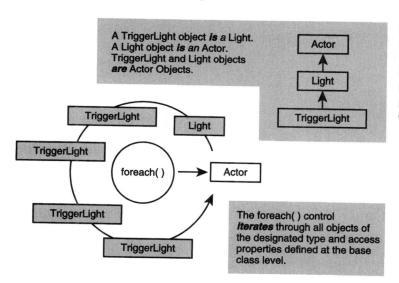

Figure 10.9 The `Light` and `TriggerLight` classes are derived from the `Actor` class, so the `foreach()` control detects them if you program it to seek all objects of the `Actor` type.

Defining the DiscoLightTrigger

To make use of the `foreach()` action, you define the `DiscoLightTrigger` class. This class incorporates the `foreach()` control to allow you to access all the `Light` and `TriggerLight` objects in your level. As you access these objects, you can change their properties. Among other things, you can turn the lights on and off.

To create the `DiscoLightTrigger` class, you specialize the `Trigger` class. Follow the usual routine to perform this task. Access the `Trigger` class in the `Actor` class hierarchy. In the New Class dialog, enter `DiscoLightTrigger` as the class name and `Ch09Disco` as the package name. Here is the code for the class.

```
//=========================================================
// DiscoLightTrigger.
// See DiscoLightTrigger.txt
//=========================================================
class DiscoLightTrigger extends Trigger placeable;
function Touch( Actor Other )
{
     // #1
     // Create a local variable for the TriggerLight class
     local TriggerLight SomeTriggerLight;
     // #2
       if ( ReTriggerDelay > 0 )
       {
            if ( Level.TimeSeconds - TriggerTime < ReTriggerDelay ){
                 return;
            }
            TriggerTime = Level.TimeSeconds;
       }
     // # 3 Iterate through the Actors (TriggerLight objects)
     foreach DynamicActors( class 'TriggerLight',
                              SomeTriggerLight, Event) {
          // # 4
          // Trigger this actor
          SomeTriggerLight.Trigger(Other, Other.Instigator);
       }// end foreach
     // #5
       if (RepeatTriggerTime > 0){
            SetTimer(RepeatTriggerTime, false);
       }
     // Note: Do not call Super.Touch(Other) here
     // This class handles the trigger event on its own.

   }
```

When you specialize the Trigger class, your work centers on the Touch() function. At comment #1, you create a local variable of the TriggerLight type, SomeTriggerLight. This variable allows you to identify objects of the TriggerLight type in your level. You could just as easily declare an object of the Light or Actor type to serve in this role, but to make the process of iteration more efficient, you designate a search object at the TriggerLight level.

At comment #2, you include a selection statement that prevents the trigger from being activated in an unwanted manner. The code first uses a selection statement to determine whether the ReTriggerDelay value is greater than 0. In the test expression, you subtract the number of system ticks allowed for the life of the trigger from the time at which the trigger is activated. If the difference is less than the time allowed for the delay of the reset of the trigger (ReTriggerDelay), then the function returns and no further actions are performed. If the time is not less, then the value assigned to TimeSeconds is assigned to TriggerTime.

The result of this action is that you can then go to the code following comment #5. This action prevents the SomeTriggerLight object from being initialized several times in succession, causing the lights to flash on and off before arriving at a steady on or off state.

At comment #3, you employ the foreach() control statement. In what amounts to the most central action of the entire class, the statement calls the DynamicActors() function, which takes three arguments. The first argument is the class that you want to discover in the process of iteration. As mentioned previously, this could be either the Light or Actor class. To make the process more efficient, you choose a level of class generality that accords with the TriggerLight class. This is the TriggerLight class itself. If you were working with several classes derived from the Trigger class, then you would use the Trigger class itself.

The next argument in the DynamicActors() function is the local variable defined above, SomeTriggerLight. The DynamicActors() function momentarily copies the class object of the type you have designated to this variable so that it can work with it. The third argument identifies a property in the object that you access. This argument identifies the Event you set in the Events tray of the TriggerLight and DiscoLightTrigger Properties dialog. You have already set the Event property for the TriggerLight objects. You will shortly set this property for the DiscoLightTrigger object.

For each type of object with the designated Event, the foreach() control initiates an action. In this instance, in the lines associated with comment #4, you define the action. The action constitutes calling the Trigger() function. The Trigger() function calls on the objects it communicates with to turn off or on.

One More TriggerLight Property

You set one more property in addition to those named in Table 10.1 for the four TriggerLight objects. This is the InitialState property in the Object tray. For each of the TriggerLight objects, open the Properties dialog and set the InitialState property to the TriggerToggle value, as Figure 10.10 illustrates. When you assign this value, the light issued by each object toggles on or off each time it is visited by the foreach action.

Figure 10.10 Set the InitialState property to TriggerToggle.

Add the DiscoLightTrigger Object

Now that you have attended to the definition of the TriggerLight class and the final configuration of the TriggerLight objects, add a TriggerLight object to your level just over the jump pad. To accomplish this, first access the Actor Class Browser and activate the DiscoLightTrigger class in the Trigger tree, as shown in Figure 10.11. Then, in the Dynamic Light viewport, position the cursor above the jump pad and right-click. Select Add DiscoLightTrigger Here.

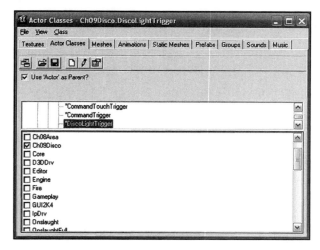

Figure 10.11 Select the DiscoLightTrigger object and place it above the jump pad.

Figure 10.12 illustrates the trigger over the type of jump pad. As you can see, the situation does not differ from what you have seen several times in previous exercises.

Figure 10.12 Position the DiscoLightTrigger above the jump pad and then configure its settings.

Settings for the DiscoLightTrigger Object

Given that you have placed a DiscoLightTrigger object above the jump pad, you can now configure its properties. First, access the Events tray. Locate the Event property in the Events tray and type DiscoLight, as illustrated in Figure 10.13. This is the Event value you have set for all the DiscoLight objects (see Table 10.1). The two property names must match exactly for the foreach control to detect their correspondence.

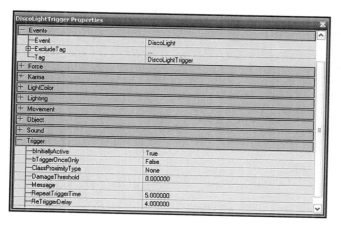

Figure 10.13 Set the Event, RepeatTriggerTime, and ReTriggerDelay properties.

In addition to the Event property, in the Trigger tray of the DiscoLightTrigger Properties dialog set the RepeatTriggerTime property to 5 and the ReTriggerDelay property to 4. These settings prolong the trigger event so that you can see the effect of the triggered action.

Note

The RepeatTriggerTime property controls the amount of time the trigger waits before it can be triggered again. The ReTriggerDelay property controls the amount of time the trigger waits from the time the actor touches it to the time it triggers an event. In this case, this time extends from the moment the player Pawn object touches the trigger and the moment you see the lights turn on or off.

Testing the New DiscoWorld

When you test run the level, it starts with the lights on, as Figure 10.14 illustrates.

Figure 10.14 The level opens with the lights on.

Move the player Pawn figure to the jump pad. At this point, the lights turn off. Now, each time the player Pawn figure initiates a new action with the DiscoLightTrigger object, the lights are toggled on or off. If you position the player Pawn object on the DiscoLightTrigger object, the lights turn off or on every few seconds. Figure 10.15 shows you the level with the lights off. The glow affiliated with the ice ball is the Light object, which is not affected by the toggling action initiated by the DiscoLightTrigger object.

Figure 10.15 The DiscoLightTrigger object turns the lights off.

Adding a Message to the DiscoLightTrigger

To increase the level of interactivity the map provides, you can modify the DiscoLightTrigger class so that it issues a message. Toward this end, implement a second version of the DiscoLightTrigger class. To accomplish this, first save the Ch10Disco01.ut2 map as Ch10Disco02.ut2. Delete the DiscoLightTrigger object and replace it with the DiscoLightTriggerB object after you implement the code and configure the object.

Continue working from the Ch09Disco package. To develop the class, follow the usual routine. In the Actor Class Browser, navigate to the Trigger listing and select New Class. In the

New Class dialog, type `Ch09Disco` as the package name and `DiscoLightTriggerB` as the class name. After you save the shell of the new class, you can then copy in the code from the `DiscoLightTrigger` class and add the few new lines required for a version that issues a message. Here is the code for the new class. The lines you add are in bold.

```
//======================================
// DiscoLightTriggerB.
// See DiscoLightTriggerB.txt
//======================================
class DiscoLightTriggerB extends Trigger placeable;

var private bool Toggle;
function Touch( Actor Other )
{
    local TriggerLight SomeTriggerLight;
    // #1 access the base class Message data member
    // Assign a value using a newly defined function
    Message = GetMessage();
    if ( ReTriggerDelay > 0 ){
        if ( Level.TimeSeconds - TriggerTime < ReTriggerDelay ){
            return;
        }
        TriggerTime = Level.TimeSeconds;
    }// end if

    foreach DynamicActors( class 'TriggerLight', SomeTriggerLight, Event){
        SomeTriggerLight.Trigger(Other, Other.Instigator);
    }
    // #2 Access the message value
    if( (Message != "") && (Other.Instigator != None) ){
        // Send a string message to the touching class object.
        Other.Instigator.ClientMessage( Message );
    }
    if (RepeatTriggerTime > 0){
        SetTimer(RepeatTriggerTime, false);
    }
}//end Touch
// #3 Provide a message
private function string GetMessage(){
    if(Toggle == False){
        return "Change the lights!";
    }
}
```

At comment #1 in the DiscoLightTriggerB, you make a call to the class member function GetMessage(). This function is defined in association with comment #3. It tests for the value of Toggle, which is an inherited class attribute. If this value is set to False, then the function returns a line of text, Change the lights!

At comment #2, you attend to a few housekeeping chores associated with messages. To accomplish this, you create an if selection statement that makes use of a compound Boolean AND operator. This determines that the value of the Message data member is not empty and the Message can be processed by an Instigator object. If this statement evaluates to True, then you send a message.

Testing DiscoLightTriggerB

As Figure 10.16 reveals, when you activate the new version of the specialized Trigger class object, the behavior of the lights is the same as before, but now you see a text message when the player Pawn object activates the trigger.

Figure 10.16 Implement the functionality to issue messages.

DiscoLightTriggerC

As an extra project, create a class called `DiscoLightTriggerC`. Use the `Ch09Disco` package. Save the Ch10Disco02.ut2 level to a new version, Ch10Disco03.ut2. Derive the class from the `Trigger` class, just as you did with the `DiscoLightTrigger` and `DiscoLightTriggerB` classes. This time around, instead of deleting the first object, duplicate the jump pad and position the duplicated jump pad so that it lies near the first one.

To implement this class, use the DiscoLightTriggerC.txt code sample. This class definition allows you to bring forward some of the work you performed with arrays and that `Rand()` function in previous chapters. In this instance, you create a class that issues messages randomly taken from a collection of quotes by Groucho Marx. Figure 10.17 shows the level with one of Groucho Marx's lines.

As with the previous class, to configure the `DiscoLightTriggerC` object, locate the `Event` property in the `Events` tray and type `DiscoLight`, as illustrated in Figure 10.14. This is the `Event` value you have set for the `DiscoLight` objects (see Table 10.1). The two property names must match exactly.

Figure 10.17 Groucho Marx adds levity to the level.

In addition to the Event property, set in the Trigger tray of the DiscoLightTriggerC Properties dialog, set the RepeatTriggerTime property to 5 and the ReTriggerDelay property to 4. These settings prolong the trigger event so that you can see the effect of the triggered action. Here is the code for the DiscoLightTriggerC class. You can find it in the DiscoLightTriggerC.txt file.

```
//============================================
// DiscoLightTriggerC.
// See DiscoLightTriggerC.txt
//============================================
class DiscoLightTriggerC extends Trigger placeable;
// #1
var private bool Toggle;
const QUOTES = 10;
var private string GrouchoSays[QUOTES];
// #2
function PostBeginPlay(){
    SetQuotes();
}
function Touch( Actor Other )
{
    local TriggerLight SomeTriggerLight;
    Message = GetMessage();
    if ( ReTriggerDelay > 0 ){
      if ( Level.TimeSeconds - TriggerTime < ReTriggerDelay ){
            return;
        }
      TriggerTime = Level.TimeSeconds;
    }// end if

    foreach DynamicActors( class 'TriggerLight', SomeTriggerLight, Event){
        SomeTriggerLight.Trigger(Other, Other.Instigator);
    }
    // Access the message value
    if( (Message != "") && (Other.Instigator != None) ){
        // Send a string message to the touching object.
        Other.Instigator.ClientMessage( Message );
    }
    if (RepeatTriggerTime > 0){
        SetTimer(RepeatTriggerTime, false);
    }
}// end Touch
```

```
// #3 Provide a message
private function string GetMessage(){
    local string Quote;
    if(Toggle == False){
        Quote = GetQuote();
    }else{
        Quote = "";
    }
    return Quote;
}
// #4
private function string GetQuote(){
    local int QuoteNumber;
    local string WhatHeSays;
    QuoteNumber = Rand(QUOTES);
    if(QuoteNumber < QUOTES ){
        WhatHeSays = GrouchoSays[QuoteNumber];
    }
    return WhatHeSays;
}
// #5
private function SetQuotes(){
    GrouchoSays[0] = "Either he's dead or my watch has stopped. ";
    GrouchoSays[1] = "And I want to thank you for all the " $
                    "enjoyment you've taken out of it. ";
    GrouchoSays[2] = "All people are born alike - " $
                    "except Republicans and Democrats. ";
    GrouchoSays[3] = "I don't care to belong to a club that " $
                    "accepts people like me as members. ";
    GrouchoSays[4] = "I must confess, I was born at a very early age. ";
    GrouchoSays[5] = "I worked my way up from nothing "$
                    "to a state of extreme poverty. ";
    GrouchoSays[6] = "Military intelligence is a contradiction in terms. ";
    GrouchoSays[7] = "No man goes before his time - " $
                    "unless the boss leaves early. ";
    GrouchoSays[8] = "The secret of life is honesty and fair dealing." $
                    " If you can fake that, you've got it made. ";
    GrouchoSays[9] = "A hospital bed is a parked" $
                    " taxi with the meter running. ";
}
```

The code for this class involves changes that are more extensive than those for the previous class but all involve familiar activities. At comment #1, you add a constant, QUOTES, and initialize it with 10. You then use the constant to create an array called GrouchoSays.

In the comments associated with comment #2, you override the PostBeginPlay() function from the base class. Within this function you call the SetQuotes() function, which you define in the lines trailing comment #5. The SetQuotes() function is private and takes no argument. Its purpose is to allow you to assign 10 quotes from Groucho Marx to the GrouchoSays array. There are much more elegant approaches to performing such operations, but this approach keeps everything on the most simple level, so it is easy to debug. The lines assigned often consist of two or more concatenated strings. This is to make it so that the code can be readily displayed in this book and more easily read in the editor.

In the lines accompanying comment #3, you call the GetQuote() method. You assign the value the function returns to a locally defined variable of the string type, Quote. You then return Quote so that it can be assigned to the Message property, as in the previous version of the class.

In the lines associated with comment #4, you define the GetQuote() function. To define the function, you declare a local variable of the int type to record random numbers. You also declare a local variable of the string type to process quotes from the GrouchoSays array. To retrieve a quote, you call the Rand() function. You use the QUOTES constant, so the function returns values extending from 0 to 9, which all lie safely in the boundaries of the GrouchoSays array. However, just to make sure, you also implement a selection statement that checks that the value generated by the Rand() function is always less than 10.

Adding a KHinge Object

Save Ch10Disco03.ut2 as Ch10Disco04.ut2 and again continue working from the CH09Disco package. This time around, you add a KHinge object to your level. To add this object, you are not required to write any new code. However, adding the object gives you a chance to explore yet another class in the class hierarchy and to explore a few new properties.

This time around, start by opening the Static Mesh Browser. Select File > Open, and search through the *.usx files until you find the Pipe_staticmeshes.usx package, as shown in Figure 10.18.

From the File menu of the Static Mesh Browser, select Open. Within the browser, you then see the contents of the package. Set the Category field to General and select the pipegear mesh, as shown in Figure 10.19.

Now move to the Dynamic Light viewport of your level. Right-click and select Add Karma Actor. The pipegear object appears in your level. Position it against the floor or against one of the walls, as shown in Figure 10.20. This figure shows you a side view of the map.

Figure 10.18 Begin by accessing a static mesh package.

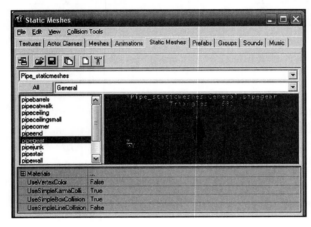

Figure 10.19 Select the pipegear mesh.

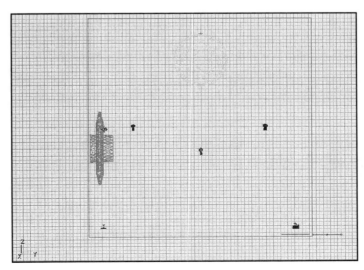

Figure 10.20 Position the pipegear mesh against one of the walls.

When you add a static mesh as a Karma object, it can process information provided by the physics engine. Karma in the Unreal Engine refers to physics, which relates to all aspects of movement in a level. When you right-click and select Add Karma Actor, you add a static mesh as a Karma object. Such an object can readily interact with the world.

To configure the Karma object, click on it to open its properties dialog. Find the Karma tray, navigate through the KarmaParams tree to the KStartEnabled property. As shown in Figure 10.21, set this property to True.

Now click Build All and Play Map and test run the map. If you have positioned the KActor object (pipegear) as shown in Figure 10.21, it falls to the floor and topples over. It then slides across the floor and comes to rest against the opposing wall.

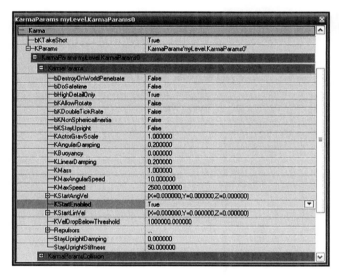

Figure 10.21 Set KStartEnabled to True.

Problems with Physics

If your Karma object does not fall to the floor or in some other fashion move when you first run your level, the problem is likely to be the Display settings for your game. There are two approaches to solving this problem. The first is to access the Settings dialog in your game. As shown in Figure 10.22, set the Display settings to High. This provides the amount of detail to allow the physics engine to operate correctly.

You can also set the Karma properties dialog for the Karma Actor object. To accomplish this, again access the Karma tray and then navigate through the KarmaParams tree until you see the hHighDetail property. Set it to False, as shown in Figure 10.23.

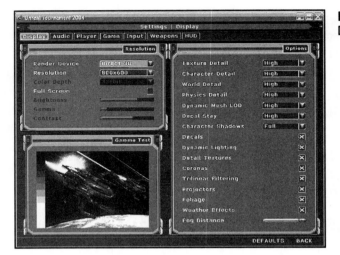

Figure 10.22 Set the Display settings to High.

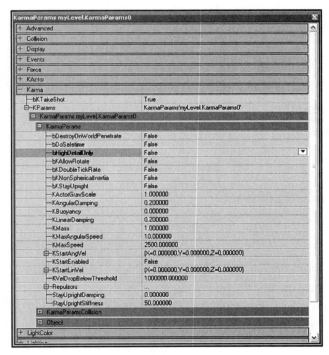

Figure 10.23 Set the bHighDetailOnly property to False.

Implementing Rotation

Given that your Karma Actor object is now in place, open the Actor Class Browser and navigate to the KActor and then the KConstraint and KHinge classes, as shown in Figure 10.24. As you might expect, a KHinge object is something that rotates. You can tie a KHinge object to a KActor object so that the motion of the KActor object centers on the KHinge object. The result is that the KActor object rotates around the hinge.

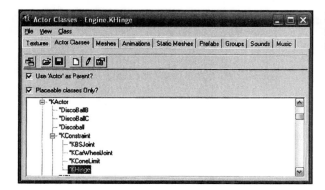

Figure 10.24 Select KHinge from the Actor Class Browser.

After selecting the KHinge class in the Actor Class Browser, find a position in front of and as close to the middle of the pipegear object as possible. Right-click and select Add KHinge Here. The icon for KHinge appears as shown in Figure 10.25. Hold down the Control button and right-click and drag the mouse to rotate the arrow extending from the KHinge until it points straight at the KActor object to create the center of rotation.

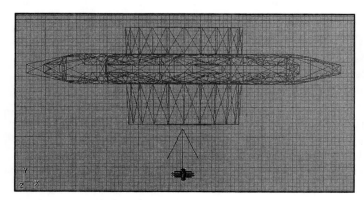

Figure 10.25 The red arrow that appears with the KHinge class shows the line of rotation for the hinge.

When you create an instance of the KHinge class, the hinge appears with a red arrow. The arrow indicates the axis of rotation. If you were putting in a KHinge for a door, then the arrow would point straight up or down. Set the properties for the KHinge as follows. Refer to Figure 10.26:

- Click the KHinge object and open its properties dialog. Find the KarmaConstraint tray. Click the KConstraintActor1 property. A field appears, as shown in Figure 10.26. Click the Use button. The name in the field changes, and you see a KActor identified.

- Move down in the list of the KarmaConstraint tray and find the KHingeType property. Set its value to HT_Motor.

- Set KDesiredAngularVel to 65536. You use this figure because the game uses UI units instead of radians or degrees. 65536 is one full rotation per unit time.

- Set KMaxTorque to 100.

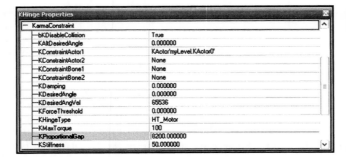

Figure 10.26 Set the KHinge properties.

Now save, Build All, and run your level. Figure 10.27 illustrates the pipegear object on the far wall. It spins as the ball goes up and down. If you use an object of the DiscoLightTriggerC class in the level, you also see messages from Groucho. Welcome to the Discotheque!

Note

You can set the desired angular velocity to be negative to make it spin the other way. The KDesiredAngVel is the KarmaConstraint tray. To reverse the spin, set the value to -65536.

To duplicate the pipegear and KHinge objects, hold down the Control key and click to select both of them. From the top UnrealEd menu, select Edit > Duplicate to make copies. You must copy both the KActor (pipegear) object and the KHinge object as a pair. If you copy only the KHinge object, then the system is confused and the spinning stops. Move this new pair to a position along the wall or ceiling. The effects of nine or so gears, four spinning one way, five the other, adds an interesting effect.

Figure 10.27 The pipegear object rotates while the ice ball goes up and down.

Finale

One further action you can take to close out your work both in this chapter and in this book involves adding your own music track. To accomplish this, from the top UnrealEd menu, select View > Level Properties. Click to open the Audio tray. In the Audio tray, you see a Song property, as shown in Figure 10.28. Type the name of a song in this field. The songs available to you are in the Songs folder under UT2004. Song files have an *.oog extension. When you type the name, leave off the file extension.

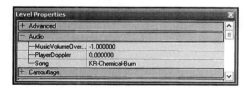

Figure 10.28 Add your own song to the level.

Conclusion

This chapter brings to an end this venture involving programming in the Unreal Level Editor. If you have worked through the examples in this book from the position of a complete beginner, then you deserve much praise for your effort. Chances are, along the line, some of the code proved difficult to implement.

It is also the case that the features of Unreal Tournament are so numerous that it is impossible to address all of them in a book of this size. As mentioned in Chapter 1, the Internet resources remain one of your best bets for continuing your development activities after you establish a grasp of the essentials. We hope this book has provided you with such a grasp. If you feel you have only made a beginning, then that is a good sign.

In this chapter, you explored development of several different classes from the class hierarchy. The classes you have worked with have constituted only a few of the many that compose the Unreal Tournament class hierarchy. Full exploration of all of the classes amounts to a task that is likely to involve you in years of programming.

This book is written as Epic is preparing to release a new version of Unreal Tournament. You need not fear that the skills you developed during this exploration of the 2004 version of the game engine will for this reason be useless. The fact is that in past releases, most of the classes in the hierarchy have remained similar to or the same as their previous versions. When changes do occur, as you might expect, they often make the classes easier to use and provide more pronounced features.

It is hoped that this book has offered you a place to start on your own path to both working with and showing others how to work with Unreal Tournament programming. As mentioned in Chapter 1, the richness of the culture can be tremendously facilitated if those who participate in it do so in the spirit of cooperation and sharing.

If it is the case that your involvement with Unreal Tournament programming extends beyond the classroom or your efforts as a hobbyist, then there is no reason to doubt that your steps might lead to a game development organization. Many companies have endorsed the Unreal Engine. Many games have been and will be built with it. The prospects are exciting. Best of luck in all you do!

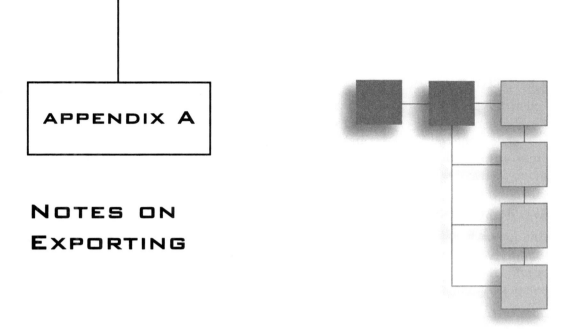

APPENDIX A

NOTES ON EXPORTING

When you create a package using the Actor Class Browser, UnrealEd creates a *.u file and places it in the Unreal Tournament System directory. Figure A.1 illustrates the Ch04Area.u file, which you created during your work session for Chapter 4.

When you create a package using UnrealEd, the only visible sign of your work is the *.u file that appears in the System directory. You see no source code other than what you see when you use the code editor to view the script for the class.

Figure A.1 The System directory hosts *.u files, among others.

Exporting Files

You can save the code you write in the code editor in UnrealEd by exporting it. Generally, you should periodically export your work so that you have backup versions of it. Exporting your code at the end of the day and then copying the exported files to an archive directory provides you with a way to recover if a package is corrupted. The following two sections show you two ways to export your code.

Export Starting from the Icon in Your Level

One approach involves exporting the code from an instance of a given class you have placed in your level. To use the StandUpTrigger object as a starting point (see Chapter 4), you might begin in the Dynamic Lighting viewport. Right-click the Trigger icon. Then in the pop-up menu, select Edit Script. See Figure A.2.

Figure A.2 Right-click and select Edit Script.

The code editor then opens, as Figure A.3 illustrates. From the main menu of the code editor, select File > Export Changed Scripts. Whether you have actually changed the script does not matter. Any open script is a "changed" script. The file is saved to a folder in the UT2004 directory named after the package.

For understanding the confirmation dialog, see the section titled "Confirming Exportation."

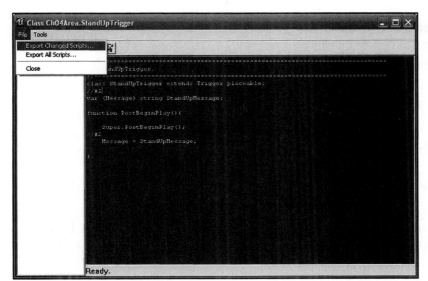

Figure A.3
Export the active script.

Export from the Actor Class Browser

As you are working in the Actor Class Browser, navigate to the class you want to export. As Figure A.4 illustrates, right-click on the name of the class. From the pop-up menu, select Edit Script. This opens the code editor. From the menu of the code editor (as shown in Figure A.3), select File > Export Changed Scripts.

For understanding the confirmation dialog, see the section titled "Confirming Exportation."

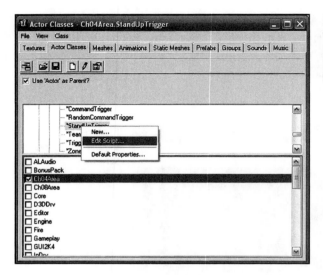

Figure A.4 Select the file and then use File > Save Changed Scripts to export the file.

Confirm the Exportation of the File

After you select Export Changed Script from the top menu of the code editor, you see the Export Classes to .uc Files dialog, as Figure A.5 shows. The crux of the matter is that you are creating an editable text (*.uc) file. This file is saved to a directory named after the package that contains your file. Click Yes. After the dialog vanishes, click to close the code editor.

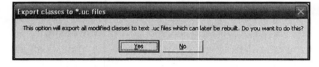

Figure A.5 You save the text of your script and can recompile it later.

Viewing Exported Files

When you export your code, UnrealEd creates a package directory for you and places your code file in it. The package directory for your StandUpTrigger file is named after the Ch04Area package, because this is the package that contains the StandUpTrigger class. To see the name of the package UnrealEd creates, view the title bar of the code editor (shown in Figure A.3).

To find the package directory, start on your default (C:) drive. If you have installed Unreal Tournament using the default installation settings, you find the UT2004 directory at the root level, as shown in Figure A.6. If you have exported a file from the Ch04Area package in UnrealEd, then it's in your Ch04Area directory in the UT2004 directory.

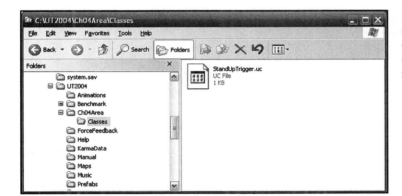

Figure A.6 When you export a script, UnrealEd generates a package directory with a Classes subdirectory.

When UnrealEd exports your script, it creates a package directory with the name you designate for the package in the Actor Class Browser. The package directory contains another directory named Classes. In the Classes directory, as shown in Figure A.6, you find all the files you have exported from a given package. In this case, you see only one file, because only one class has been exported. This is the source code file for your StandUpTrigger class. Such files have a *.uc file. You can open them with Notepad.

Note

You can open the file with any text editor. One popular editor is ConTEXT. You can find out many ways to use this editor in *UnrealScript Game Programming All in One* (Thomson, 2006).

When you open the *.uc file using Notepad, you see the same code you have seen in the code editor, as Figure A.7 shows.

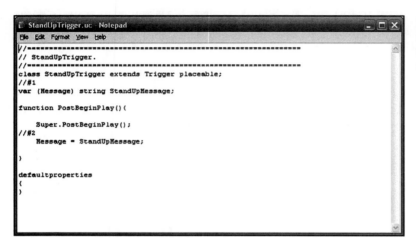

Figure A.7 Notepad displays your *.uc files after you have exported it.

Exporting Packages

Another approach to working with your code involves exporting a complete package of classes. Exporting entire packages is often the best policy, because it is almost always the case that dependencies exist between classes in a given package. In the Ch08Area package, for example, the CommandGoalTrigger class depends on the Story and CodePlay classes.

To export the classes in a package, start in the Actor Class tab. If the packages field of the tab is not visible, select View > Show Packages.

Note

It is not necessary for any given level to be open in UnrealEd. Also, if you do not see the package you want to export, then select File > Open Package. Select the package from the directory.

In the bottom field of the Actor Class tab, scroll to the package you want to export. In Figure A.8, you see the Ch08Area package. To select this package, click the adjacent check box.

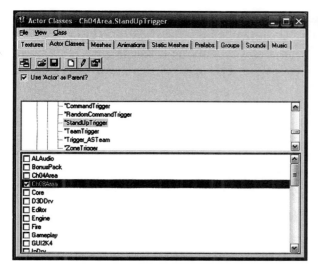

Figure A.8 Check the box next to the package you want to archive.

When you select the package, you select all the classes it contains. Now proceed to the top menu. Select File > Export Changed Scripts. True, as Figure A.9 reveals, you do not see a reference to packages, only to "changed scripts," but the package is implied. The classes are in the package.

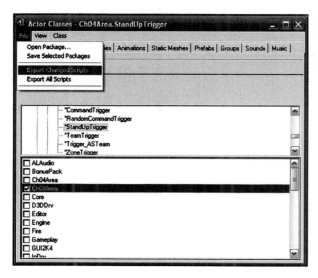

Figure A.9 Exporting the package will export all files within the package.

As Figure A.10 illustrates, you then seen a dialog that asks you to confirm that you are exporting classes to *.uc files. The dialog is confusing because it seems to be saying that you are doing something that disrupts your ability to continue to use the package. As it is, you are just copying the code to files outside the *.u file used by the Unreal Level Editor. Click Yes.

Figure A.10 Click Yes to confirm you want to copy the code to *.uc files.

Viewing Exported Package Files

To find the files that constitute the exported package, navigate to the UT2004 directory. Assuming you have exported one of your packages, find a folder UnrealEd has created. The folder has the same name as the package you exported.

Click to open this folder. You see a Classes folder within the package folder. Click to open the Classes folder. As Figure A.11 illustrates, you now see the *.uc files UnrealEd has created for your classes.

UnrealEd does not delete directories, so if you have exported a class from a given package before, the same package directory is used. The code files are overwritten.

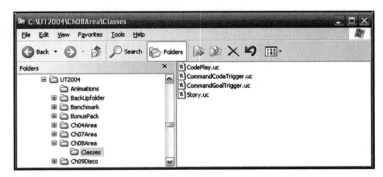

Figure A.11
After you export your classes, you see them in a Classes subdirectory.

Recovery

You compile a *.uc file using class files, but this activity lies beyond the scope of this appendix. See *UnrealScript Game Programming All in One* (Thomson, 2006) for precise, step-by-step procedures for compiling packages. After you have compiled a package, you select File > Open package from the top menu of the Actor Class Browser.

In this setting, if you export your files, you can copy them to a backup or archive directory and have them on hand if things go wrong. As shown in several chapters, if you open the files in Notepad and set the font to 12 pt Courier, you can use the Alt + C and Alt + V keys to copy the text into the code editor of the Unreal Level Editor.

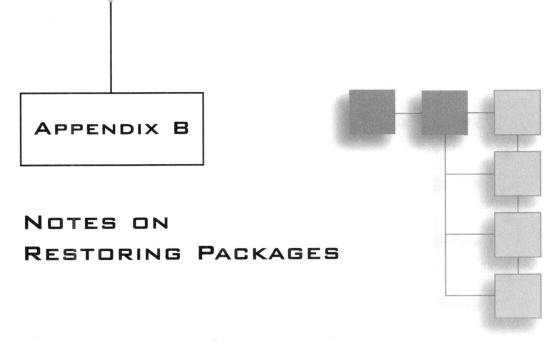

NOTES ON RESTORING PACKAGES

Files Used for Unreal Tournament

In this appendix, you see a few types of files mentioned repeatedly. Table B.1 provides a summary of these files. Refer to it in subsequent sections to orient yourself.

Note

Before you perform any of the actions in this appendix, close Unreal Tournament and the Unreal Level Editor.

Figure B.1 shows you the directories in which you find the files of the different types. The UT2004 directory contains all others. In the Maps directory, you find the files you create for your levels. These are of the *.ut2 type. In the StaticMeshes directory, you find package files for your static meshes. You create static meshes in Chapters 9 and 10. The files used to configure Unreal Tournament (*.ini) and to store the compiled versions of your class files (*.u) you find in the System directory. The *.uc files are the source code files. These reside in directories you can create when you export class files (discussed in Appendix A). You can also create such directories manually.

Table B.1 Important File Types

File Type	Description
*.ini	Files of this type contain a list of all the packages included when you build Unreal Tournament. The UT2004.ini file is located in the System directory. It is essential to be very careful when you work with this file. Make a backup version of the file called UT2004.ini_backup before you perform the tasks named in this appendix.
*.uc	Files of this type contain the text of UnrealScript programs. The discussion in Appendix A covers how to create such files. This appendix (B) shows you how to use them to create a new package file. Such files reside in the Classes directory in the package directory. Such directories do not exist unless you create them. You can create them manually through Windows or using the Unreal Level Editor (as discussed in Appendix A).
*.usx	This is a static mesh file. This file resides in the Static Meshes directory. For the final chapters of the book, you encounter errors if this file is not present or has been corrupted. You create the files from scratch, but if you use material from the CD, you must place the static mesh files in the Static Mesh directory before you can build your level.
*.ut2	This is the level file. It contains most of what you use for your basic level. However, if you have customized UnrealScript files (class files) or assets, such as dynamic meshes, then you must also have these at hand in the right directories before you can open the *.ut2 file.
*.u	Files of this type are your package files. In this appendix (B) you explore how to create this file using the ucc make command. Using this command, you compile the *.uc files for your package to generate a *.u file. You can then manually load the *.u file into the Unreal Level Editor by using the File menu option of the Actor Classes tab of the browser.

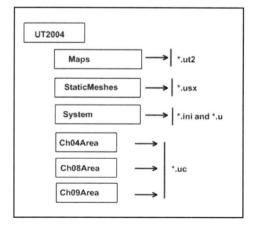

Figure B.1 While the System directory contains several types of files, other directories are characterized by the single type of file they contain.

Restoring Corrupted Packages

Here is a general view of the tasks you perform to restore a package. Subsequent sections of this appendix discuss these tasks in detail:

- Set up a package directory that includes a Classes subdirectory. Place the backup UnrealScript files in this directory. See "Placing Source Files in a Package Directory" for specific directions.

- Delete the corrupted package (*.u) file. This file resides in the System folder. See "Deleting a Corrupted *.u File" for specific instructions.

- Add or Verify the EditPackages line in the initialization file. See "Verify the Edit-Packages Line."

- In the Unreal Level Editor, open the newly generated package. See "Accessing the New Package."

Placing Source Files in a Package Directory

Let's assume that you have a package called Ch04Area and that somehow it has become corrupted. If it is corrupted, you can tell if you try to open the level that uses the package. Among other things, the level does not open and you get a message that says that a given class is missing or that the package is corrupted. The level (*.ut2 files) is still fine. It is just that the package containing the classes you have developed has been corrupted.

You have on hand a set of files that contain the code for the classes in the Ch04Area package either from having saved the package as shown in Appendix A or as provided on the CD. These files are in the Classes directory under the Ch04Area directory. They are all *.uc files.

You use the *.uc files to generate a new package file. To accomplish this, you must compile them using a compiler program that Unreal Tournament provides.

To begin this work, you first create a package directory under the UT2004 directory. If you are restoring the Ch04Area package, then you name this directory Ch04Area. If a directory by this name already exists, you can rename the previously existing directory or move it to an archive directory. Within the package directory, you create a directory named Classes, as shown in Figure B.2. In the Classes subdirectory you place your code (*.uc) files.

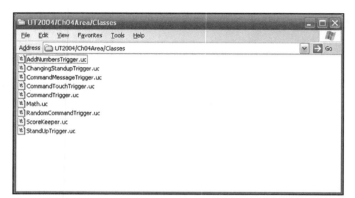

Figure B.2 Set up directories for your package and the classes it contains.

Renaming a Corrupted *.u File

When you create a package in the Unreal Level Editor, you create a *.u file. This file contains the primary code for all of your classes. If this file becomes outdated or in some other way corrupted, then you can no longer open the level associated with it.

To make is so that you can again use your level, you must restore the *.u file. To restore the *.u file, you first find the corrupted version of the file in the UT2004 system directory. To find this file, navigate to the C: drive of your computer and find the UT2004 directory. (You find the UT2004 directory on the C: drive if you have followed the standard installation routine for Unreal Tournament.)

Figure B.3 illustrates the positions of the UT2004/System after a standard installation. At the top of the list is the Ch04Area.u file. To find a specific *.u file, scroll through the files in the directory. If you do not find the *.u file you are looking for, it is probably the case that it has been deleted. If it has been deleted, you can replace it, as the next section shows.

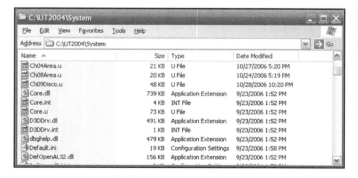

Figure B.3 The UT2004\System directory contains the *.u files.

If the corrupted version of the package file is in the System folder, then start by renaming it with an "_old" extension. Suppose, for example, that you have a corrupted file with this name:

    Ch04Area.u

To rename it in Windows, click on it to activate the change option and then modify its name so that it appears this way:

    Ch04Area.u_old

Windows might issue a warning that you are changing the file type, but this is okay. At this point, you can create a new *.u file. To accomplish this task, it is necessary to work in a DOS window using a command prompt. The next section details this activity.

Note

Rather than deleting files, rename them. Avoid deleting files. As long as you have not deleted your original files if you fail to perform a restoration procedure correctly, you can always go back to where you started. As a general policy, until you know exactly what you are doing, it is best to rename and place files you want out of the way in an archive directory.

Generating a New Package (*.u) File

You cannot successfully complete the actions discussed in this section unless you have completed the action detailed in the previous two sections. If you have not completed those actions, do so now. At this point, it is assumed that you have completed the following tasks:

- Placed copies of all the class files you want to restore in a package directory for the package you want to re-create. For instructions on how to accomplish this task, see the section titled "Restoring Corrupted Packages."
- In the System directory of Unreal Tournament, rename the *.u file for the corrupted package. In this book, this is likely to be the HelloWorld.u, Ch04Area.u, Ch08Area.u, or Ch09Area.u. As an example, you rename Ch04Area.u as Ch04Area.u_old.

Now you are ready to regenerate a new *.u file. The next section describes this activity in detail. It is a bit involved, so follow the discussion closely. Try to review it in its entirety before you start work. The main steps are as follows:

Verify the existence of the EditPackages line in the UT2004.ini file. See the section titled "Verify the EditPackages Line."

Use the appropriate command to generate a new package. See the section titled "Compiling a New Package File."

Verify the EditPackages Line

Before you can regenerate the package (*.u) file, check to see that the Unreal Level Editor knows that the package exists. To accomplish this, navigate to the System directory and find the UT2004.ini file, as shown in Figure B.4.

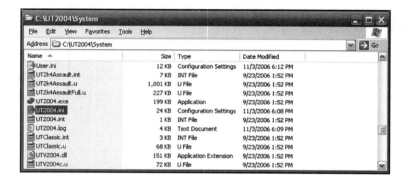

Figure B.4 Find the UT2004.ini file in the UT2004\System directory.

In Windows, right click on the UT2004.ini file and select Notepad to open the file. Then select File > Find and search for EditPackages, as shown in Figure B.5.

EditPackages is a special term that Unreal Tournament uses to identify the packages it includes when you run it. In Figure B.5, you see that a line is included for the Ch04Area package.

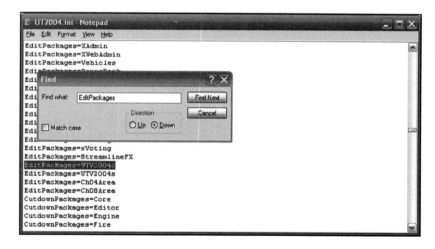

Figure B.5 Verify or add an EditPackages line.

If you are working with the ChO4Area package, then the line you are looking for looks like this:

```
EditPackages=ChO4Area
```

Scroll up and down to find the line in the UT2004.ini file. If you see the line for your package already included, verify that the spelling is correct for your package. Then close the file.

If you do not see an EditPackages file for your package, then you must add one.

To add an EditPackages line, first position the cursor at the end of the last EditPackages line and press Enter. This action positions your cursor on the next line.

Now that you have a blank line, verify that the cursor is at the start of the blank line, and type the EditPackages statement for your package. If you are working with the ChO4Area package, here is what you type:

```
EditPackages=ChO4Area
```

Figure B.6 shows you how this line appears after you have typed it. The cursor resides in the position after the last character typed.

After you add the EditPackages line, carefully check it to confirm that every character in the line is correct. Then select File > Save from the top Notepad menu and close the Ut2004.ini file. Now you are ready to recompile your package.

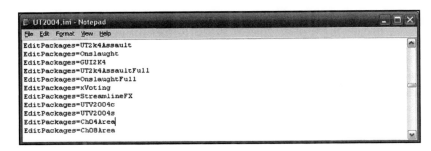

Figure B.6 An EditPackages directive exists for each package included in the build.

Compiling a New Package File

To complete this bit of work, you must first complete all of the work detailed in the previous sections of this appendix. Review these sections to confirm that you have completed the preliminary work. This work involves these steps:

- You have set up a Classes directory for your package and have included in this directory all the class files you want to include in your package.

- You have renamed the old package file in the System directory if such a file exists.

- You have verified that the UT2004.ini file contains an EditPackages line for the package you want to generate.

Now you can regenerate a new package (*.u) file for your classes. Toward this end, go to your desktop in Windows and open a DOS window. To open a DOS window, from the Start button of Windows, select Run. In the Run field, type **cmd**, as shown in Figure B.7.

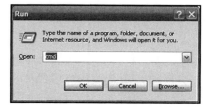

Figure B.7 Select Start > Run and type **cmd** to open a DOS window.

Note

The screenshots of the DOS window in the figures that follow feature a white background. You can set the background to white and the text to blank if you use the Properties options of the DOS window. These are accessed through the control button in the upper left of the window. For more information about configuring windows, see John Flynt, *UnrealScript Game Programming All in One* (Thomson, 2006).

Figure B.8 illustrates the DOS window. After you have invoked the DOS window, type a series of CD commands to change directories to activate the Unreal Tournament System directory. Figure B.8 illustrates these commands. The first is CD ../.. which moves the directory location up two directory levels to the C: (or root) directory. Your system is likely to show a similar opening window. You type this command alone to move up a directory:

    CD ..

To move down a directory, you type `CD` and then the name of the directory, as shown in the commands, to move down from the root directory to the UT2004 and System directories in Figure B.8.

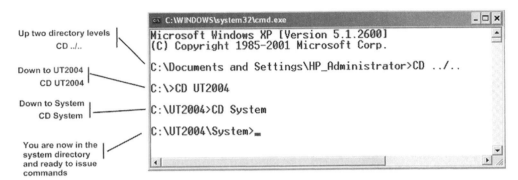

Figure B.8 Issue `CD` commands to navigate to the UT2004\System directory.

Now that you have activated the System directory, you can issue a command that regenerates your package. The specific details how this happens are beyond the scope of this book. For more information, see the book named previously.

You need to issue only one command. Here is the command you issue.

```
ucc make
```

Type it as shown in Figure B.9 and press Enter. Note that you can type the command in either lowercase or uppercase letters.

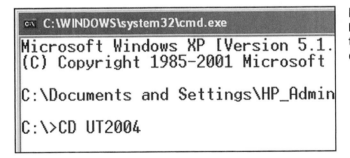

Figure B.9 The UCC MAKE command invokes the Unreal Tournament compiler.

After you issue the `UCC MAKE` command, the compiler for Unreal Tournament begins to execute. The classes you have placed in the Ch04Area directory (for example) are accessed. A new *.u file for the `Ch04Area` package is generated.

The process of regenerating files for your program takes a short while, usually less than a minute. The time depends on the speed of your computer. While the compiler is running, you see a series of messages displayed in the DOS window. In this context, the only one of interest is the one that reports your package has been generated. Figure B.10 illustrates what you see if you regenerated the Ch04Area package. In this case, you see Ch04Area - Release, showing that the compiler has accessed your package. Other lines show the successful compilation of other packages you might have created (such as Ch08Area in Figure B.10).

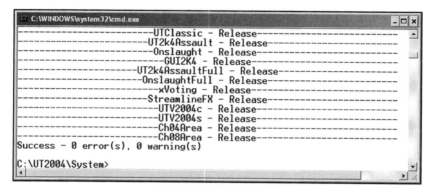

Figure B.10 You see a report for your newly compiled package.

To verify the existence of the new package (*.u) file in the System directory, issue this command:

    DIR *.u

Figure B.11 illustrates the command and the report that follows. The DIR command causes the system to display the contents of a directory. After the report is issued, scroll up the DOS window to find the *.u file.

```
C:\WINDOWS\system32\cmd.exe                                          _ □ x

C:\UT2004\System>DIR *.u
 Volume in drive C is HP_PAVILION
 Volume Serial Number is 73BC-4457

 Directory of C:\UT2004\System

09/23/2006  01:52 PM           161,173 BonusPack.u
10/18/2006  02:55 AM             2,608 Bumper.u
10/27/2006  05:20 PM            21,121 Ch04Area.u
10/24/2006  05:19 PM            20,213 Ch08Area.u
10/28/2006  10:20 PM            48,443 Ch09Disco.u
09/23/2006  01:52 PM            73,774 Core.u
09/23/2006  01:52 PM           458,259 Editor.u
09/23/2006  01:52 PM         2,666,248 Engine.u
```

Figure B.11 The new *.u file appears in the System directory.

Accessing the New Package

After you regenerate a package, open the Unreal Level Editor and access the Actor Class Browser.

Do not yet open the level in which you encountered difficulties. Use the blank level that appears by default.

From the View menu, select Show Packages. Then select File > Open Package, and select your newly generated *.u file (Ch04Area.u, for example) from the list, as shown in Figure B.12. Even if you can already see the package in the list, this action allows you to verify the existence of the package and refreshes the settings in the Unreal Level Editor.

At this point, you can again try to access the level in which you have encountered difficulties. The next section provides points you might use for troubleshooting.

Figure B.12 If your new package is not visible in the Package list, select File > Open Package and select it from the System directory.

Troubleshooting

Errors usually appear to you in two ways. One way is less nerve-wracking than the other. The gentler path involves encountering an error dialog that tells you that a given object is corrupt. The less gentle path involves trying to start the Unreal Level Editor or Unreal Tournament and encountering a "general protection" fault. You cannot even start the editor or the game. The next few sections discuss things you might try if you encounter errors.

Do This First

First, do not always trust an error message if you have opened the Unreal Level Editor and everything has been working well. You might get a dialog that tells you that a level or package file is corrupted. It could be that this is not so. It might be that a parameter in the Unreal Level Editor has not been updated. To test this case, save and close your level and then the Unreal Level Editor and then reopen them. The problem might go away. What happens in reality is that many values are refreshed in the Editor, and this is what solves the problem.

Bad Objects

When you place an object in a level, it can become "bad" if you do not have a compiled package that supports it. This can happen in a number of ways. One way is that the object in your level is no longer "synchronized" with the compiled class. This basically means that the object you are trying to use represents an outdated version of the class in a given package.

A level with a bad object often opens. Only when you try to run or build it do you encounter an error message or a general protection fault. If you see an error dialog that warns you about the missing object, stop there.

The dialog might tell you that a class is not synchronized or that a class is corrupted. The message is very complex and convoluted, but if you read it closely, you can find a reference to a missing or defective class.

Do not try to run (play) your level. Do not try to rebuild your level. Instead, first find the objects in the level of the type identified as defective, delete them, and replace them from your new package.

After you have replaced the objects, save your level. Close it and reopen it. With luck, the error dialog no longer appears, and you can proceed with builds.

Unreal Tournament or the Level Editor Refuse to Open

When Unreal Tournament or the Level Editor refuses to open, you usually see a general protection fault. This usually happens if you have inadvertently deleted a package (*.u) file.

As mentioned above, the UT2004.ini file lists all the *.u files the System directory is supposed to contain. If one of these has been deleted, then Unreal Tournament refuses to open.

Assume, for instance, that you have been working with the Ch04Area.u file. You close a session and then a day later try to go back to work. You encounter a general protection fault when you try to open either Unreal Tournament or the Unreal Level Editor.

The error message usually identifies the missing package. If not, you can reason through your actions to discover where you might have accidentally deleted a package.

You can check for a missing package if you navigate to the System directory in a DOS session and issue the `Dir *.u` command, as shown above. Or you can just go into Windows Explorer and check the file list. If you have deleted a package, it does not appear in the file list for the System directory.

Even then, this might not be the problem. You need to perform an additional action to make certain that the missing package file is the real problem. It is a problem only if Unreal Tournament is really trying to access it. As mentioned previously, you find out what files Unreal Tournament is trying to access by inspecting lines in the EditPackages section of the UT2004.ini file.

To proceed, use Notepad to open the UT2004.ini file. This file resides, as you know, in the UT2004\System directory. Use the Find utility to search for the EditPackages lines.

If the line that calls to a missing package is there, then you have found the problem. To eliminate the problem, comment out the line that calls the nonexistent package.

To comment out the line, type a semicolon at the beginning of the line. Here is an example of how you might comment out the EditPackages line for the `Ch04Area` package:

```
EditPackages=UTV2004c
EditPackages=UTV2004s
;EditPackages=Ch04Area
EditPackages=Ch08Area
CutdownPackages=Core
```

After commenting out the line, save and close the UT2004.ini file.

Then in the System directory, issue the `UCC MAKE` command. This rebuilds Unreal Tournament. At this point, you are likely to be able to again open the game and the Editor.

For instructions on how to re-create the package you have accidentally deleted and include it back in the game, go to the beginning of this appendix and follow the instructions. The procedure is exactly the same, except, obviously, you have no old or corrupted package (*.u) file to delete.

Missing Asset Files

A sound, texture, mesh, or other file is known as an *asset* file. For the projects you work with in this book, you usually work with just *.uc and *.ut2 files, but in Chapters 8, 9, and 10, this situation changes. For these projects, your work extends to using static mesh files. You generate these files from your projects for this book, but if you use the levels on the CD without working through the steps needed to construct them, then you must place the static mesh files (*.usx) in the Static Meshes directory.

INDEX

License Agreement/Notice of Limited Warranty

By opening the sealed disc container in this book, you agree to the following terms and conditions. If, upon reading the following license agreement and notice of limited warranty, you cannot agree to the terms and conditions set forth, return the unused book with unopened disc to the place where you purchased it for a refund.

License:
The enclosed software is copyrighted by the copyright holder(s) indicated on the software disc. You are licensed to copy the software onto a single computer for use by a single user and to a backup disc. You may not reproduce, make copies, or distribute copies or rent or lease the software in whole or in part, except with written permission of the copyright holder(s). You may transfer the enclosed disc only together with this license, and only if you destroy all other copies of the software and the transferee agrees to the terms of the license. You may not decompile, reverse assemble, or reverse engineer the software.

Notice of Limited Warranty:
The enclosed disc is warranted by Thomson Course Technology PTR to be free of physical defects in materials and workmanship for a period of sixty (60) days from end user's purchase of the book/disc combination. During the sixty-day term of the limited warranty, Thomson Course Technology PTR will provide a replacement disc upon the return of a defective disc.

Limited Liability:
THE SOLE REMEDY FOR BREACH OF THIS LIMITED WARRANTY SHALL CONSIST ENTIRELY OF REPLACEMENT OF THE DEFECTIVE DISC. IN NO EVENT SHALL THOMSON COURSE TECHNOLOGY PTR OR THE AUTHOR BE LIABLE FOR ANY OTHER DAMAGES, INCLUDING LOSS OR CORRUPTION OF DATA, CHANGES IN THE FUNCTIONAL CHARACTERISTICS OF THE HARDWARE OR OPERATING SYSTEM, DELETERIOUS INTERACTION WITH OTHER SOFT-WARE, OR ANY OTHER SPECIAL, INCIDENTAL, OR CONSEQUENTIAL DAMAGES THAT MAY ARISE, EVEN IF THOMSON COURSE TECHNOLOGY PTR AND/OR THE AUTHOR HAS PREVI-OUSLY BEEN NOTIFIED THAT THE POSSIBILITY OF SUCH DAMAGES EXISTS.

Disclaimer of Warranties:
THOMSON COURSE TECHNOLOGY PTR AND THE AUTHOR SPECIFICALLY DISCLAIM ANY AND ALL OTHER WARRANTIES, EITHER EXPRESS OR IMPLIED, INCLUDING WARRANTIES OF MERCHANTABILITY, SUITABILITY TO A PARTICULAR TASK OR PURPOSE, OR FREEDOM FROM ERRORS. SOME STATES DO NOT ALLOW FOR EXCLUSION OF IMPLIED WARRANTIES OR LIM-ITATION OF INCIDENTAL OR CONSEQUENTIAL DAMAGES, SO THESE LIMITATIONS MIGHT NOT APPLY TO YOU.

Other:
This Agreement is governed by the laws of the State of Massachusetts without regard to choice of law principles. The United Convention of Contracts for the International Sale of Goods is specifically disclaimed. This Agreement constitutes the entire agreement between you and Thomson Course Technology PTR regarding use of the software.